INVENTING SOUTHERN
LITERATURE

INVENTING SOUTHERN LITERATURE

Michael Kreyling

University Press of Mississippi *Jackson*

Parts of this book have appeared, in different versions, in *Mississippi Quarterly*, *The Southern Review*, and *The South as an American Problem* (published by the University of Georgia Press). We thank the editors for permission to use this material.

The paper in this book meets the guidelines for permanence and durability of the Committee on Production Guidelines for Book Longevity of the Council on Library Resources.

Library of Congress Cataloging-in-Publication Data

Kreyling, Michael, 1948–

    Inventing southern literature / Michael Kreyling.

      p.   cm.

    Includes bibliographical references and index.

    ISBN 1-57806-044-3 (cloth : alk. paper). — ISBN 1-57806-045-1 (pbk. : alk. paper)

    1. American literature — Southern States — History and criticism — Theory, etc. 2. American literature — Southern States — History and criticism. 3. Criticism — Southern States — History — 20th century. 4. Southern States — Intellectual life. 5. Southern States — In literature. 6. Group identity in literature. 7. Regionalism in literature. I. Title.

PS261.K7   1998

810.9'975 — DC21   97-42139
                                                           CIP

British Library Cataloging in Publication data available

CONTENTS

ACKNOWLEDGMENTS

This book has been several years in the making, and along the way I have counted upon the kindness of several people for advice and simple attention while I literally talked out loud about a topic that seemed all too often to make sense only to me.

Graduate and undergraduate students at Vanderbilt, and one class of undergraduates at Millsaps College in Jackson, Mississippi, have been subjected to this slant on southern literature. Their willingness to agree and disagree has sustained my commitment to the project. As long as it made sense to my students, I kept working.

Colleagues at meetings of the Society for the Study of Southern Literature, the St. George Tucker Society, and the Southern Intellectual History Circle have listened to versions of this work as it evolved— not always in a clear and coherent direction. The good news is that you will not have to listen any longer; you can read the book. This, of course, goes double for my colleagues in the English and history departments at Vanderbilt. Individual members of these organizations have been especially helpful and tolerant: Richard King, Susan Donaldson, Anne G. Jones.

Noel Polk read the manuscript voluntarily and gave me some much-needed advice. Michael O'Brien has been interested in this work for at least a decade, waiting for it to find its real trail. Throughout my work I used O'Brien's as a standard, and I hope this lives up to it. Lewis P. Simpson read and commented on parts of the project in its early stages. His willingness to be costumed as an early postmodernist for my argument is only one indication of his intellectual and professional generosity and scope.

The people at the University Press of Mississippi have been incredibly supportive. Joycelyn Trigg did copyediting that any author prays for. Seetha Srinivasan, editor-in-chief, believed in this book when it was not much more than disconnected pieces and promises; I'm happy that it is finally a tangible product of the University Press of Mississippi.

Chris, my wife, a writer herself, robbed time from her own work to read and critique this. In the low days when going on with it did not seem to matter much, she showed why and how it should be done.

Nashville, Tennessee
August, 1997

INTRODUCTION

Awareness of being imbedded in secular, serial time, with all its implications of continuity, yet of "forgetting" the experience of this continuity. . . . engenders the need for a narrative of "identity."
BENEDICT ANDERSON, *Imagined Communities*

Southern literature—an amalgam of literary history, interpretive traditions, and a canon—is a cultural product, or "artefact," to be understood just as Benedict Anderson understands the "nations" that fill up the history of the modern era (205). "Identity," in Anderson's study, is not an innate phenomenon but a product culturally and historically fabricated to local specifications by narratives that are more or less cooperative (the narrative of literature cooperative with the narrative of history, for example) and more or less conscious. This is not a breath-taking insight; contemporary literary critics and historians are weaned on the idea of the constructedness of meanings. Students and critics of southern literature, however, have been more rigorously schooled than others in the orthodox faith that our subject is not invented by our discussions of it but rather is revealed by a constant southern identity. From the polemical writings of the Agrarians to recent works of criticism, biography, literary history, and even film reviews, the established formula is repeated, the narrative of forgetting and making continued. It is not so much southern literature that changes in collision with history but history that is subtly changed in collision with southern literature. *Inventing Southern Literature* is, then, not a counternarrative that seeks to dynamite the rails on which the official narrative runs; rather, it is a metanarrative, touching upon crucial moments when and where the official narrative is made or problematically redirected. Readings of individual novels, when they occur in this work, are not intended primarily as acts of interpretation but rather as illustrations of the fabricating process at work. I propose to demonstrate that such-and-such an interpretation does not have to be the way it is but is contingent upon a working literary-cultural process of identity.

What makes Benedict Anderson's study of "nationness" useful for this study of southernness in American literature from the "pre-" creation of the southern renaissance by the Agrarians to its monumental commemoration in *The History of Southern Literature* (1985) is that Anderson gives reverent place for "nonartefactual" values and realities: "love" (141), self-sacrifice (7, 144), and the possibility of a "metaphysical conception of man" (10, n. 3). *Imagined Communities* oscillates between a skeptical pole—history (sometimes *history*)—and a kind of melancholy acknowledgment of what must not be thought in a post-Foucault age, that there is substance in concepts that have resisted and continue to resist our will to believe in their constructedness: "In an age when it is so common for progressive, cosmopolitan intellectuals (particularly in Europe?) to insist on the near-pathological character of nationalism, its roots in fear and hatred of the Other, and its affinities with racism, it is useful to remind ourselves that nations inspire love, and often profoundly self-sacrificing love. The cultural products of nationalism—poetry, prose fiction, music, plastic arts—show this love very clearly in thousands of different forms and styles" (141).

The following argument concerning southernness in literature and literary history, using mostly prose fiction as "cultural products," should be understood within the arc described by Anderson's extremes of skepticism and love. Anderson's (and much related scholarly) work on the formation of nations and nationalisms shows great influence in southern literary study just now. For example, Barbara Ladd's *Nationalism and the Color Line in George W. Cable, Mark Twain, and William Faulkner* (1996) is founded on lines of inquiry promulgated by Anderson and others working in the field of nation formation. Ladd tends to see the post-Reconstruction United States reimagining itself in largely unsavory nationalistic terms while southern writers strive to preserve something of an earlier, less nationalistic, perhaps less racist, less imperialistic culture (xii). She chose her trio of writers for their common attractions to literary form and to history.

On the one hand there is the passionate skepticism represented by the Robert Penn Warren of the foreword to his "New Version" of *Brother to Dragons*. "Historical sense and poetic sense," Warren writes, "should not, in the end, be contradictory, for if poetry is the little myth we make, history is the

big myth we live, and in our living, constantly remake" (xiii). "Should not"—
but as the tragic conflict of *Brother to Dragons* makes clear, more often than
not actually is. "Poetry" is the name we customarily give to cultural products
that are privileged, by canons of reading and interpretation, to boast the closure, meaning, finishedness that lived history negates. Warren conceived of
Thomas Jefferson as the southern mind affirming of history the same privilege we reserve for poetry. The portico of Monticello, sadly, extended just so
far into the wilderness, and then fell off into chaos. Warren knew that Jefferson's poetic reach far exceeded his historical grasp.

On the other, nonskeptical hand there is Louis D. Rubin, Jr.'s, confident
affirmation in the introduction to *The History of Southern Literature* (1985):
"The facts are that there existed in the past, and there continues to exist today, an entity within American society known as the South, and that for
better or for worse the habit of viewing one's experience in terms of one's relationship to that entity is still a meaningful characteristic of both writers
and readers who are or have been part of it" (5). Rubin's statement, with its
firm and assertive "South" beyond the reach of skepticism, is the foundation
for generations of southern literary study. *Contra* Anderson, Rubin sees historical continuity as nonproblematical, seamless, untroubled by "forgetting,"
and immune from vexing questions of gender, sexuality, race, and class. What
is southern literature will always be recognizable by a formula as constant as
the thing itself, for the South and its history are "facts" and "entities" that
remain intact in and impervious to literary representation.

Such constancy is one of the perennial claims of the South and its literature. When I began teaching southern literature, at the Meridian branch of
Mississippi State University in the spring of 1976, the works of Rubin and
others of like mind were as welcome as runway lights on a midnight approach.
In my first class I used without hesitation Cleanth Brooks's "Southern Literature: The Well-Springs of Its Vitality" as a charm to banish the night. But
the night always returned. The Bulldog van left at 9:30 P.M. sharp, faithfully
retracing its path to Starkville up state route 19 through Philadelphia.
Somewhere near the town the driver, an assistant coach, slowed down
(for this newcomer's benefit, I think) and pointed to a pitch-black road
leading off to the west. "Back there's where they found those boys," he
reminded us. Schwerner, Chaney, and Goodwin—how many Mississippi
ghosts or burning movies later?—still dead, and still powerful. Here was the
problem that Warren struggled with: a historical South vying in the (neo-
phyte academic) mind with a poetic one, neither dismissible as unreal.

Over a couple of months of those nighttime rides up SR19, the question arose: how does the southern literature that I taught so confidently from 7:00–9:30 P.M. accommodate the murder and secret burial of Civil Rights activists, or a thousand other nonloving acts that seemed to have no place in its "vitality"? Was the darkness I always saw surrounding Philadelphia, Mississippi, somehow an element in the wellsprings of southern literary vitality? This book is a long-deferred attempt to answer those questions. It is not an exploration of the problem of evil, however, but a study of the inventions and reinventions of the South in literature as ways of keeping history at bay.

Inventing Southern Literature aims to interrogate the positivist position, represented by Rubin, Brooks, and many others in southern literary criticism and literary history who viewed southern literature as an untroubled rendition of the "facts" of southern life, by retrieving some of what seems lost in the amnesia characterizing the making of the orthodox narrative of identity. To this end, I will begin with a reappraisal of the literary and cultural movement led by the Vanderbilt Agrarians in the late 1920s and punctuated by the publication of their manifesto, *I'll Take My Stand* in 1930 (Twelve Southerners). *Not* finding adequate material causes for the southern renaissance, as historian C. Vann Woodward has implicitly argued in his essay "Why the Southern Renaissance?" (1975), is more important than finding them. The inadequacy of the historical cause reinforces the case for the transcendent one.

Richard King, in *A Southern Renaissance* (1980), has taken an alternate route inward, tracing the (Freudian) mind of the South in its narrative workings from the Agrarian project into the literature-anchored renaissance. King's work ably maps the patterns of repression in the southern renaissance voice. I take instead an outward route, arguing that the Agrarian project was and must be seen as a willed campaign on the part of one elite to establish and control "the South" in a period of intense cultural maneuvering. The principal organizers of *I'll Take My Stand* knew full well there were other "Souths" than the one they touted; they deliberately presented a fabricated South as the one and only real thing. On their left was the near-legendary scrutiny of the Sahara of the Bozart triggered by the Scopes trial in the mid-1920s. On the right was a movement to institutionalize nostalgia for the Old South, expressed in the inauguration of annual spring pilgrimages in several southern towns and lodged in the Agrarian literary imagination as the wholly unacceptable voice of such local-color redoubts as the Poetry Society of South Carolina. The Agrarians picked their shot carefully, aided by accident and conscious planning. The legacy for all who study southern literature, however, is a secure faith that it could not have happened any other way: the Agrarians were prophets speaking an inspired message. Heretical though it may be, my reading of *I'll Take My Stand* strives to position it as a text that in fact might have turned out otherwise.

The Agrarians, however sharp as polemicists, were not literary historians. Literary history, as an academic pursuit, was a mausoleum they imagined in the custody of professional grave wardens, not literary critics such as themselves. Edwin Mims, the chair of the English department at Vanderbilt and their most immediate antagonist, embodied most of what they wished to avoid in their careers. Mims and his ilk were the overseers of a genteel and politely progressive southern literary history. The Agrarians could see themselves in no such role. Mim's identification with New South "progressivism" probably had more to do with the Agrarians (especially Tate) adopting an aggressive "reactionary" stance than the actual conceptual content of either label.

Nevertheless, adapting their inchoate literary history and critical practice to an actual project was vital for the survival of the movement. As the second chapter shows, Richard M. Weaver (1910–63), a self-avowed disciple of the original group (having studied under Ransom at Vanderbilt and Brooks—adjunct to the originals—at Louisiana State University), was the intellectual who made southern culture the basis of his literary and social thought in the years when New Criticism was moving literary criticism away from historical scholarship. Brooks, Warren, and legions of critics and teachers of less renown took to the streets against the historical scholars from the late 1940s through the 1960s. Weaver, working in comparative obscurity (his major book-length study of southern intellectual and literary history was published posthumously in 1963) essentially held southern literary history in escrow until the techniques of New Criticism could be recoupled to its southern subject matter.

The work of Louis D. Rubin, which provided the venue for this recoupling, or may have itself accomplished it, is the subject of the third chapter. Rubin's academic career, beginning in American Studies with Robert Spiller in the late 1940s, indicates a temperament disposed to embed literary criticism in historical circumstance but to privilege the literary text as "best evidence." The omnipresent historical circumstances of Rubin's career (1945–90s) were the desegregation of southern culture and society, and the impress of "theory" upon aesthetic formalism (New Criticism). His literary work shows—in many ways, is—the process by which history was detoxified and recoupled with literary criticism as part of the conservative reaction against desegregation in society and theory in literary study. Not that Louis Rubin would have signed "The Southern Manifesto" (1956). He was a political liberal with culturally conservative tendencies, and that tension makes his work a fascinating record of professional literary negotiation between his felt need to include more history (in this case, race) and the establishment's conservative tendency to recognize only essentialized form.

Following the chapter on Rubin's work is a discussion of the development, over approximately the same period, of classroom anthologies of southern literature. It is intended as the second panel of a diptych, Rubin himself being so influential in the compiling and publishing of nearly all these anthologies that it would be foolish as well as meaningless to try to separate him from their history. Anthologies do not teach southern literature, of course, but they do constitute the primary means by which the paradigmatic modes of understanding the South are promulgated. From *The Library of Southern Literature* (1908–13) to our present moment in a fashionable fin de siècle, the story of the South is recorded in the history of its anthologies. And that history is never concluded: between the writing of this book and its publication, at least two new major anthologies have emerged — one from Oxford University Press and another from W.W. Norton.

Paradigm invention and reinvention do not occur instantaneously, but rather over time and incrementally. As I mentioned earlier, one of the purposes of *Inventing Southern Literature* is to suggest that what we have inherited as this entity need not have been this way. By way of making good on that assertion, I take up at this point in the book three of the most pressing issues arising in southern literary study: construing the African-American male writer as southern; pursuing gender equity by likewise construing the white southern woman writer's tradition(s) as affirming the orthodox idea of southernness; and speculating on the uses and abuses of William Faulkner as our "Major Figure," the Michelangelo around whose achievement a cultural identity can be organized. My argument is frankly adversarial: if the critical thinking supporting any or all of these positions can be shown not to be inevitable — to be reversible, flawed, or simply one among several viable interpretations of the material — then continuing in the orthodox paths becomes, at best, but a partial fulfillment of the critic's and the teacher's responsibility.

The gradual negotiation by which the African-American voice and view were admitted to the southern canon, illustrated in my interpretation of Louis Rubin's work, resulted in a mixed blessing. Admitting Ralph Ellison made Richard Wright's provisional recognition as a writer more important to the social record than to the literary one, for most of Wright's works had been in print before the publication of *Invisible Man* in 1952. If they were recognized later rather than earlier, then the change did not occur in the works but in our ways of or reasons for (or for not) reading them. The Ellison-Irving Howe debate of the 1950s has been overlooked by critics of southern literature anxious to demonstrate liberal bona fides through admission of black southern literature to the canon. Lest this literature might not be fully construed using the southern interpretive paradigm, Ernest Gaines's work is often mentioned as the strong shoulders on which southern literature will be carried to its next phase. Counterreadings of Gaines's works, especially *In My Father's House* (1978) and *A Lesson before Dying* (1993), suggest that Gaines's southern, male, and racialized thematics do not run in the channels carved by the critical consensus for (white) southern literature. When the critical net is widened, to include works such as Raymond Andrews's *Appalachee Red* (1978), the drive to preserve the consensus intact is definitely blunted.

Thinking the African-American male writer into the southern canon is not the only reinvention project underway. The traditional southern canon, the inclusion of Eudora Welty, Katherine Anne Porter, and Caroline Gordon notwithstanding, has not accommodated gender issues comfortably either. Prior to the southern renaissance, as the work of Anne Goodwyn Jones in *Tomorrow Is Another Day: The Woman Writer in the South, 1859–1936* (1981) makes clear, the categories of woman and writer were not automatically thought to coincide. Faulkner, the major figure of the renaissance, left a clear trail of misogyny in his work. The aftershocks have proven serious obstacles: the "feminine" voice seems so clearly at odds with the prototypical southern one as established by Faulkner as to set at odds the visions of both. Balancing readings of representative works by white southern women (Lee Smith's *Oral History* [1983], Josephine Humphreys's *Rich in Love* [1987], and Jill McCorkle's *Tending to Virginia* [1987]) upon the traditional interpretive foundation discloses a precarious redistribution of meaning and weight. As more radically antagonistic works such as Dorothy Allison's *Bastard out of Carolina* (1992) and its burgeoning critical commentary make clear, the interests of southern women writers and the survival of the orthodox canon do not walk hand-in-hand.

The certitude that Faulkner said it all for southern literature has been both benediction and curse. Clearly, without the near-universal acknowledgment of his literary power at the time of the publication of *The Portable Faulkner* (1946) and the bestowal of the Nobel Prize (1950), there would have been much shorter coattails for the southern literature movement. If Faulknerian power could inflate southern literature as a whole, it could also suck the air out of the jar, leaving writers starving for autonomy. Two related chapters in *Inventing Southern Literature* investigate the pros and cons, to Faulkner and to southern literature, of his status as the major figure. One builds on work by John Irwin, Philip Weinstein, Gary Stonum, and others who have been drawn to the absolutely savage self-consuming patterns in Faulkner's life and work. The arguments seem to hinge on the degree of self-awareness that we can posit at any given moment in the writer's life and career. Launching an argument from the premise that all of Faulkner's work can and must be read with attention to his suspicion of that work's efficacy in any other corner of his human existence, I try to develop an appreciation for the irony in the ways (we) southern literary critics and teachers have turned Faulkner inside-out and made of a singularly private man a public writer and literary icon.

That writers in the shadow of Faulkner have been both chilled in the penumbra and motivated to shrug it off is a situation explored in the related chapter on Faulkner's influence. This chapter enlists a host of southern writers—Eudora Welty, Reynolds Price, Barry Hannah, Flannery O'Connor, Peter Taylor, and others—who have, through strategies of irony and patient endurance, made space for themselves in Faulkner's wide and heavy literary shadow.

The conclusion to *Inventing Southern Literature* departs the realm of exclusively literary study for the intersection of that world and the world of cultural politics: the arena in which we perennially wrestle for control of the meanings by which we organize reality. That is, parting words address the ongoing debate on the survivability of the South and the place of literary study in public discourse. As I write, the opinion and editorial page of the Nashville *Tennessean* carries an essay by a Nashville citizen arguing that a local high school should not be compelled to change its mascot from the "Rebels" to something else—unnamed but presumably more palatable culturally and historically. The argument is rousing. "Always remember: America was founded on rebellion. Before we were Americans, we were rebels first." The defense of a high school mascot in Nashville leads the essayist to the debate over the Confederate flag on a southern Statehouse and eventually to a defense of southern history in toto. Less than 5 percent of southerners, in 1861, owned slaves, the *Tennessean* writer claims: "Must we condemn all things touched by slavery?" His answer is, of course, no (Shofner).

As if to prove Robert Penn Warren no less than prophetic in the local as well as the universal, a response to the call to dismiss history comes from a doctoral student in history at Vanderbilt University. His rejoinder, simply summarized, is that history cannot be shouted down in the debate over the meaning of the South (McMichael). Our cultural productions need constant maintenance.

The die-hard southern defender's chief supports in his argument are Alexis de Tocqueville, Lord Acton, and Eugene D. Genovese. Leaving the first two for another engagement, my conclusion focuses on responding to Eugene D. Genovese, not least because the prohistory rejoinder also invokes Genovese — not the later Genovese of conservative reaction but the Marxist and anti-Vietnam historian of the 1960s and 1970s, whose landmark *Roll, Jordan, Roll* (1974) still makes a very big dent in the southern claim to immunity from history. Genovese's recent published works, *The Slaveholders' Dilemma: Freedom and Progress in Southern Conservative Thought, 1820–1860* (1992), *The Southern Tradition: The Achievement and Limitations of an American Conservatism* (1994), and *The Southern Front: History and Politics in the Culture War* (1995), constitute a major conservative response to revisions of southern intellectual and literary history. From his earlier work on the history of southern slavery Genovese has turned to an argument for the separability of southern habits of thought and imagination from the material conditions of southern society. The pro-Rebel voice in the *Tennessean* is heartily confident that the "we" to whom it refers can be rallied under Genovese's more prestigious banner, and that measly fractions of historical circumstance carry no weight when incommensurable "tradition" is on the scales.

Genovese reaches back to the Agrarian stalwarts for the literary component of his battle array, and by relying on such reinforcements he is vulnerable. Returning to the early chapter on the Agrarians, I suggest a reading of their message and practice as culture critics that counters Genovese's assertions of an all-for-one southern identity and a one-for-all southern tradition. Such a debate is neither antiquarian in its parameters nor idly "academic" in promised outcomes. As the dueling opinions in my local newspaper attest, no amount of argument on the nature and usage of the South exhausts our need for it as the vehicle of psychomachia. Considerably more than determining just how many angels can dance on the head of a pin is at stake. Citizens have died in our postmodern decade of simulacra for waving the wrong symbols in the wrong places. My conclusion treats one such case and the project in reactionary southern nationalism perched upon it by the Southern League, a small, self-conscious organization of southern culture warriors who have tried since the early 1990s to direct southern cultural feeling into political action.

Inventing Southern Literature must, ultimately, come down on some side. The classroom where southern literature is taught is one of the most politicized on the campus. Teaching and learning southern literature has ever been political, whether the pursuit required an accounting for the graves of the three civil rights activists in Philadelphia, Mississippi, or something more than witty cocktail-party comment on films like *Ghosts of Mississippi* (1996) or *Rosewood* (1997). Against heavy odds I continue to resist the verdict of Quentin Compson. If one must be born in the South to participate meaningfully in its dialogue, then there is in fact only a monologue. On the other hand, Quentin's roommate is no cultural prize either. Authentic cultural debate in any human community must do what Benedict Anderson suggests: keep the conversation going, and keep it balanced between the artefactual and non-artefactual realities. Understanding the South without attempting to understand the projects that have created, indicted, refurbished, or rebirthed it is impossible. The history of southern literature is not the history of an "entity," of "fact" understood to be within time but not of time. Warren had it right, from the start. The myth and the history feed one another; together they make consciousness a process, and we are in it, body and mind.

INVENTING SOUTHERN
LITERATURE

I

THE SOUTH OF
THE AGRARIANS

Communities are to be distinguished, not
by their falsity/genuineness, but by the
style in which they are imagined.
BENEDICT ANDERSON

Beyond certain professional boundaries, the study of the literary and
intellectual history of the American
South still invites a shadow of skepticism — tired skepticism, but skep-
ticism nonetheless. Either there was no relevant history of either type
there in the first place, or it was all part of a larger and more significant history. Mencken had a belly laugh in "The Sahara of the
Bozart." What literature? What intellect? "You might be a redneck
if..." you thought the South could boast a poet, a symphony orches-
tra, or a drypoint etcher. A slightly older Yankee critic, Henry Adams,
observed moodily in his *Education* (1918, but written earlier) that the
southerners of his acquaintance did not possess intellect; they were
possessed by temperaments (56–60). Consequently, southerners did
not think but rather passed through emotional phases, like the moon
or the weather. Their cultural works (Adams did not mention any)
were therefore devoid of actual content. To be a southerner was to
live a style.

On another hand, there might be no content one could safely con-
fess. Even a defender like U. B. Phillips scarcely made the work of
owning up to the southern mind and its productions any easier: "Gas-
tronomic resource is fostered by the climate, to stimulate appetites
which the hot weather makes languid. Indeed most of the habits of
life are affected. In the tedious heat work is hard, indolence easy;
speech is likely to be slow and somewhat slurred; manners are soft; and
except when tempers are hot, the trend is toward easy-going practices
even among healthy people" (5). You are what you eat and what you
breathe: the southern mind might be well seasoned, but it is thick, like

gumbo. The constructions of social relations undergirding this community were no less viscous than the mind and its intellectual products. According to William Graham Sumner, the social relations of the South (read: white racial supremacy) were mired in the swamp of "folkways" while most of the rest of the enlightened world had won the high ground of "stateways." Phillips was a friend, and Sumner took no cane to southern institutions; yet with friends like these, the South might have been better off with its enemies.

The literary arena had little to offer in defense. George Washington Cable (1844–1925) had objected to certain southern folkways, but a majority in his home region had effectively muffled his criticism with the silent treatment in the 1880s and 1890s. After *The Grandissimes* (1880), a success probably because of its rich evocation of southern folkways, came *Dr. Sevier* (1885) and *John March, Southerner* (1894), assigned to mediocrity probably because of their calls for reform. Abandoning his socially critical themes, Cable opted for romantic escape. Thomas Nelson Page (1853–1922) and Mary Johnston (1870–1936) held sway in that market; their dominance postponed Ellen Glasgow's (1873–1945) call for "blood and irony" in southern literature for, perhaps, decades. In *The History of Southern Literature* Glasgow's work is discussed in "Part III: The Southern Renascence, 1920–1950" even though 1920 was midcareer for her. In other words, Glasgow's critique of the South defers to the literary renaissance. Quentin Compson, then, is the southern defender who gets the credit for stopping up the spout of stereotype, joke, and pseudo-wisdom. In "The Endeavor of Southern Intellectual History," the introduction to *Rethinking the South*, Michael O'Brien argues that most of our professional energies are still largely spent in trying to shut Shreve up. As what follows will show, even with the resolve to ignore Quentin and Shreve, it is next to impossible to talk about the South without them.

The defensive posture is not surprising; anyone who set out to study the mind of the South in the decades of Adams, Mencken, Page, Phillips, and their contemporaries (1890–1930) shouldered a very heavy burden up a very steep hill. Even such encouragement as Miss Rosa Coldfield extends to Quentin has its backlash: "So maybe you will enter the literary profession as so many Southern gentlemen and gentlewomen too are doing now and maybe some day you will remember this and write about it. You will be married then I expect and perhaps your wife will want a new gown or a new chair for the house and you can write this and submit it to the magazines" (Faulkner, *Absalom, Absalom!* 9–10). The William Faulkner who wrote *Absalom, Absalom!* (1936) had no intention of following Rosa Coldfield's advice into literary oblivion with the likes of Page or Johnston. He had Quentin choose suicide instead, giving his survivors in the study of the South our central, agonistic, split-personality model. Quentin swings from sacred memory to profane present, consistently failing to imagine a community save one riven by miscegenation, incest, racial guilt, and shame.

The literary nucleus of the Fugitive-Agrarian brotherhood (John Crowe Ransom, Donald Davidson, Andrew Lytle, Allen Tate, Robert Penn Warren: poet-critics, poet-historians) confronted the fractured process of imagining the South with less ostensible befuddlement than Quentin. They were not as "tragically" damaged as Faulkner's *alter ego,* although Warren seems to have been no stranger to the gut feeling of dividedness and the others surely bore their hurts. Their individual and collective contributions to southern intellectual and literary history have determined the currents followed for most of this century by demarcating before/after, neo-/post-, renaissance/other. So strong and successful has this "style" of imagining been that we seldom question its sources, rapids, submerged snags—the network of assumptions, negotiations, and local interests—that had to be navigated (or ignored) to get us to this point. One current example of the durability of this myth or origin is Joseph Blotner's repetition of it in *Robert Penn Warren: A Biography* (105–06). In an attitude of revision, then, this study takes its starting position. The challenge begins with a reconsideration of a few of the "manifestants" of *I'll Take My Stand.*

As O'Brien observes, apropos of the intellectual history of the South (the enterprise or project of the Fugitive-Agrarians included), "all cultures are provincial; that is, their ideas are indigenously fashioned for local usages" (2). To identify oneself as a provincial, as these inventors did as a matter of course, is not so much to declare a fact as to perform a style. The Agrarian movement was caused less by what, retrospectively, participants like Allen Tate officially remembered their stresses to have been (the whiplash caused by the collision of a traditional culture with a modern one) than by local usages the Agrarians and reenactors of the movement tend to obfuscate.

Like all dedicated elites, the Agrarians more or less manipulated the image of the problem their time and place embodied so that their solution seemed unavoidable. Anthropologists studying such groups interpret these manipulations as typical ritual. "It is only by exaggerating the difference," anthropologist Mary Douglas has written, "between within and without, above and below, male and female, with and against, that a semblance of order is created" (4). Or, as Benedict Anderson observes, "in everything 'natural' there is always something unchosen" that must be pointed out as such (143). Orthodox studies of the Agrarians tend to conclude that these poets and critics did not construct a "semblance of order" but discovered a "natural" order. Nor did they sort the chosen from the unchosen; rather, they saw with prophetic clarity the inherent unity of the South. Southern literary history, claiming the Agrarian group as its root system, has portrayed the founders as defensive rather than aggressive, as acted upon rather than acting, as free from ideological fashioning and inclination rather than steeped in both. Such is not necessarily the case. Perhaps it was not so much "the South" that triggered *I'll Take My Stand* as the presence in the cultural/historical arena of competing "orders" of cultural power that threatened to imagine the South in other ways, ways that would have disenfranchised the Agrarian elite. And they fought back.

The explanation of the threat perceived and the concerted reaction begins with the construction of "the South" in the Agrarian manifesto *I'll Take My Stand* as part of an annus mirabilis, 1930. One version of the story has been told and stylized many times, usually under the assumption that "the South" existed as an object independent of these twelve southern intellects before each had conceived an intention to write and that in all its reality it called them into articulation like a burning bush. The standard argument admits to no local usages to pollute the purity of the work.

In contrast, I propose that the Agrarians produced the South in the same way that all historically indigenous social elites produce ideological realities: out of strategies for seizing and retaining power (cultural, political, sexual, economic, and so on) that are then reproduced as "natural."* Quentin Compson alludes to this always-disappearing stage of the creation of ideological reality when he counters Shreve's intrusion into southern history with the claim, "You cant understand it [the South]. You would have to be born there." According to Quentin's rules, only a southerner can dispute a southerner, and so no dialectic is ever possible. Shreve is a sort of reckless Althusserian, accusing his roommate of being not much more than the "imaginary" created by an arbitrary set of social formations (the South) intent on keeping itself in business. For long stretches in *Absalom, Absalom!* Shreve seems to be correct. Quentin's Faulknerian doom is that he thinks so too.

---

*For this brief discussion of ideology I am using the essay "Ideology and Ideological State Apparatuses (Notes toward an Investigation)" in Louis Althusser's *Essays and Ideology* ([1]–60).

The 1920s seems to have been a propitious time for thinking aloud about the simultaneity of contemplating and producing culture. Karl Mannheim's *Ideology and Utopia* was first published in German in 1929, the crucial year the southern Agrarians worked to assemble and publish their manifesto. Mannheim studies "the sociology of knowledge" rather than its content, and he is especially interested in the formation of intellectual elites, self-formed social groups "whose special task it is to provide an interpretation of the world," an ideology, in the midst of and for a larger cultural group from which they (the elite) will then draw off power (10). Mannheim's work provides useful general guidelines for rethinking the formation of "the South's" history by the Agrarian elite: "This type of thought [that of professional intellectual elites] does not arise primarily from the struggle with concrete problems of life, nor from trial and error, nor from experiences in mastering nature and society, but rather much more from its own need for systematization, which always refers the facts which emerge in the religious as well as in other spheres of life back to given traditional and intellectually uncontrolled premises" (11).

The survival in power of such a particular group takes precedence over empirical data; cultural power, not "the search for truth," is the primary motivation for intellectual production. The group that succeeds in naming the system therefore controls those who seek entrance to or maintenance within it. The group that establishes the most resilient "traditional and intellectually uncontrolled premises" wins the sweepstakes. In post-Bozart free-fall, the Agrarians were one of several elites (in the South and in the United States at large) seeking to make their system the template for a regional or national culture. This was a period of culture wars perhaps as fierce as our own, and "the South" was as engaged then as it is now.

"In the battle of ideas," wrote Irving Babbitt, chief of a rival elite, archenemy of the first twentieth-century cadre of southern intellectuals, "as in other forms of warfare, the advantage is on the side of those who take the offensive" (44). Babbitt and his Humanist allies (especially Norman Foerster and Paul Elmer More) had seized the advantage in a battle of ideas that could, in Foerster's clarion call, define the "needs of America as the dominant world power and adequate model of civilization in the twentieth century" (Foerster xvi). The campaign of the Humanists, fusing ancient Greek, Confucian, and Christian philosophies against romantic naturalism percolating below in human instinct, and in enthused, revealed religion above, had made great progress in the public mind of the 1920s while those who would take arms against it were writing poetry and publishing *The Fugitive*. In May 1930 three thousand people attended a discussion of the New Humanism in Carnegie Hall (Hoeveler 25).

Donald Davidson, at Yaddo in upstate New York almost a year earlier, heard rumors of the Humanist offensive. He wrote to John Crowe Ransom with the breathless urgency of a lookout: "It seems that More, Babbitt, and other Humanists are about to bring out a symposium on Humanism in America....and this is expected to give their movement a concrete source to expand from" (5 July 1929). Davidson had seen only a part of the enemy offensive. *Humanism and America: Essays on the Outlook of Modern Civilization,* edited by Foerster, would be published in 1930, along with a counterpunch: *The Critique of Humanism: A Symposium,* edited by C. Hartley Grattan. Work on an Agrarian symposium, as yet untitled, had not progressed far enough to get in on the first round. Allen Tate, the driving force, was in France on a Guggenheim Foundation fellowship. Davidson feared that the advantage of surprise had been lost, but he saw another southern quality that, if exploited, might even the contest by exaggerating differences between two similar, conservative camps: "[T]he lack of these Humanists is their failure to have intimate touch, to be really a coherent body. They can only write and hope vaguely, whereas we, though constituting a group of less majestic proportions, really form a unit of mutual understanding and actively are in touch with a specific Cause" (5 July 1929). Davidson was a culture warrior, if nothing else, and his report from the frontier bears his distinctive mark of attack, attack, attack. If Michael Hill is correct in his thesis that the southern habit of warfare owes its character to Celtic forebears with a penchant for direct, frontal, furious assault upon more numerous and better-equipped foes, then Davidson is the type of the southern laird (*Celtic* 173–81 passim).

Davidson's reconnaissance captures the southern intellectual movement early in its formation as concerned chiefly with "its own need for systematization" in a struggle between very similar intellectual elites for cultural advantage. Both groups, for instance, downgraded romanticism as a respectable cultural and literary era, and both held religion at arm's length. "Styling," then, grew in importance. Mannheim's study of intellectual elites had led him to generalize in "The Third Form of the Utopian Mentality: The Conservative Idea," a chapter in *Ideology and Utopia,* that the conservative idea of Utopia seldom rises to the surface unless and until pushed. "Goaded on by opposing theories," he writes, "conservative mentality discovers its *idea* only *ex post facto*" (230; emphasis in original). The Agrarian-defined South, early in this process of developing socially formed ideologies, appears as the Cause because it is that historically resonant style that distinguishes it from a movement basically similar but run by others. Here is an indication of the workings of local usages to which O'Brien refers. Both the Humanists and the inchoate group of southern reactionaries in Nashville were "looking for a new set of controlling ideas capable of restoring value to human existence" (Foerster vi). Each group needed an Other against which to strike differences. For the Agrarians, the Humanists were the first such antagonist.

There was a second threat, however, one closer to home, that pressed the Agrarian group to clarify its rules of warfare and the idea of the South around which it would rally. Howard Mumford Jones, then a professor of English at the University of North Carolina, Chapel Hill, had approached both Davidson and Ransom in the summer of 1929 for advice and contributions to a symposium he proposed to edit for the University of North Carolina Press. In nearly identical letters to both Ransom and Davidson (25 July 1929), Jones described the proposed volume and sought their comment and participation. Davidson eventually agreed; Ransom did not. The working title was "Culture below the Potomac," a phrase reminiscent of Mencken's prejudicial positioning, in "The Sahara of the Bozart," of Dixie below the waistline of cultural propriety. Although Jones and Davidson had corresponded cordially, and although Davidson eventually wrote an essay on trends in modern southern literature for the volume (published as *Culture in the South* [1934] with W. T. Couch as editor), there was little more than formal politeness between the two men and their camps. Jones was seen as too "progressive" in his own views, as were his associates. In a letter to Tate, Davidson showed the other face of the Agrarian movement, its tendency to exclusiveness and internal systematization:

> But I also enclose a copy of a letter from Howard Mumford Jones which just reached me and is self-explanatory. It upset me!
>
> You will see, after reading it, what is before us. If Jones, whom I like and respect in many ways, put his scheme on foot, the "progressive" note will be accented very much, I greatly fear. You can imagine, for instance, what a man like [Howard] Odum would have to say about the negro question. For us, the issue is: Will we let the Progressives (some of whom are "immigrant" Southerners) capture the field and walk off with public opinion [?] But they have great strength on their side — prestige, resources, etc. They can get eminent contributors. They may even cut the ground out from under us. (29 July 1929; Fain and Young 228)

The rhetoric of battle, Davidson's favorite, suggests that this southern true believer was intent upon "exaggerating difference" in order to establish a South over which he and not some carpetbagger like Jones or sociologist like Odum would hold control. Although the progressive southern symposium was delayed several years, the threat of it triggered in Davidson a reaction to control and define the South in the process of cultural contest. Tate, still in France, was not blasé either. He wrote Davidson agreeing that Jones was indeed a Yankee who had adopted "southernism as a means to academic preferment" and added that he (Tate) was full of energy for the southern cause (10 August 1929; in Fain and Young 231).

With a sense of arriving belatedly on the field, Davidson, Ransom, and Tate rushed *I'll Take My Stand* to completion. With latter-day Puritans like Babbitt to the right of them and carpetbaggers like Jones and racial "progressives" like Odum to the left, there was little room to maneuver. So much the better. Although close quarters bequeathed to the southern intellectual elite a defensiveness toward foes and a strictness with their own comrades in arms, a pantheon of Confederate heroes was ready-at-arms for support. Snide hostility toward Mencken's tirade in "The Sahara of the Bozart" in 1917 had metamorphosed by 1930 into a formidable and systematized intellectual and cultural counterattack.

Tate's calls for strictness in the ranks were due in large part to his sense of being outnumbered and outhustled. In any case, the crisis as it appeared late in 1929 was fortuitous. He had made his debut as an international literary and cultural critic in T. S. Eliot's *Criterion* (a journal generally friendly to Babbitt, More, and their crowd) in July 1929 with an attack on the philosophy of the New Humanists, "Humanism and Naturalism." Tate's charge against Babbitt and his followers was that their thought lacked "a living center of judgment and feeling" (179). "Until this center is found," Tate continued, "and not pieced together eclectically at the surface, humanism is an attempt to do mechanically—that is, naturalistically—what should be done morally" (180). Had Tate known Mannheim's work, he might have seen his own image in it. Mannheim proposes that the conservative critique of the so-called liberal idea will charge that the latter lacks foundation, is "mere opinion," and that by contrast the conservative idea is "rooted in and express[es] itself concretely in the living reality of the here and now" (232). The crucial assumptions underpinning Tate's thought, assumptions he injected into the full southern ideology as it took form under the impress of his intellect, were that the center was an entity to be "found"—"present in this world" (232)—and that false prophets were to be tarred with the charge that their values were "pieced together," which is to say, man-made.

These were not ideas that Tate had formed on his own. Ransom, his elder and professor, had been developing such a cultural critique in his own theology-based attack on the modern age, *God without Thunder*, also published in

1930. Two major elements of the southern manifesto come from Ransom's argument into Tate's and then into the main current of orthodox southern thought: the assertion that the South as cultural ideal is apprehended with the same human faculties with which religion is acknowledged and the notion that intellectual, critical thought proceeds through binary oppositions. The idea is that only two positions are possible in any moment of debate or inquiry — the one you hold and its opposite. Compromise is bad faith, or "impurity," to return to anthropologist Mary Douglas's terminology.

Ransom's term for the content, structure, and means of apprehending the message or fact of religion was "myth." His definition in *God without Thunder* is cumulative, illuminating in its progress the binary, cleaving habit of his thought — a habit he passed on in his two contributions to *I'll Take My Stand*, "Statement of Principles" and "Reconstructed but Unregenerate."

"Religious doctrines," he wrote, "are embodied in myths, and myths attempt to express truths which are not accessible to science" (11–12). As the definition of myth is launched, so is the cleaving: religion *or* science. Then Ransom adds, by stages, more culturally specific elements: "Myths are construed very simply by the hard Occidental mind: they are lies. It is supposed that everything that is written in serious prose ought to be historical or scientific; that is, devoted either to authenticated facts or to sober generalizations about these facts. Myths, like fairy tales, like poems, are neither. They are therefore absurd" (55). So saith the modern mind, according to Ransom. But the older "Hebraic, oriental, symbolistic" mind sees knowledge differently. This rival mind predates the "Occidental, scientific, modern, and anthropological [i.e., man-centered]" mind and is not indentured to history or to science (55–57). Imagining, then, a mind prior to (historically) the one in which he himself is thinking, Ransom imagines a self and a community (the South) inherently stymied and conflicted. In his own poetry, images and techniques of blocking and countervailing movement are plentiful. "Old Mansion," for example, narrates a situation of denied admission to a symbolic structure, and "Captain Carpenter" pits rollicking, ballad style against a serious theme — the dismembering of tradition.

At this point in his seminal essay Ransom attacks history as the language of the modern usurper of religion. What has been usurped, to allude to Ransom's title, is God's "thunder," His power and meaning. Modern man has quieted it by seeing the human record of existence from his own point of view, or, anthropologically: "Let us define history as strictly as we can... The primary role of the historian is to establish the 'facts'... His effort was always to get as near to an eye-witness account as he could. And this permits us to define what fact meant to Herodotus, and what it has meant to historians ever since. A fact for him was evidently the impression of an event which he could establish as having been registered upon the senses of an honest and sound observer. . . . *Fact is the sensible event*" (Ransom 57–58; emphasis in original). Then the historian forsook his "primary role," Ransom continues, and succumbed to the method of science. He gave up "sensible event" and embraced "law" and "principle" as constituents of an interpretive system. System then turned miracles—Jonah, Joshua, the Virgin Birth—into metaphors. Thus was myth sold down the river of history: "The myth of an object is its proper name, private, unique, untranslatable, overflowing, of a demonic energy that cannot be reduced by the poverty of the class-concept [not social class, but "class" in the sense of sorting by affinity]. The myth of an event is a story, which invests the natural with a supernatural background, and with a more-than-historical history" (66–67). With a simple rotation of focus, South becomes myth, and Ransom's quarrel with modern apostasy becomes the foundation of his imagining of the South. Anderson argues a similar line when he concludes that much "nationalist imagining" bears "a strong affinity with religious imagining" (10).

Ransom held forth unapologetically for miracles, for the subordination of human reason to faith, for Anglicanism as the only approved sect, and against Paul Elmer More as being too metaphorical and secular in his understanding of Christianity. This position thrilled one of his students at Vanderbilt, Richard Weaver, whose filtering of Ransom's message through southern matter is the subject of the next chapter.

Ransom's crucial thinking on the South, however, is the focus of the present chapter, and it germinates here, in a devotion to religion so strong that he took "fundamentalism" (despite his own Anglican proclivities) as right and proper. His thinking on the betrayal of history to science is crucial as well, for the meaning and function of "history" in the literary history of the South is the central question. Ransom achieved these positions by a ruthless process of excluding one term in each juxtaposition of opposites. Religion is set opposite secular, social "economics" (118), fundamentalism against modern cultural sophistication (97ff.), love against lust in [hetero]sexual relationships (140). The pattern is so strong that it spills over into his essays in *I'll Take My Stand*: European (southern) against American, traditional against modern, industrial against agrarian, and so on. His pattern of inquiry leaves no middle ground, no site for the miscegenation of ideas, no compromises.

More than most of his comrades in the southern reactionary movement, Tate absorbed Ransom's habits of thought, but he assimilated them to a mind in the late 1920s and 1930s not as ready to acknowledge the empirical fact of miracles or to prescribe a particular religious denomination as the antidote to the spiritual malaise. Tate was more deeply saturated in the century of the malaise than his professor, and apt to accept the murky condition of poised opposites rather than Ransom's definitive resolutions. Tate knew that in thinking about the One, the center, he could not also be sure it was safely outside (his very own) human thought. The ironies of this fix seem to have invigorated him intellectually. Not until his conversion to Roman Catholicism in 1950, perhaps, was Tate sure that the object of his belief was indeed prior to and beyond human thought and construction. The act of violence he called for in "Remarks on the Southern Religion" (his contribution to *I'll Take My Stand*, and in several ways his homage to *God without Thunder*) is an act of intellectual violence — a sort of self-maiming: one simply o'er-leaped the limits of human thought, sure in faith of landing in the moral center. The South was Tate's temporary center until he found another (Roman Catholicism) he could believe to be absolute.

For Davidson and his friends back home in 1929–30, Tate had a full-scale plan of battle worthy of Stonewall Jackson, whose biography he had written a few years earlier. He proposed the "formation of a society, or an academy of southern positive reactionaries made up at first of people of our own group," the recruitment of an auxiliary of "inactive" members from professional classes outside academia, a constitution that "should set forth, under our leading idea, a complete social, philosophical, literary, economic, and religious system," and an eventual publication to promulgate the group's agenda (Fain and Young 229–30). It is tantalizing to imagine what Tate would have thought of the Southern League, founded in 1994, for just such purposes.

Tate's zeal, however, was not for the second coming of the South in concrete historical terms, for his own nuanced self-consciousness led him to the precipice of suspecting that his own thought was a function of the historical circumstances it strove to surmount. There had been hints a few years earlier in letters he and Davidson had exchanged about Tate's long poem "Ode to the Confederate Dead." Davidson had complained, "Your elegy is not for the Confederate dead, but for your own dead emotion, or mine (you think)" (Fain and Young 186). Tate did not disagree: "My attempt is to see the present from the past, yet remain immersed in the present and committed to it.

I think it is suicide to do anything else" (Fain and Young 189). It is certainly living on the edge to split oneself into the present and the past, as the Quentin of *Absalom, Absalom!* will attest. Tate, though, had the energizing dilemma he needed. The program he suggested for the Agrarians would likewise be divided in its structure.

Mannheim segregates liberal and conservative along the lines of reason: the liberal position is aligned to an idea "rationally conjured up . . . as the best among a number of possibilities" while the conservatives hold that their controlling idea has "unfolded itself in the collective creations of the community . . . as an inner form" (233). Tate's plan would accomplish the latter by an act of rational conjuring: "[T]his program would create an intellectual situation interior to the South. I underscore it because, to me, it contains the heart of the matter" (Fain and Young 230). Tate, in a subtle and breath-taking act of thought, would create his and the South's own Mind *and* create the reality-sense of its prior existence, well before thought and naming defined it. As Lewis P. Simpson and others have argued, he almost got away with it.

Tate also supplied a tentative table of contents for the Agrarian book; his controlling idea was that the Agrarians could recoup through intense coherence what they stood to lose through tardiness. Like Stonewall, he might pull off a lightning march and salvage the battle. Nothing less than cultural survival was at stake: "for this end we must have a certain discipline; we must crush minor differences of doctrine under a single idea" (Fain and Young 230).

The "single idea" and the "intellectually uncontrolled premises" were never specifically named — "you couldn't understand it; you would have to be born there." A few months later, as he became more familiar with the character of Davidson's belief in the single idea, Tate clarified and retreated from the crusading rhetoric and the notion of implied belief:

> There is one feature of our movement that calls for comment. We are not in the least divided, but we exhibit two sorts of minds. You and Andrew [Lytle] seem to constitute one sort — the belief in the eventual success, in the practical sense, of the movement. The other mind is that of Ransom and Warren and myself. I gather that Ransom agrees with me that the issue on the plane of action is uncertain. At least I am wholly sceptical on that point; but the scepticism is one of hoping to be convinced, not by standing aside to watch the spectacle, but by exerting myself. In other words, I believe that there is enough value to satisfy me in the affirmation, in all its consequences, including action, of value. If other goods proceed from that, all the better. My position is that since I see the value, I am morally obligated to affirm it. That sounds pretty grand, but I can think of no other phrase. (Fain and Young 240–41)

Tate could see the practical and the myth; in his mind the South ran on both tracks, was party to both kinds of discourse, was both a priori constant of discourse and manipulated image. He played the agnostic role; he said his prayers in case a God happened to exist after all. As he acknowledged to Davidson, his position was neither easy to explain nor readily susceptible of quick and fervent belief. His position lay somewhere between the hallowed silence of the Davidsonian view and the concrete historical view of the progressives. Tate tried to explain the differences and to hold them in intellectual tension in his essay for *I'll Take My Stand*. In *Who Owns America?*, the sequel to the Agrarian volume (published in 1936 with Herbert Agar), Tate tried more explicitly to turn the concrete-historical, property and exchange, into the metaphysical; by his own admission, he failed (Fain and Young 295).

Whereas the "progressives" (for example, most of the contributors to *Culture in the South*) habitually described the South in objective terms—as distribution of income, agricultural zones, races and classes, census and tax figures—and (as Mannheim had also observed) cherished the future as the time in which the meaning of social experience could and would be perfected, the Agrarians, having invented themselves as "positive reactionaries," clung to their belief in the past: "Consequently not only is [conservative utopian] attention turned to the past and the attempt made to rescue it from oblivion, but the presentness and immediacy of the whole past becomes an actual experience" (235).

For example, essays that eventually appeared in *Culture in the South* consistently positioned the south (as it were, deliberately lowercased) as a historical phenomenon like many others; the formulation "culture in the south" supposed that "south" had little or nothing to do with "culture" itself, as the individual blossom has no necessary claim to the butterfly that lands on it. In his preface to the volume of thirty-one essays, William Terry Couch, who had replaced Jones, set the tone for the whole volume by taking for granted that "the fundamental issues in southern life . . . are much the same as elsewhere" (vii). The Agrarians absorbed criticism of their own volume by consoling themselves that those on the other side had utterly missed the "immanent, intrinsic value" (236–37) of the South by following the things of this world.

Rupert Vance's essay, for example, treats the South as a set of circumstances susceptible of improvement by "regional planning" (Couch 38) and Broadus Mitchell, the bete noire of Davidson (who could think of no more appropriate punishment for him than "hanging" [Fain and Young 289]), made the bold assertion that "[o]ur religion, letters, laws, arts, social amenities, and race relations are all functions of our economic life" (Couch 80). Reductive statements such as these understandably made the Agrarians disinclined to attribute much merit to their antagonists' volume or the agenda on which it was built.

Howard Mumford Jones, who surrendered "Culture below the Potomac" when he moved from Chapel Hill to Ann Arbor in 1930, had already taken opposing intellectual and literary ground, a few months before the Agrarian manifesto appeared, in an essay in Stringfellow Barr's *Virginia Quarterly Review*, "Is There a Southern Renaissance?" (April 1930). His answer to the question of his title was negative, but his means of arguing to the verdict are more revealing, perhaps, than the verdict itself. Jones contrasts the theological underpinnings of the northern (that is, puritan) literary culture and those of the South. He can find no evidence that the South could ever come up with a cultural renaissance since it could not match the vigorous intellectual life created by generations of New England Puritans from Bradford to Emerson. And in a subsequent essay, "The Future of Southern Culture," Jones faintly praised "the neo-Confederate wing" (154) of southern intellectuals for the power of their manifesto, yet he held their feet to the fire of concrete historical circumstances by consistently injecting Negro slavery, the continuing race problem, and such real-life conditions as single-crop agriculture into their utopia. By such indirect means, history and race gradually became functioning synonyms in southern discourse.

It was easier to distance the Agrarian South from charges of fascism than, in the longer run, to pull away from race. Jones enlisted under Stringfellow Barr's critical banner: "the apotheosis of the hoe" was a pretty myth but left out too much history for intellectual safety. The Agrarian intellectuals were not very effective in rebuttal, for they were loath to submit their imagining to analytical discourse. Davidson's negotiations with Jones over his essay for the University of North Carolina volume, "The Trend of Literature: A Partisan View," provide a case in point. Jones accepted Davidson's work before he left the project to Couch, but he had some reservations: "My main — indeed, my only — quarrel with it is that I seem to go around in a circle since you nowhere explicitly state what it is you mean by the southern quality of Southern literature" (Jones to Davidson, 7 October 1930). Davidson stood fast, refusing to be drawn into the trap of definition; that trap would force him to lower (as he saw it) southernness to the level of historical corroboration. His essay as published is quite certain what is not southern about the literature under survey: social satire, propaganda, Faulknerian decadence, Cabellian whimsy. He is opaque as to what is southern: "It would be hard to pick out definitely southern characteristics in any given number of southern poets, but it would be equally hard to prove that they are un-southern" ("Trend" 207) The "immanent and intrinsic" would be known to initiates, those born into the knowledge, and would confound those outside the circle. To explain southernness, Davidson argued, "would require a second essay" (Davidson to Jones, 21 October 1930), a project he had no intention of undertaking. If Jones would play the part of Shreve, Davidson would oblige by acting Quentin.

As steadfastly as Davidson guarded the sanctuary, Warren raised a ruckus in it. From the distance of England, where he was a Rhodes Scholar, he broke ranks. Davidson's reaction to "The Briar Patch," Warren's essay for *I'll Take My Stand,* shows just how radically Warren's break seemed to be. Davidson was so troubled that his cry of objection to Tate deserves lengthy quotation:

> I'm sending you herewith — as I should have done before this — Red's essay. Will you read it and give your frank opinion of it? At first, after reading it hastily, I had thought it would be quite all right, though not a very strong essay. Since reading it this morning again, very carefully, and after having gone through Lanier's and Lytle's fine pieces, I was rather shocked with Red's essay. It hardly seems worthy of Red, or worthy of the subject. And it certainly is not very closely related to the main theme of our book. It goes off at a tangent to discuss the negro [sic] problem in general (which, I take it, is not our main concern in the book), and it makes only two or three points that bear on our principles at all. Furthermore, the ideas advanced about the negro don't seem to chime with our ideas as I understand them. Behind the essay, too, are implications which I am sure we don't accept — they are "progressive" implications with a pretty strong smack of latter-day sociology. Furthermore, I think there are some things that would irritate and dismay the very Southern people to whom we are appealing. (Have made certain changes in Red's wording here and there.)
>
> I simply can't understand what Red is after here. It doesn't sound like Red at all — at least not the Red Warren I know. The very language, the catchwords, don't seem to fit. I am almost inclined to doubt whether RED ACTUALLY WROTE THIS ESSAY! (21 July 1930; Fain and Young 250–52)

It is, perhaps, too easy to focus exclusively on Warren's very moderate views on racial reform as the detonator for Davidson's explosion. Even in terms of his 1930s milieu, Warren was cautious, moderate-to-conservative, antiradical, and "gradualist." Still, his understanding of "the negro problem" was historical, far from Tate's preference for relegating it to the frame of cultural "image." Moreover, Warren's analysis directly challenged the southern utopian ideology that Tate, Ransom, and Davidson had agreed to impose on the ranks. "If the Southern white man feels that the Agrarian life has a certain irreplaceable value in his society, and if he hopes to maintain its integrity in the face of industrialism or its dignity in the face of agricultural depression [the other eleven could not have failed to feel themselves directly addressed], he must find a place for the negro in his scheme" ("Briar" 263). And Warren left no doubt that the place to be found must be real, that is, found within and made of economic, political, legal, and historical circumstances. He went so far as to suggest that organized labor and a planned economy might offer some positive solutions (258–60).

These "'progressive' implications with a pretty strong smack of latter-day sociology" troubled the orthodox Agrarian mind as much or more than race. Fain and Young, however, do not include Tate's response to Davidson — if one exists. Warren had run the blockade against history, had mixed the either/or that Ransom had declared pure and impure. Such, though, is Warren's way of thinking, and it gives his fiction and poetry, his essays (*Segregation: The Inner Conflict of the South* [1956]), and his American Literature anthology a bite and tension that the orthodox line unfortunately lacks. The orthodox line was, however, the first to issue from the main concern of *I'll Take My Stand*. Warren's roiling lay dormant.

No "second essay" defining southernness was ever undertaken, as such, by any of the founding generation of the southern intellectual elite, the Agrarians. For various reasons, those in positions to do the work passed it by. Ransom moved into literary theory. Tate went back to poetry and criticism. Warren wrote poems, novels, and criticism; taught at various universities; and developed New Criticism with Cleanth Brooks along practical lines in such projects as the *Southern Review* and *Understanding Fiction*. Tate was temperamentally suited, perhaps, to a study of the intellectual situation interior to the South, since he had striven to create one, but he was also less anxious to search the historical record for the traces of one that might have preceded his entrance into the history. He could, after all, tolerate only one southern writer of the nineteenth century — Edgar Allan Poe — and Poe was not the right foundation for much of a culture beyond himself. The work of constructing this precursor intellectual and literary culture waited for Richard M. Weaver in the next generation.

II

RICHARD WEAVER AND THE OUTLINE OF SOUTHERN LITERARY HISTORY

Rather, the literati were adepts, strategic strata in a cosmological hierarchy of which the apex was divine.
BENEDICT ANDERSON

When Richard M. Weaver (1910–63) came to Vanderbilt University for a master's degree in 1932 (he had applied, without success, for a fellowship to the University of North Carolina at Chapel Hill), the fervor of the Agrarian movement was beginning to ebb. The soldiers in the Cause were occupied with thoughts of life after crisis. Tate, the envy of his friend Davidson, had always been able to turn down the polemic and turn up poetry in an instant. That flexibility now became a goal of Davidson's: "And how I do envy you that you can still turn to poetry, again and again, and let all your feelings out; while I remain stopped-up, raging speechlessly when I should be raging in verse" (Fain and Young 262). Personal and professional hardships dogged Davidson's tracks. Soon he became disenchanted with the movement because it seemed to be the cause of so many personal disappointments: "We like to think of ourselves as crusaders; in our minds' eye, we can see ourselves doing a kind of Pickett's charge against industrial breastworks, only a successful charge this time. But we don't actually do the crusading" (Fain and Young 276).

By 1937 Davidson longed to get back to "the literary side" of intellectual work (Fain and Young 302). Pseudo-Confederates like Couch appeared to have won the field. Ransom, always too cool and intellectually distant for Davidson's taste, had discontinued his call (in "Land!") for "an agrarian agitation," direct political action in the name of the Cause. He was on the brink of moving to Kenyon College and into literary criticism, aiming his ruthless binary thinking at "pure and impure poetry" ("Poets without Laurels") and more or less trading in the ontological constant "South" for its successor, "Literature." Dissatisfaction with the way Vanderbilt's administration had managed negotiations with Ransom left Davidson with a sense of estrangement from his own institution. For various reasons, but with one general result, the core of the first generation of Agrarian intellectuals passed up the challenge to undertake a southern literary history. For the time being, the cause of literature was not the cause of southern literature.

The burdens of the Agrarian cause had become unbearably onerous when Seward Collins, whose *American Review* had served as a pulpit for Agrarian essayists, proclaimed in an interview with Grace Lumpkin, "Yes, I am a fascist," and dug the group grave even deeper by stating that both Jews and Negroes were troublemakers who deserved racial segregation (Lumpkin, [3]). Even Tate, as much as he felt the practical need for an organ of public discourse, wanted to put some distance between the Cause and Collins, so he cut *American Review* loose. But the damage had been done. What fatigue and low professional morale had not weakened in the Agrarian intellectual fiber, the loose lips of Seward Collins had scuttled. By the latter 1930s the southern intellectual movement faced a more formidable opponent than Mencken's derision: it was in the pits of political incorrectness. Franklin Delano Roosevelt had proclaimed the South America's number one economic problem in 1938, and very few turned to the now-dispersed Agrarians for coaching in how to raise the ranking. Erskine Caldwell had "made" the South on stage and in his fiction. The "decadent" Faulkner of the 1930s helped push the South even deeper into imagined ill-repute with novels like *Sanctuary* (1932) and *Light in August* (1936); critics named him the founder and first graduate of "The School of Cruelty." Margaret Mitchell's "epic romance" closed out the decade with a return to the Old South in all its ruffles and flounces.

Richard Weaver took up the Agrarian heritage under such conditions. Like most of the Agrarian initiates, Weaver—ultimately—cared less for the many facts of history than he did for the unifying, religious myth he saw at the foundation of Western civilization. Unlike the previous generation, however, he knew more of the actual intellectual and literary history of the South prior to the twentieth century. While they could profess literature, Weaver could profess literary history. Unlike his elders, Weaver was neither poet, novelist, nor literary critic. Granting his substantial work in literary and intellectual history, Weaver was a rhetorician who saw his mission on the frontiers of philosophy; debate was his way of life. As Karl Mannheim had defined the terms, Weaver was a conservative ideologue, and his most important work in this vocation was to adapt the undone, inchoate literary-historical project of his "fathers" to the circumstances of history—a history he saw as damaged by advanced empirical rationalism. Mannheim's words describe the gist of Weaver's work: "Conservative experience merges the spirit, which at one time came upon us from beyond and to which we gave expression, with what already is, allowing that to become objective, to expand in all dimensions, and thereby endowing every event with an immanent, intrinsic value" (236–37). In Weaver's conservative philosophy, "spirit," which he saw as the immanence of transcendental value in the material world, came upon human experience in a series of transubstantiating moments, most recently in the American South. This merging of spirit "with what already is" lasted for a time and then was destroyed by overwhelming material, historical forces. In the case of the South, the catastrophe of the Civil War was to be seen as the reinstatement of history. The immanent and intrinsic value conferred upon history, however, had not been entirely obliterated by the return of circumstances. It had been driven deep into Mind, where it existed as a "metaphysical dream." It was this dream or idea that projected "consequences" into the menu of human action. Weaver did not allow the possibility that this interaction is reciprocal, that these wished-for consequences generated ideas, one of them being "the South" that he invented in his literary-historical work.

Weaver was the extractor of this dream; if it could be thought of as an ore, then he refined it and forged it into weapons with which to battle the illegitimate victors—false prophets of what, in *Ideas Have Consequences* (1948), he called "hysterical optimism" in the goodness of man and the perfectibility of his projects (10). In public policy, the miscreants derive their postwar energy from the New Deal, seen as an assault on "the last metaphysical right"—to own property autonomously. In diplomacy, they are the supporters of such internationalist ideas as the United Nations, seen as projects seeking to destroy the organicism of local community. Philosophically, Weaver was a legitimate descendant of the original Agrarian brethren.

From the generation of the fathers in the late 1920s and 1930s to Richard Weaver in the 1940s until his death in 1963, the work of Agrarian southern intellectuals was to lift the South out of what Mannheim had called the "concrete problems of life" (where Shreve's improvisatory mode of explanation seems as good as any other stab at meaning) and return it (in Weaver's words) to the "ceremony of innocence ... that clearness of vision and knowledge of form which enables us to sense ... what is alien or destructive, what does not comport with our moral ambition" (11). Lewis P. Simpson, sympathetic with Weaver's Voegelinian desire for the first unity, and skeptical, at the same time, that such a unity was/is ever available to mortal man, recognized Weaver's act of thought in language that connects Weaver's project to Ransom's: "In fiction and in poetry — in poetry in the most complete signification of the term — a vision of the South had emerged which defined the meaning of the history of the South more fundamentally than reasoned discourse has the capacity to do" ("South" xvi) . In Weaver's work, the process by which vision cast out history in the discourse of the South was deliberate. Ransom had gestured toward the objective in such works as God without Thunder and his southern essays. Weaver was of a more pugnacious temperament. With no poetry or fiction to write, he was unencumbered. His rhetorical strategy was intentional, for Weaver recuperated several of the significant themes and tropes of the argument of I'll Take My Stand and used the general program of that symposium on specific political and cultural "problems." Unlike the original Twelve, who had learned the hard way to dislike confrontation (drawing or losing so many public encounters), Weaver the debater sought clashes deliberately.

Like Paul following the Messiah, Weaver was an apostle too late for the original calling. I'll Take My Stand had been planned, written, and published while he was an undergraduate at the University of Kentucky (1928–32) and still, by his own account, under the baleful heresy of progressive, liberal utopians — what Mannheim, in his scheme, calls "The Liberal-Humanitarian Idea" (219–29). Briefly, this utopian ideal is genealogically rooted in the bourgeois rebellion against feudal and clerical restrictions on self-knowledge, self-fulfillment, and thought generally associated with the Middle Ages. In many historical reconstructions (including Weaver's), this humanitarian order deposed its "natural" and unified precursor in the fourteenth century when Baconian realism overtook Thomistic "logical realism." William of Occam was the chief, premodern Jack the Ripper; nominalism was his weapon of choice. From Occam it was a clear but downward path to Cartesians, Darwinians, psychoanalysts, and finally communists (1–17). Weaver, entering the public arena during World War II, saw Stalinist communists as the ultimate legacy of the bourgeois-inspired desertion of Thomistic universals (*Ideas* 9). As a consequence of the triumph of deracination under the hegemony of empirical rationalism, mankind had been slouching to the brink of disintegration for five centuries. It had been a slow trip, but Weaver was convinced (as is Eugene Genovese in the 1990s; see the conclusion to this book) that we have finally arrived. A return to the few, universal propositions of a classical culture was needed, Weaver believed. He saw the American South as this cultural salvation, and he invented — as a consequence of this idea — its literary-intellectual history accordingly.

In his twenties, after the crash of the stock market, Weaver lived by the false creed of liberalism, he later confessed. Such delusions, he implies in his memoir, "Up from Liberalism," were natural. The national economic and social structures had been shaken by the Great Depression, and academic men flocked to the new political correctness: "science, liberalism, and equalitarianism" (22). This was, as the Paul of the Letters might have called it, the philosophy of the age, promulgated in classrooms, textbooks, lectures, and essays. Not much has changed in seventy years; a conservative faction still believes media and academia to be the enclave of left-liberal bias. Weaver looked back on this philosophy as the used-up flotsam of Humanism, and like Tate before him he made his debut, of sorts, in his master's thesis under Ransom with an attack on the ideology to which, during his undergraduate years, he had been devoted. The act of conversion was therapeutic.

It was Ransom's influence in the mid-1930s, the Ransom of *God without Thunder* and the Agrarian social essays, that pushed Weaver to decry the feet of clay on his modern, liberal idol. "I had tried some of the Leftist solution and had found it not to my taste," Weaver wrote; "it was possible that I had been turned away from the older, more traditional solutions because they wore an antiquarian aspect and insisted upon oppositions which seemed irrelevancies in the modern context" (23). The "older, more traditional solutions" increasingly answered the modern problems, for Weaver saw a redeemed future in the defeated past more clearly than did his teachers. The past assumed the character of the One as the present slid into the chaos of the Many.

Weaver's sense of historical time loosened as he began to assemble a narrative that explained the fall from traditional immanence into modern abstraction. The fourteenth century (his version of Mannheim's feudal-clerical utopia) marked, for Weaver, the last pinnacle of metaphysical clarity — the five (now six) centuries since had been but a long decline into the empirical wasteland. In classic conservative (and, not incidentally, literary-modernist) fashion, Weaver jettisoned the future and embraced the past, erasing from historical significance the times (middle-class and mercantile) that had given him birth and character (235). Weaver also entered into a sense of history that dispensed with the "it" and rather conceived of meaning in history as the struggle between a once-and-future spirit and a temporary materiality with which it was perennially at odds under the guise of the ideal and the local.

Weaver did in fact find himself intellectually at Vanderbilt, for his master's thesis contains in embryonic form most of the ideas and attitudes he later refined. "The Revolt against Humanism" is Weaver's first major swerve away from his liberal youth. The essay traces the fall of the ideal from Protagoras, the first mind in the West to be corrupted by the empirical, to Henry Adams and thence to Weaver's own mentor Ransom, the man of courage who took up "the hated word 'orthodoxy' and defended it" (42). In Ransom's return to the unity of the Platonic tradition, Weaver found his own path.

Weaver left Vanderbilt with a master of arts degree in 1934, taking college teaching jobs that eventually led to a position teaching English at Texas Agricultural & Mechanical University, College Station, Texas, which was ready for his kind of missionary outreach: "I encountered a rampant philistinism, abetted by technology, large-scale organization, and a complacent acceptance of success as the goal of life" ("Up" 24). After a couple of years parched by the "naturalism" of Texas and the Aggie worldview, Weaver was ripe for conversion. His calling so closely parallels that of Saul (Acts 9: 3–19) that it deserves full quotation:

> I recall very sharply how, in the Autumn of 1939, as I was driving one afternoon across the monotonous prairies of Texas to begin my third year in this post it came to me like a revelation that I did not have to go on professing the clichés of liberalism, which were becoming meaningless to me. I saw that my opinions had been formed out of a timorous regard for what was supposed to be intellectually respectable, and that I had always been looking over my shoulder to find out what certain others, whose concern with truth I was beginning to believe to be not very intense, were doing or thinking. It is a great experience to wake up at a critical juncture to the fact that one does have a free will, and that giving up the worship of false idols is a quite practicable proceeding. (24)

He turned the car around and headed for Baton Rouge, where, perhaps, Cleanth Brooks, like Ananias in Damascus, was having a dream that a man named Weaver had need of his teaching.

Weaver went to Louisiana State University to study southern literary thought and expression of the nineteenth century in the doctoral program. With his dedication to a Platonic orthodoxy and his aversion to rationalism, he meant to find a "reified" southern Mind unfettered by particular circumstances and embodied for the most part in literary form. "The study and appreciation of a lost cause," he wrote retrospectively of that decision, "have some effect of turning history into philosophy" ("Up" 25). Turning history into philosophy, the many into the one, could only be accomplished under the sign of an ideal unity, a Platonic dream, such as Weaver predicated of the South: "that unified and preponderating mind" (*Tradition* 30) that he believed he had found not only in the American South but prior to it in the works of his heroes: Aquinas, Milton, Plato, Ransom. Weaver's transformation from liberal to conservative intellectual follows the route traced by Mannheim with hardly a variation.

Weaver's doctoral dissertation, written in 1943 under Brooks's supervision, carries the title "The Confederate South, 1865–1910: A Study in the Survival of a Mind and a Culture." The aim of the work is to document the "cultural and spiritual unity of the South as it revealed itself after the Civil War" (v). The work was unsuccessful in finding a publisher in Weaver's lifetime; it went out to university presses just a few years after W. J. Cash's *The Mind of the South* (1941) had, perhaps, cornered the southern market and scanned the southern Mind. It was posthumously published in 1968 under the title *The Southern Tradition at Bay*, with an introduction by a still-unreconstructed southerner, Donald Davidson, who must have recognized some of Weaver's ideas and relished his use of the rhetoric of battle.

Weaver's book is an amalgam of polemic and scholarship, literary history and unadorned ideology. He profiles the inchoate Mind of the South that operated as the template for the individual minds and temperaments of the contributors to *I'll Take My Stand*. That is, he goes into postbellum southern intellectual life to identify the culture of the fathers' fathers. Like Plato rather than Protagoras, Weaver finds an ideal — the South as a poetic constant — to serve as the measure of human social and literary endeavor. *The Southern Tradition at Bay* asserts the existence of an intellectual culture in the South based on a few universal, transcendent propositions: community, tradition, nature, and God woven over time into a "metaphysical dream" (40). Unlike many other modern historians of southern thought, who generally channel southern history through agonistic paradigms such as Faulkner or Warren (for example, Woodward and many of like mind, who tend to see the definitive southern experience as a coming-to-terms with a burden of racial guilt), Weaver routes his study through the myth of the Agrarian message. That is, he finds its origins in the stasis of ontology rather than in the turmoil of history.

Whether knowingly or not, Weaver's literary-historical work provided just the right "docking mechanism" for a southern literary critical project formalistically disciplined by New Criticism to see the individual work ontologically rather than historically. The Agrarian poet-historians had left some pointers to the historical situation in thematic readings of individual literary works, but they always started and ended with literature. Weaver leaves us with the history and the paradigm that invests it with meaning.

Weaver himself seems to have been just the intellectual hybrid, scholar-crusader, to undertake such work: rhetoric was his lance, and he was prepared to fight, to lose, and to flourish in defeat. In the introduction and epilogue to *The Southern Tradition at Bay*, Weaver sounds the same alarm Davidson had trumpeted when he saw the Humanist host in 1929: "I should list first of all the fact that the South, alone among the sections, has persisted in regarding science as a false messiah. This by itself indicates that the Southern tradition has a center of resistance to the most powerful force of corruption in our age. While the Western world has gone after false gods it [the South] has clung, often at the cost of scorn and insult, to its lares of the field. More concretely, it has not, in the same measure as 'progressive' sections of the country, become engrossed in means to the exclusion of ends" (30–31). Critics of the program embedded in *I'll Take My Stand* had already made it clear that many southerners had gone the way of progress happily. In fact, the late 1920s and 1930s saw huge migrations from southern rural areas to the cities and towns. Contrary to much Agrarian rhetoric and hope, southern rural populations expressed a desire for such modern and progressive products as motorized tractors, electricity, and paved farm-to-town roads that helped them escape isolated communities. The Agrarian writers must have known that they were recommending a wish contrary to fact, that they were already losers in the battle for the hearts and minds of rural southerners. Even Davidson, the hardest and most resolute soldier of them all, was convinced (in 1938) that the battle had been lost and he himself left dismembered on the field, like Ransom's Captain Carpenter. He was already prepared for retrospective and memorial rituals (Fain and Young 310).

Weaver, however, who had had no first-hand experience of the battles Davidson remembered, was well qualified to carry on the battle in rhetoric if not in actual public policy. If particulars had always been the bane of Agrarian metaphysics, then he would argue strenuously that particulars had nothing to do with the metaphysical center anyway. The mind of every genuine southerner was the "preponderating" mind of the South. Here was Cash's "Man at the Center," but shorn of behavioral split ends such as the tendency to violence, hedonism, proto-Dorian pride, and—of course—racism. Weaver's southerner was even more likely than Cash's to exist in myth. Whereas for Cash, myth carried pejorative connotations, for Weaver, picking up the term from *God without Thunder,* myth carried the highest approbation.

Weaver's "mythy" mind of the South, moreover, had not grown out of local conditions, southern or American, but had been carried across history and deposited in the pre-Confederate South as part of a series of inspirations of spirit in time. In his "Epilogue" Weaver reveals this essential sequence and its relationship to the South: "That the fall of Rome, the dissolution of medieval Catholicism, the overthrow of Napoleon, the destruction of the Old South were purposeful and just are conclusions that only the tough-minded will question" ([388]). Lewis Simpson chooses this passage as "a summary moment" in Weaver's meditation on the mind and culture of the South ("South" xv–xvi). By clustering these four historical moments, Weaver implicitly argues for the transhistorical, transubstantial significance of the South: the fall of Rome to the barbarians had lost the world of the West its tradition of civil and domestic piety; the destruction of medieval Catholicism by middle-class reformers had cost the West its metaphysical moorings and a model for a social hierarchy; the overthrow of Napoleon and the Jacobin takeover in France had given the Enlightenment the political foothold needed for the entry of industrial capitalism into world history. Each setback was just because the precursor culture, starting out pure, had trafficked too recklessly with its particular barbarians. Defeat and destruction were necessary and just, but not necessarily prima facie evidence of innate flaw. The flaw was in the mortals, not in the Unity.

The defeat of the South summed up the history of the cumulative tragedy of the Western, Christian ideal, and conferred instant longevity and authority on the South. By Weaver's reconfiguration of history, the South was now part of a meaning far older than any that could possibly be claimed by mere American history. Defeat in the Civil War meant the demise of *"the last non-materialist civilization in the Western World"* (391; Weaver's emphasis), a fortunate defeat in that it promoted the South from phenomenon in history to ideal above it.

As Weaver highlighted that line, rethinking the meaning of the history of the West, Western civilization was in the midst of its second world war in thirty years — a war that would present its survivors with the facts of technological genocide by the eventual losers and a technological apocalypse in the arsenal of the winners. The South as Weaver imagined it had a powerful ideological part to play in the cultural apocalypse of his time, the redefining of good and evil in the aftermath of the Second World War.

Most of Weaver's "southern essays" are situated in this ideological milieu; unlike the Agrarian manifesto, they are more immediately aimed at a local political and ideological opponent. The impassioned faithful to whom Weaver steered his message — "sons of the Confederacy" bound by a particular regional and class piety, to paraphrase George Core and the late M.E. Bradford in their preface to *The Southern Tradition at Bay* ([9]) — consisted of a conservative, white, heterosexual male South that, at least since the years of the Agrarian movement, had thought of itself as a cultural elite with the increasingly difficult mission of reminding the whole South of "who we are" (to adapt one of Bradford's titles). Their "we" was under attack from within and without by minorities previously excluded, and the "are" was shifting tenses with disturbingly intractable acceleration into the past. Weaver the conservative ideologue was, to this group and cause, the southern Aquinas.

Weaver's first published essay establishes the line of reasoning that runs consistently through all his work. "The Older Religiousness in the South" was published in *Sewanee Review* in 1943, just before Allen Tate assumed the editorship. The essay bears marks of strong influence by Tate's essay on southern "religion" in *I'll Take My Stand* and further back by the defense of orthodoxy in Ransom's *God Without Thunder*. Consciously or not, Weaver was following the tracks of the battles that had preceded him. That those battles had been "lost" was of course the crown of their value.

Religiousness is a carefully chosen term, for it refers to an attitude or temperament rather than to a body of doctrine, to the idea of religion rather than to the social history of a particular sect. Like Tate, Weaver would avoid naming a particular denomination — in contrast to Ransom's recommendation of Anglicanism. Weaver the rhetorician probably intended such a distinction, as his essay gradually reveals. A body of doctrine, offering several propositions for assent or for dispute, invites rational examination and discourse. That, in turn, exalts reason over faith, and the decay of religion inevitably follows. Weaver's point is that such rational religion (doctrine rather than faith) is a northern vice. Emerson and Unitarianism made "assent a matter of intellectual conviction" and persuaded an individual "to explore principles" rather than to submit will and intellect to "that general respect for order, natural and institutional, which is piety" (135–36). Babbitt's Humanism was nothing more, in this context, than the spirit of Puritanism without its religious trappings; and Weaver belatedly attacked one of Tate's foes who had long since departed the arena. Southern society, by virtue of its innate religiousness and its comparative laxity as to doctrine, presented, somewhat paradoxically, a more stable and natural society than any New England might boast (a thrust at another former opponent, Howard Mumford Jones, who had argued New England's superiority in this respect). "The necessity of having some form of knowledge which will stand above the welter of earthly change," Weaver wrote, "and bear witness that God is superior to accident led Thomas Aquinas to establish his famous dichotomy, which says, briefly, that whereas some things may be learned through investigation and the exercise of the reasoning powers, others must be given or 'revealed' by God" (142). Weaver, echoing Tate's horse-horsepower analogy in "Remarks on the Southern Religion," advanced a similar Thomist dichotomy: on one side (the side of earthly change) he put the "egotistical and self-willed people" (136) of the Puritan tradition; nearer to God he put the South. Southern history was, in Weaver's strict view, the history of God's true religion on earth: "And when that army [Lee's Army of Northern Virginia] went down in defeat, the last barrier to the secular spirit of science, materialism, and pragmatism was swept away" (146). History cast out metaphysics when Grant accepted the sword of Lee. And metaphysics, Weaver's whole body of work strongly insists, is the only legitimate foundation for a culture and its art. The Emersonian North, pace Howard Mumford Jones, has less claim to a meaningful culture the more it mixes reason with piety. Ransom's intellectual example warns repeatedly of the error of mixing modes of thinking. Weaver not only imitated his elders in the outlines of his intellectual work but he also fought the old antagonists over the old ground.

Weaver's subsequent essays continue to argue that human history made a fatal wrong turn when it crushed the Confederate South. He was scrupulous in maintaining, however, that the metaphysical dream of history had not been touched even though the material civilization had been defeated. In his wartime and Cold War southern essays, he continued the transfusion of southern ideology into the contemporary cultural body. Albert Taylor Bledsoe, an antebellum southern intellectual, theologian, and lawyer appeared, to

Weaver, the perfect model of resistance to the "pragmatic liberalism" (169) that had done so much damage to the West since the French Revolution (and promised to continue that vandalism through the acts of the Earl Warren Supreme Court). History was merely a riot of accident; essences remained unmoved. Bledsoe's proslavery arguments merely needed a simple updating for use in the growing desegregation turmoil of the late 1940s. The cultural improvisors dismantling southern discrimination could not answer the essential argument: that all societies maintain themselves by discrimination, choosing whom to admit and whom to exclude. Could not answer, that is, except with force, and that only highlighted the correctness of Weaver's (the loser's) stand.

In yet another southern essay of the time, "Southern Chivalry and Total War," Weaver argued that the proper corrective to the horrors of World War II (specifically the deaths of civilians in Dresden and in the Nazi camps) was to be found in the institution of southern chivalry — or would have been had the Union armies not annihilated it, and the victors' histories ideologically stigmatized it. True to his Platonic belief in unity, Weaver found the enemy of 1861–65 to be the enemy of 1939–45: "It scarcely needs pointing out that from the military policies of Sherman and Sheridan there lies but an easy step to the total war of the Nazis, the greatest affront to Western civilization since its founding" (169). Nor was it the Union military leadership alone who fell into Weaver's relentless paradigm. Since southern society, in its fundamental form, is a feudal-clerical organization, it functions as the antidote to nazism. The middle-class society of the urban North is, to Weaver, a much more frightening specter than the slave system of the South: "The Nazi movement has been sponsored by the lower middle class, and all of its so-called innovations are but projections of the middle-class mentality. . . . And total war [as perfected by Hitler and Sherman] is a typical middle-class concept because this class, with its materialistic bias, is unable to see that there is involved in war anything other than complete destruction of the enemy, so that, as the popular thought has it, we won't be at the expense of having to do this again" (169). Blessedly free of a middle class, low or otherwise, Weaver's imagined South is uniquely capable of mercy and foresight.

Had the critics of the Agrarian manifesto attempted to tar them with fascism because of Collins's interview with Grace Lumpkin? Weaver was now on the scene to turn the tables, to link fascism, the middle class, and the heroes of the Grand Army of the Republic in a grand conspiracy to rob mankind of redeeming value. In his southern essays specifically, as in his other work generally, Weaver imagined the South consistently if extremely from an original design his elders had shelved.

Weaver's historical sense, always selective, seems to have been eventually smothered by the bell jar of his southern ideology. Although he meant such statements as, "But a nation is made what it is by its past; there is no identity without historicity" (251), his own commitment to the "metaphysical dream" of the South urged him to eliminate unfavorable aspects of "historicity"— matters of fact that tended to mar the shapely contours of the myth. He was, according to Hayden White's definition, a metahistorian. Data was always of less importance to Weaver than ideology—the "set of prescriptions for taking a position in the present world of social praxis" (White 22). The South was not and never had been, for Weaver, "the present world of social praxis." The South was rather the legitimate successor to the ontological and moral authority husbanded in the "Platonic-Christian tradition," the enhanced but essential South in which Weaver took his stand.

Weaver insisted on a pure line of descent, heeding the strong but implicit instructions of *I'll Take My Stand*. The intellectual project he furthered fits within the religious vision of history to be found in the work of Eric Voegelin, for whom history was a more or less "adequate symbolization" of a presence transcending human reality. In the preface to *Order and History*, Voegelin asserts a paradigm into which Weaver and the conservative tradition of southern intellectual history snugly fit. Simply add "the South" to the societies herein acknowledged: "For the great societies, beginning with the civilizations of the Ancient Near East, have created a sequence of orders, intelligibly connected with one another as advances toward, or recessions from, an adequate symbolization of truth concerning the order of being of which the order of society is a part" (ix). Deep in its cultural cortex, the mind of Richard Weaver's South insists upon its oneness with the whole that surpasses the part.

From the first deliberate and concerted work of the Twelve Southerners in the late 1920s to Weaver's work in the 1940s and 1950s, the genealogy of a conservative southern intellectual and literary history runs true. In warning of its imminent destruction, Eugene Genovese has reinvigorated a traditional southern ideology. The purist tradition is not, however, the only intellectual history to be derived from the Agrarian source, merely the first and the truest to its intellectual genesis. Louis D. Rubin, Jr., represents another cultural interest, a liberal or, rather, liberalizing intellectual and literary history of the South, with greater debts to Thomas Wolfe and W. J. Cash, greater allowance for African-American cultural expression, a greater generosity of interest in finding consensus in a diverse South. The circumstances under which the liberal "tradition" in southern intellectual and literary history was invented, and the formula by which it was reconciled with the elder and more conservative source, are the subject of the next parts of this narrative.

▌▌▌

RACE, LITERATURE, AND HISTORY IN THE WORK OF LOUIS D. RUBIN, JR.

That literature may usefully be viewed in terms of its historical unfolding, its changing relationships to changing time and place, is not universally acknowledged in contemporary critical thought.
LOUIS D. RUBIN, JR. (1984)

One problem facing the literary historian/critic of the South is that the significant southern literary figures of this century—those with the means, motive, and opportunity to write a southern literary history (the Fugitive-Agrarian brotherhood, their heirs and successors [chiefly Richard Weaver, as we have seen])—have shown little or no desire or inclination to sit still for the unfolding of historical change and to map its impact on "literature." Louis Rubin's statement above is significant for the year of its utterance. Arguably, only a southern literary critic—one schooled in the textual formalism of New Criticism as a literary as well as a regional discourse—would survey the professional landscape and think that coupling literature and history was, in 1984, a bold departure for the literary critic. Even the renegade critic—for example, Jefferson Humphries, in his introduction to *Southern Literature & Literary Theory* (1990)—in the act of acknowledging "history" transforms it, by theoretical meditation, into "literature," thereby rescuing the beast he had set forth to slay (xii–xiii).

Often in the history of its invention, the demands of southernness, like those of nationness, drove one way while history unfolded in quite another. Benedict Anderson offers a formulation that approximates the situation: "The fact of the matter is that nationalism thinks in terms of historical destinies, while racism dreams of eternal contaminations, transmitted from the origins of time through an endless sequence of loathsome copulations outside history" (149). Anderson's positioning of racism contra nationalism (the former "dreams," the latter "thinks"; the former is ontological, the latter is teleological) is rough but useful in that it informs my argument, in this chapter, that the South's racial folkways and changes to them function as the advance guard of history, compromising the integrity of the text and of the literary history composed of such inviolate texts. Although the scorecard inning-by-inning may not be the same, the players are: race, history, southernness (nationness).

New Criticism, created and nourished by critics from the 1940s to the early 1970s, consciously at odds with literary historians of their generation, made history in effect a fallacy — as crippling to aesthetics as the intentional or the pathetic. A collision of "the metaphysical dream" and history seems now to have been inevitable. How long could the literature of the South be excused from owning up to the culture's racial praxis? Donald Davidson's shock at and rejection of Warren's essay in *I'll Take My Stand* is symptomatic: so appalled was he at the "loathsome copulation" of race with the program of southern definition in the symposium that he rallied to the hallucinatory position that Warren never "ACTUALLY WROTE THIS ESSAY!" (Fain and Young 252).

Race was a roomy vehicle for all the ramifications of history — especially in the midcentury years when the transition from aesthetic formalism to literary history was grudgingly acknowledged. In the early 1950s, as *Brown v. Board of Education* (1954) made its inexorable way to the Supreme Court and then into public policy, the myth of the organic integrity of the southern community ran head-on into sociological and political powers determined to adjust its design, its ways of operating, its very metabolism. Du Bois's prediction that the history of the twentieth century would be the history of the color line seemed so infallibly accurate as to identify "color line" and "history" (vii). When driven partisans of massive resistance, like the signatories to the "Southern Manifesto" (1956) or Herbert Ravenel Sass of South Carolina, for example, fulminated against the "miscegenation and widespread racial amalgamation" that they feared would be the outcome of desegregated classrooms (45), behind their hysteria was the larger fear of the "loathsome copulation" of history and the southern (white) dream of identity. Denial, a direct or fortuitous offshoot of southern-sponsored aesthetic formalism (New Criticism), could not hold out for long. All the more, then, was history a problem for literary critics working in the shadow of the Agrarian legacy. George B. Tindall was not the first nor the last to note that the Agrarian manifesto of 1930 (*I'll Take My Stand*) deliberately aimed to manifest "regional loyalties in situations dissociated from an emphasis on the issue of race" (Tindall 126). Louis Rubin enters the picture at this point, aiming to repair the "dissociation" of literature and history.

The dissociation of race from the Agrarian myth of the South, at least in the literary mind, was never more clearly illustrated than by Allen Tate, who turned the African-American experience in the South into a more or less effective "image" and thereby yanked it from history (and vice versa): "All great cultures have been rooted in peasantries, in free peasantries, I believe, such as the English yeomanry before the fourteenth century: they have been the growth of the soil....The white man got nothing from the Negro, no profound image of himself in terms of the soil" ("Profession," 525). In its obligation to the "great [white] culture," the lesser African-American, according to Tate, had failed. "Image" became a kind of magic word by which the asymmetrical shapes of historical experience were converted to myth. Literature was made of images; life, on the other hand, was subject to experiences. If one's art were perceived by the literary powers as too full of experience (as was Richard Wright's or Douglass's or Du Bois's), it was barred from literature as being too mortgaged to the fallacy of history.

Because Tate and his cohorts among southern literary critics have assumed themselves victors in the race to invent the South, history gave way to image. Wilbur J. Cash, no Agrarian but not immune to the power of image himself, saw present and potential problems in a people whose collective "mind...is continuous with the past" (x). "The past," Cash argued, is not the same as "history," and those who elevate the former (as image) neglect the latter. Specifically this is the case, Cash trenchantly observed, if history is composed of experience rather than image:

> Primarily this group [the Agrarians] was one which turned its gaze sentimentally backward. Its appearance just as the South was moving toward the crisis of the depression, just as Progress was apparently sweeping the field, just as the new critics and writers were beginning to swing lustily against the old legend and the old pattern, was significant. In a real fashion these men were mouthpieces of the fundamental, if sometimes only subterranean, will of the South to hold to the old way: the spiritual heirs of Thomas Nelson Page. And their first joint declaration, *I'll Take My Stand*, was, like their earlier prose works in general, essentially a determined reassertion of the validity of the legend of the Old South, an attempt to revive and fully restore the identification of that Old South with Cloud-Cuckoo Town, or at any rate to render it as a Theocritean idyl. (389–90)

By yoking the Agrarians to Thomas Nelson Page, Cash could not have made a more annoying charge — as he probably knew full well. He had also placed the Agrarian imaginary — more subtly than its harsher left-wing critics who openly proclaimed its alleged fascism — in a defensive position vis-à-vis history. Progress is on the march (one can almost hear the Lowell Thomas cadence in Cash's prose), and "legend" can mount only a puny defense.

Almost no one played southern literary history by Cash's rules in the 1940s and 1950s. Surprised now and then by traces of the legend in his own argument (especially when he takes up the subject of women, the white belle and the "compliant" slave woman), neither did Cash himself (56 passim). The "old pattern" of the New Critics has held sway until the current age of "theory," the advent of which has opened cracks in heretofore solid literary edifices. Southern literary study seems to have resisted theory with particular fervor. To be sure, theory (like any "new" strategy for looking at the familiar — like New Criticism itself in the 1930s and 1940s) is a threat. But to what?

American literary historian Lawrence Buell has examined the problems in writing and in reading literary history as a truth-bearing, rather than performative, genre. What he has said of American literary history goes double for southern: "The anxiety provoked by such factors [as changes in the ways literary history is understood and in the persons who write it] may weigh harder on Americanists than on British literature specialists because of certain complications endemic to the former field, which for one thing relies for its self-definition more heavily on extratextual claims about the distinctiveness of the nation's social structure, physical environment, and so forth. Therefore Americanists may be destined to make a particularly conflicted contribution to the debate over how to do literary history in a time of undoing" (217).

There is no more instructive "case of the conflicted contributor" than Louis D. Rubin, Jr. No one has done more to "naturalize" the literary critical techniques of New Criticism (which forbade the "extratextual") to the politics and thematics inherent in Agrarianism itself and in his own times. And no one has done more (not even the Agrarian Fathers) to try to accommodate "the distinctivenss of the [region's] social structure" to the needs of a literary-historical counternarrative that specifically addresses the problem of race as the chief, albeit negative, mark of its distinctiveness. Beginning in the early 1950s (at a "time of undoing" for the South) and continuing into the 1990s, Louis Rubin has forged, modified, and polished a truce aimed at addressing the needs of race, literature, and history in a southern literary-historical narrative that resists all such "contagion." He has not always thrown himself on the barbed wire, but he has been pivotal to the battle.

In two provocative essays, literary theorist Paul A. Bové has accused Agrarianism and its devotees of transforming a "politics into the political quietism or conservatism of New Critical orthodoxy" that effectively "forgot" any and all connections to history by stressing the formal, aesthetic qualities of literary works over their social and cultural conditions (115). "PROFESSIONAL SOUTHERNERS," Bové's label for the purveyors of the formalist aesthetic, induced cultural amnesia, not the historical knowledge they claimed to be explaining (116). Examples are plentiful and relatively well known. The instructions to Brooks and Warren's *Understanding Fiction* (originally published in 1943) rule out most of the cultural/historical context of a work of literature. Agrarian critic Andrew Lytle's essay-review of Faulkner's *Intruder in the Dust* (1948) actually denies that the novel is about the racial mores of the South. Such enforced amnesia, Bové asserts, makes the game too easy for the powers that be. Clearly, Bové feels there is a penalty due; not surprisingly he rules in favor of the claims of history and southern racial policies.

There is merit in Bové's allegation; before there was an Agrarian literary history (or a narrative derived from it) there was, as I have tried to show in previous chapters, a strategy for protecting its sanctity. In "Remarks on the Southern Religion," Tate's "remarks" adumbrate literary theory by painting a dark line between "history" and "image," by ruling out as nonsouthern and unthinkable anything hybrid. If "horsepower" is unthinkable as a notion because it conjoins the concrete (the horse) and the abstract (the concept of power), he suggests, how can literary history (as a similarly hybrid genre) be thought, much less written?

"Take the far more complex image of history, if indeed it may be called an image at all," Tate writes (Twelve Southerners 160). Images constitute the vocabulary of the stable, traditionalist, religious community: the ideal condition of life-in-the-group as the Agrarian formula would have it. As integers of traditional thought, images do not bond well with the contingent grammar of history. A mind thinking in images is not, Tate suggests, apt to think historically as well, at least not historically in such a way as to be long-viewing or narrativizing: "These more concrete minds may be said to look at their history in a definite and now quite unfashionable way. They look at it as a concrete series that has taken place in a very real time—by which I mean, without too much definition, a time as sensible, as full of sensation, and as replete with accident and uncertainty as the time they themselves are living in, moment by moment" (Twelve Southerners 160). History, as the record of meaning-conferring acts, tries to impose a narrative Long View on the "moment by moment." By definition, then, history is a game nobody inside the sanctuary may consent to play. "[I]f you take history not as an image or many images, you have to take it as an idea, an abstraction, a concept," Tate complains, using the fierce Agrarian either/or rule he had learned from Ransom (160). Readers familiar with Tate and the Agrarian dogma will recognize "idea," "abstraction," "concept" as the poisonous heresy of the deracinated modern mind. Like Cartesian zombies, moderns think in the Long View, arrogantly granting precedence to the abstract series over the concrete moment. They (we — Tate included himself) see horsepower rather than the horse, empty structures of experience rather than the "whole, separate, and unique" moment (162). Without formal attribution, Tate had borrowed Ransom's argument and some of his examples from *God without Thunder*. Unlike his professor, however, Tate avoided an overt denominationalism, opting instead for southern "religious sense."

Bové's indictment aims to recover what must be forgotten in order to make the religious view sufficient. The problems facing a southern literary historian writing from the inside (where else?) were formidable. Louis Rubin saw the tip of this paradox in the problematic relationship between an empirical historical entity (the South) and belief in the ontological distinctiveness of aesthetic works produced by its artists. In an early essay, he notes with apparent equanimity that "the modern South has produced a distinguished body of criticism based squarely on the premise of the entire autonomy of the individual story and poem" (*South* 11). The problem of making a collection of "entire autonomies" into a coherent literary canon troubled the Agrarian fathers not at all, for with few exceptions they held the South itself to be the sovereign autonomy guaranteeing the unity of individual works reproducing its image in them, matter and form. Often Rubin paid homage to this critical imperative, but his tendency was almost always equally, and surreptitiously, historical. One could read serious understatement in the epigraph to this chapter: no one knew better than Rubin himself southern resistance to history. Under the rhetorical cover of common sense and reasonableness, Rubin built a southern literature that the Fugitive-Agrarian disciples could not have made. Beginning just a few years later than Weaver, Rubin was light years ahead of Weaver in trying to reconcile history and literature in the hybrid genre of literary history.

Rubin's precursors had produced volumes like Beatty and Fidler's *Contemporary Southern Prose* (1940) — dominated by essays and reviews arguing the ideological virtues of unreconstructed southernism (a kind of massive resistance before its time) — and Tate's *A Southern Vanguard* (1947), a rather loose collection of essays, poems, and stories submitted to a literary contest in memory of John Peale Bishop, who had died a few years earlier. Works available for classroom and scholarly use, such as *Southern Prose and Poetry for Schools*, compiled by Edwin Mims (the bane of the Fugitives) and Bruce Payne (1910), were clearly unacceptable, at least to true believers of Weaver's stripe. Such "constructive" pedagogical books contained propaganda aimed at affirming the New South agenda: horsepower rather than the horse, scientific history rather than the miracles of "sensible fact" Ransom preferred. There was no comprehensive work that developed a literary-historical narrative yet based its critical discipline on the antithetical principle of textual autonomy until Rubin undertook the project.

How successfully could a canon of autonomous works form or be formed into a history, a narrative? New Criticism would need a fundamental adjustment to support a literary history, and none of its originators seemed poised to make it. Ransom, as the decade of the 1930s waned, divorced himself from poetry and from the politics of his region, to the dismay of some of the original brethren. He turned to "theory" and moved to Ohio. Tate, interested in history to the extent that it could be made to disclose its sweeping conceptual principles, likewise showed little or no interest. Davidson, from his roost as Vanderbilt University professor and book reviewer for a local daily newspaper, wrote essays on the current state of southern literature; he might have taken on the work of literary history, but his energies were consumed in social and political controversies in the 1950s. Warren, because of his devotion to History and history (the big fateful pattern and the individual event), seems a likely candidate for the work. He put his massive energies, instead, into an anthology of American literature for the classroom. Owing to individual personalities and circumstances, and to the stress on the autonomy of the text, the Agrarian/New Critics never actually accomplished a literary history.

A classroom anthology, however, did appear in 1952, *The Literature of the South*, with general editor Randall Stewart (Warren's fellow graduate student at Yale University in the 1920s and chair of the Vanderbilt University English department in the 1950s, after Mims had retired) and associate editors Richmond Room Beatty, Floyd C. Watkins, and Thomas Daniel Young. The following chapter contains a detailed discussion of *The Literature of the South*, both the original and revised editions. Here, it will be sufficient to explain that the anthology acknowledges a canon that is predominantly modernist ("The Modern [Southern] Renaissance" consumes nearly one-half the anthology's space) and editorially argues the point that southern institutions, mores, morals, based on "ancient virtues," are superior to those doubtfully based on "modern gains" (*Literature*, xix, xxi). The historical context for Stewart's polemic must not be underestimated: southern literature would make the case in favor of southern culture and history under severe questioning by such existing assaults as Gunnar Myrdal's *An American Dilemma: The Negro Problem and Modern Democracy* (1944), almost exclusively restricted to the South in its reading of "the problem," and by anticipated onslaughts such as the sociological and legal text and footnotes to *Brown v. Board of Education*. The first edition of *The Literature of the South* is an overwhelmingly white literature, as a comparison with its 1968 edition (in Chapter IV) will show. In a defensive, circle-the-wagons mode, southern literary inventions produced communities of letters that affirmed the dream over historical unfolding and change.

This reinforced consensus, though, is not exactly the one Louis Rubin, starting out professionally in American Studies in the 1950s, adopted. As several of his works show, Rubin is an admirer and sympathetic interpreter of H.L. Mencken, the one-man wrecking crew of the Bozart. Moreover, Rubin, in the late 1940s and early 1950s, was working with Robert Spiller on American Studies projects that supported *The Literary History of the United States* (1948) and Spiller's own *The Cycle of American Literature* (1955). These significant texts are regional in focus (New England) and historical to the backbone. One cannot, it seems, serve both Mencken/Spiller and the religiously tilted literary historical poetics of Weaver and the Agrarian tradition — at least, not for long.

As an early champion of Thomas Wolfe, whose writing got him hooked on southern literature in the first place, Rubin also had trouble trying to crash the Agrarian parade. Their preference for aesthetic formalism in poetics exiled Wolfe's hirsute novels to the literary boondocks. Rubin's essay "Thomas Wolfe in Time and Place," one of his contributions to his own symposium, *Southern Renascence* (a kind of answer, in 1952–53, to *The Literature of the South*), argues for the "desegregation" of the fledgling modern southern canon to accommodate Rubin's hero: "It was these Nashville Agrarians of *I'll Take My Stand* who in large measure formulated the credos and the critical foundation basic to most modern Southern literature. Participating membership in the Nashville group, however, is hardly a requirement for the Southern author" (*Renascence* 290–91). Nor, need it be said, for the southern literary critic. Crashing the sanctuary guarded by "these Nashville Agrarians" was more difficult than negotiating a truce with the Agrarian-New Critical axis; or, at least, Rubin chose joining over trying to beat them. In following years, as Rubin published many of his books and essays, he worked to co-opt the ancient consensus to a modern program. *The History of Southern Literature* (*History*, 1985), of which Rubin is chief editor, stands as a monument to his takeover.

The *History* seems to have been constructed in a kind of charmed obliviousness to its existence in "a time of undoing" (217). The year 1984 was an uncommonly auspicious one for the work (as Rubin wrote his introduction to the completed project), but he makes nothing of the Orwellian coincidence.* There have been symposia, readers, anthologies of various breeds, but nothing before the *History* has given southern literary history so much legitimacy in one volume. It even claims to supercede Jay Hubbell's *The South in American Literature* (1953) by extending its survey into modern and contemporary ground, by withdrawing southern literary study from the larger field of "American Literature" (inasmuch as no such compromise is carried in the *History*'s title, nor is any detectable in the editorial policy and practice), and by transferring the handling of southern literature from the scholars to the critics (Rubin, "Way" 149ff.). This point seems more valid when one notes the absence of any of the kinds of writing Weaver included (or that some anthologists now deplore): works by Calhoun and other antebellum proslavery advocates, for example. With the exception of Lewis P. Simpson's contributions to Part I, there is little in the *History* about the intellectual life of the South except its literature.

Few will dispute the claim that Rubin is the primary architect and developer of southern literary study in this century and that the *History* is his

---

* Andrew Lytle, by way of contrast, wrote a retrospective introduction to a reissue of his *Bedford Forrest and His Critter Company* (1930) in 1984 in which he drummed the theme of modern apocalypse with fervor.

monument. Some have added ornament, or even a wing, to the basic structure, but the blueprint is Rubin's, extended or polished or interpreted by "the Rubin generation," many of whom are Chapel Hill Ph.D.'s, and by the fraternity of friends whom Rubin has often acknowledged.* From inside the building, though, we cannot always tell what the structure looks like.

Rubin himself is a source of some clues as to design choices. In "The Way It Was with Southern Literary Study: A Reminiscence," Rubin shows that he has been a self-conscious (albeit not wholly consistent) conciliatory and liberal presence in fluctuating rapport with the essentially conservative (if not reactionary-and-proud-of-it) right wing of southern literary history.

Rubin takes as his foundation the assumption that a realistic relationship between human history and aesthetic works is the premise from which literary criticism/history begins. Buell, in a related context, has described such a foundation assumption as representative of an older vintage: "Literary history's mission was once well understood. Its task was to conjoin intrinsic and extrinsic, literary texts and their historical settings, in narrative that represented history's actual course. Literary history was a hybrid but recognizable genre that coordinated literary criticism, biography, and intellectual/social background within a narrative of development" (216). The Fugitive-Agrarian narrative, insofar as one is adumbrated in their several works, is not progressively developmental but disintegrative: things fall apart as history brings change to an original, utopian state of organic stability. "Loathsome copulations" dilute the purity of the original. Rubin faced multiple challenges reconciling intrinsic with extrinsic, when the extrinsic was mostly race and the intrinsic was trained to ignore it. He revived the word "image" as a way of placating one master but coupled it with "history" and tried to make room for race as ways of placating another.

In his "The Curious Death of the Novel: Or, What to Do about Tired Literary Critics," Rubin assents to the premise that art is "the ordering of human experience into a meaningful pattern, dependent not on its faithfulness

---

*"The Rubin generation" was first used by Jefferson Humphries in his introduction to *Southern Literature & Literary Theory* (Athens: University of Georgia Press, 1990), pp. vii–xviii. Rubin denied the existence of such a generation in "A Letter to the Editor," *Mississippi Quarterly*, 1992. A partial list of the scholars and critics who have been associated with Rubin either as his students or colleagues at Chapel Hill is impressive: Thadious Davis, Fred Hobson, Anne Goodwyn Jones, Lucinda MacKethan. If one adds the names or those whose books have appeared in series Rubin has edited for Louisiana State University Press, the list grows like Topsy—and includes the author of this work.

to 'real life' but on the validity of its own representation for its impact" (15). Southern literature gets its validation as "image" from the ontological claim made by Ransom (for religion) and transferred to "South" by Tate, Weaver, and others. This suprahistorical identity is not contingent on the validity of representations of "real life" or actual history (although they might help) for manifesting itself in a literary text. Aesthetic works by southern authors (for example, novels, short stories, plays, poems, some forms of biography, and criticism itself), carry an added or supercharged degree of order because they are generated by a community that itself dwells in the suprahistorical. Like a religion, this imaginary is more than the sum of its parts. In subject matter as well as in form, southern literature reflects the "active and palpable *force*" of the community in which the individual producers have their lives (Memo, [1]; emphasis in original).

In fact, such work increases in literariness in proportion as its agreement with "community" increases and its reliance on historical fact decreases. Studying communal literature communally renews the imaginary's bonding capability: "[W]hy do southern writers write the way they do?" Rubin asks in the preface to *William Elliott Shoots a Bear*. "If one grants that there is and has been a body of literature identifiable as southern, then what is there about the place and the time that has played so noticeable a role in shaping the literature?" (ix). Rubin's starting position is often this slippery; he finds bedrock where others find a hall of mirrors. In granting that there is a "literature identifiable as southern," have we not begged the question of distinctiveness that the as-yet-uncompleted literary study is to determine? Do we not, by the circular dynamics of this argument, substitute the effect for the cause, and risk dismissing or mistaking certain problematic literary work for reasons that will never be known? In our current climate, one that recovers and brings to the foreground voices previously excluded, Rubin's practice is obviously vulnerable.

Take, as an example of this closing hermeneutical circle, the following excerpt from Robert B. Heilman's "The Southern Temper." This is the essay in definition that leads off *Southern Renascence* (1953) and, reprinted, bats second in *South: Modern Southern Literature in Its Cultural Setting* (1961), another of Rubin's projects. Heilman's assertion of natural and seamless continuity from southern society to southern literature lies deep in the DNA of southern literary study: "The sense of the concrete, as an attribute of the fiction writer, is so emphatically apparent in Faulkner, Warren, and Wolfe, so subtly and variously apparent in Porter, Welty, and Gordon, and so flamboyantly so in someone like Capote (who hardly belongs here at all) that everybody knows it's there" ("Temper" 3). Since "everybody knows it's there," nobody need really define what "it" is. It is the constantly affirmed center of a discourse protected from inquiry by assumptions about its "mythic" or organic nature. It is the trace left by the imaginary as it gets teasingly close to being the object of inquiry. Because of Heilman's reliance on this center, then, "the sense of the ornamental" and its apparent opposite, "functionalism," in literary criticism, can both signify the southern temper (7). Furthermore, the southern temper can be denoted by a sense of the concrete as well as by a sense of the symbolic, even though these two terms appear to be opposites. There is a fundamental conservatism in a critical discourse that makes itself immune to certain kinds of questions; it enforces "quietism,"one of Bové's complaints; or, resorting to Anderson's lexicon, it creates the "amnesia" required for all narrations of identity after the fact (204).

It is not as if the "through-the-looking-glass" character of Heilman's essay and of *Southern Renascence* in general was lost on its original audience. Its skeptical reception is forgotten when, as Bové charges, PROFESSIONAL SOUTHERNERS are in charge of remembering it. Norman Podhoretz (a fledgling New York Intellectual in the early 1950s, who represented one of the chief coteries also competing for mastery of the intellectual culture of the United States) detected the political aspects of *Southern Renascence* immediately in a review Rubin has been slow to forget. "One would like to think," Podhoretz begins, "that the whole thing [*Southern Renascence*] is a case of innocent literary misjudgment. But we are already dealing here not with a group of people so impressed by Southern literature that they feel impelled to study it, but rather with something closer to a political movement" (119). And that political movement can have, in Podhoretz's view, no other object than to thwart change in the legal and social relations between the races in the South.

Southern literary history, during its early years with Rubin, struggled with the challenge to acknowledge the presence of race just as Tate and others had tried to fight off accusations of fascism in the 1930s. Rubin tried to address the challenge of defending a conservative poetics rather than a reactionary politics. He saw the issue as subject matter, not as a language or condition of thought. Podhoretz, on the other hand, like many critics of the South before and since, saw race as an issue of cultural self-consciousness, protected at the highest levels: "But the Faulknerian attitude to the Negro problem—that it is a deep moral turbulence in the blood of the South which

can only work itself out in agony, guilt, and expiation—soon becomes a received idea, and the urgency disappears" (122). Reading a defense of the racial
status quo as a function of literary stylizing (that is, Faulknerian attitudiniz-
ing), Podhoretz implies, moves it from the arena of historical-political action
into a frame of aesthetic contemplation where "the urgency [to protest, to defend, to push for social change, and so forth] disappears." The canon-building
function of *Southern Renascence* is, he argues, ideologically conservative
whether or not any of the contributors confesses a particular political stance,
and it works to "disappear" the need for social action by absorbing history
into the literary, the "Faulknerian."

Rubin's writings occupy a complex position in this web of political confrontation, both loyal to the (unstated) conservative agenda and inclined
toward change. Serving the former goal, his work strives toward the establishment of the South as an "image," a keyword in the New Critical lexicon
denoting a condition of existence, or mode of being immune to historical
contingency and the call to action. In an essay of 1956, "The Historical
Image of Modern Southern Writing," Rubin collapses distinctions separating
the various meanings of "history," "the past," "the South," and "real." "History—defeat, the war, the past—in the South these were not abstractions,"
he writes. "To a child growing up in the South, they were very real. Southerners knew that history was not merely something in books" (150). And
yet, for the writers of the southern renaissance, Rubin explains, "the image
of the war and the past," their birthright, was all they had in place of first-
hand history (150). They could only know it second-hand, as an image carried mainly in books. And, as the current events of the 1950s made clear,
the book image was preferable to the contemporary reality.

Although Rubin seems unaware, his sense of the play of history in the
southern imagination is linked very closely to Allen Tate's concept of the simultaneity of past and present in the mind of the modern southerner. This
paradox and double bind made for crackling ironies in Tate's work, but Rubin is less contorted: "The writers of the Southern renascence were able to
re-create the life around them, about which they were writing, not simply
because they were blessed with somewhat superior powers of description. They
saw it as if they had been gifted with a kind of historical perspective, which
translated what they saw in terms of what *had been* as well as what now was. . . .
The present was focused into perspective by the image of the past lying behind it. Their own contemporary life was seen not only for its own sake but
as formed and influenced by the life that had preceded it" (154; emphasis in

original). It is not always so easy to measure the relative weights of the southern past as "image" and "contemporary life." More often than not, in practice, Rubin tends to privilege representations of the present viewed through the focus of the tragic past as legitimate southern literature. For instance, Rubin credits the Faulknerian voices of Chick Mallison or Quentin Compson as (in the former case) a legitimate southern voice on the question of federal intervention in southern ways of community life or (in the latter) on the oppressive nearness of the heroic past. As we shall see in Chapter V, Richard Wright's or Ralph Ellison's voices, conflicted on the other side of the racial issue, are more difficult to naturalize to the "I dont hate it. I dont hate it!" version of southernness, for they expose the "both/and" choice as avoidance of the "either/or."

Rubin's bind seems clearer in another essay on image, one that he contributed to a collection of essays coedited with longtime conservative southern advocate James J. Kilpatrick, *The Lasting South: Fourteen Southerners Look at Their Home* (1957). The subtitle is no accidental echo of *I'll Take My Stand* (1930) and of its authors, the original Twelve Southerners. Political change in the 1950s (this collection had been begun only months after the announcement of *Brown v. Board of Education* in May 1954) threatened the image of the South, and had made it unlikely that such agreement on a "specific platform and bill of particulars" as the original Twelve had enjoyed (and tried to enforce) would be possible in 1957. Yet in their preface Kilpatrick and Rubin claimed that "the South's identity is worth preserving" in the aftermath of *Brown*, during the furor of the "Southern Manifesto," and a few months before the troubles at Central High School in Little Rock.

"A good deal of what is contained in this book," Kilpatrick and Rubin write in their joint preface, "relates to [the segregation issue]" (x) even though no single essay specifically addresses it. The fourteen southerners might hold differing views on the issue; in fact, "the editors themselves" hold divergent views, although Kilpatrick, in the final essay of the book, is the only one to state his position. Not surprisingly, he is against judicial dismantling of "separate but equal" (203). His statement leaves Rubin as the "liberal" by default. It is from this "Faulknerian" position of undeclared declaration that Rubin, once again, attempts to clarify the South's image.

In "An Image of the South," the first essay of the book, Rubin walks the fine line between change and reaction. Bowing to the traditional conservatism of the southern "community," Rubin laments that "[t]he South is in danger today of losing its most precious possession, that regional quality, and the enemy is just as much within as without" (2). The cold war rhetoric of "enemies within" signals the deployment of the South in the rhetorical battles of the Red-fearing 1950s — not the last time it would be so used.

The collective impact of the essays in *The Lasting South* is to line up the southern community for a broadside attack on its deracinated mirror image: postwar American "society," a mixture of visible and invisible threats, of aliens and weak patriots, of losers of China and pinko softees on communism, of lonely crowds and hidden persuaders in business. The South was the antidote to that modern nightmare, according to Rubin. The southerner naturally got "to know and enjoy almost everyone in his community, because by the very nature of small town life he is thrown in with them day after day, at work and at play" ("Image" 4). Body snatchers could not succeed in the southern community.

New York is the familiar image of the place where the nefarious forces of destruction nest. As a counterimage to the South, Rubin claims, New York shows no desire to "encumber" itself with a history ("Image" 3). Preferring southern myth to any alternative program of existence, the Rubin of *The Lasting South* argues that the South's relatively narrow range of social activities and few but happy social classes leads to an intensity of relationship among all members of the "imaged" community. Any infiltrator would be instantly recognized. And even though there was, in the South, something of a class hierarchy, Rubin claims that no jealousy or friction created a basis for class conflict ("Image" 7). The plantation economy, Rubin goes further to assert, entailed very little mobility in buying and selling or in actual migrations from place to place (6). The broad, indirect hint seems clear: the southern community is the American answer to the Marxist paradigm of society as locked in class conflict and mortgaged to capitalistic forces. Why would a nation in danger, as the United States was in the midst of the Cold War, want to tamper with the internal systems of a region that could be its salvation? The emphasis on the image of the South induces an amnesia that makes it possible to forget, for instance, that in the actual South the buying and selling of human beings as slaves was pivotal to the plantation economy and rendered the community as capitalistic as any coven of Wall Street traders in wheat or varnish or cotton futures. Or that, while *The Lasting South* was in production, a southern community lynched Emmitt Till and acquitted those accused of the crime. Under the power of the image, the South in the 1950s becomes, not a historical result or outcome of social problems dating from the beginnings of chattel slavery in North America but rather a timeless or mythic collision between the ever-integrative community and the ever-disintegrative modern society.

Race is ever the spoiler, though — the historical slap on the face that breaks the amnesia, the hold of myth. Ironically, Rubin admits that the precursors who handed down the well-wrought image of the South also transmitted the sin. His own tortured position during this time owes something, if not all, to the racial past that is so vital to the South's identity: "Had the Southerner been willing, in the 1910's, the 1920's, the 1930's, to adjust his thinking to the Negroes' growing development and to make the necessary accommodations, a situation need never have arisen where a Supreme Court could declare that 'separate' and 'equal' were contradictory terms" (11). The southerners of the 1910s, 1920s, and 1930s were the fathers of the southern renaissance, those who created that image, that unity, that idea of the South that Rubin feels called upon to defend in other parts of his essay. Only Warren, of the core group, suggested "adjustment." The Twelve Southerners had indeed woven a nifty web of ideological heritage: they caught those who wished to perpetuate their work, but they left no fingerprints that Rubin could detect.

This entrapment is easier to see in a close look at Rubin's guardianship of the southern canon, his revisions and admissions, and the credentials he insisted upon. Between the early moment in which he expressed frustration at being shut out by "these Nashville Agrarians" and his eventual possession of *the* history of southern literature, Rubin walked and talked shifting paths. The stone in the path was always race.

To be sure, *Southern Renascence* did include an essay by a black critic, Irene Edmunds's essay on Faulkner. But that piece did not keep the volume as a whole and the literature it stood for from escaping charges of parochialism and special pleading. Willard Thorpe, reviewing the book in *American Literature*, did not mention the presence or absence of race in the table of contents or in the essays, but he did find fault in too much Fugitive-Agrarian "logrolling" (575). The anonymous reviewer in the *Nation* was more direct, faulting the volume for omitting "younger" authors (presumably those younger than Warren or Welty, who were in their early forties at the time) and "Negro authors" altogether ("Southern Authors").

The issue of race-as-literary was sensitive. Rubin had at least two masters to serve: the massed presence of his precursors in southern literature (who had left no recipe for including African-American authors among the southern community and who were still very much alive) and the gradually building conviction that some change had to occur in the segregated canon.

In a subsequent essay in his series on image, "Southern Literature: The Historical Image," in *South: Modern Southern Literature in Its Cultural Setting*, Rubin tried to reconcile the forces contending within himself and in the emerging academic field of southern literature. On the one hand, as a literary modernist by temperament and training, Rubin had held certain beliefs about the separate spheres of literature and "ideological convictions" that were more prevalent then than now (12). He read the chief black American author of the day, Richard Wright, as impeded by "social purpose" that diverted his fiction from "aesthetic grounds" into propaganda (19). Rubin was not alone in his conclusion, as a survey of the critical reception of *Native Son* or *Black Boy* will show. In the 1950s the word *propaganda* carried a stronger charge than it does today. Wright's membership in the Communist Party (USA) as well as the manifest denial, in all his works, of the splendor of the white southern community and its claim on all traditions, made his admission to the canon impossible. Elsewhere in the same essay, however, Rubin found that Erskine Caldwell's ideological convictions did not offset Jeter Lester's "individuality" as a southerner and as a literary creation (12). By the skin of his (Caldwell's) teeth, and by some surreptitious politicking with the language of literary criticism, Caldwell—who also flirted with Communism and communists—was admitted into Rubin's canon when many of Rubin's own brother critics excluded him.

The problem of African-American membership appeared to be resolved with the appearance of Ralph Ellison's *Invisible Man* (1952). Here was a "Negro novelist," Rubin wrote, who could keep the emphasis on "novelist" and who could deploy the full regalia of the literary modernist movement as well as address "recent social and political developments" (13, 20ff.). That Rubin (and so many of his readers) did not read the manifest and complex politics of *Invisible Man* as partly denial of southern imaginings of blackness is one of the amnesias of southern literary history that supports indictments such as Bové's. Nor did Rubin and his cohort read Ellison's essays in controversy, eventually collected in *Shadow and Act* (1964). If they (we) had, there would have been less tendency to see *Invisible Man*, in New Critical terms, as untainted by politics or sociology.

One African-American writer in the canon, on the grounds of literary merit, however problematical, established a precedent. Others could now be seen, usually in retrospect, as forerunners struggling toward the plateau of literature through the briar patch of social, political, cultural "setting." The enterprise of developing southern (or any other) literary history is a retrospective process; we build a past from the present with certain devices and desires. In the anthologies Rubin was later (1970, 1979) to edit himself or with associates, African-American writing gained an ever-increasing presence: first Booker T. Washington (Rubin, like many of his fellows, saw DuBois not so much as author but rather as NAACP "agitator" ["Image" 12]), Chesnutt, Ellison; then Douglass, James Weldon Johnson, Zora Neale Hurston, Wright, and others.

While the reigning teaching anthology for southern literature courses, *Literature in the South* (see Chapter IV), kept a resistant silence on the issue of race (Washington was permitted to speak, but Douglass had to wait for the revised edition), Rubin kept the subject on the table. In "Notes on a Rear-Guard Action" (1964) he surveys the history of southern literature (much of which he had assembled) from the coupled vantage points of the death of William Faulkner in the summer of 1962 and the enrollment of James Meredith at Ole Miss the following fall. His device in this essay is to enlist the Abraham of southern and American literature, Faulkner, in the cause of moderate-to-liberal involvement in the acknowledgment of race in the southern community of ideas. Rubin, thereby, returns to the "Faulknerian" thickets complained of by Podhoretz a decade earlier. This essay was written at a difficult time for southern literature, for the pressure to join the bandwagon of change had heavily influenced the southern writer, reducing the range of choices he or she felt possible and narrowing the acceptable sweep of "the tradition." These were the years of the Voting Rights Act of 1964, of freedom marches and assassinations, of Eudora Welty's "Must the Novelist Crusade?" (1965) and its muted answer "no."

Rubin's response as the leading literary historian of the South is indirect. He does not advocate a specific position on *the* political issue; that would violate his own rule of separation of the literary and the political. Rather he imagines a southern literary past using the lives and works of selected literary men whose positions in the South (and on the South) might serve cumulatively as a model for the present. Using the prestige of the major figure of the present (Faulkner), Rubin undertakes to recover corresponding major figures in the ante- and postbellum periods of southern literary history—Poe and Samuel Clemens, respectively—whose examples establish the tradition of passionate ambivalence in situations of racial conflict involving the community. This design creates and perpetuates the Faulknerian tradition of feeling much but doing little when race and the image of the South collide.

Rubin's engagement with Poe, and through Poe with the tradition of Co-leridgean unity as at its core southern, is a long and intricate story; Rubin has come back to it relatively recently in *The Edge of the Swamp* (1989). Here, let me just outline the engagement with Clemens as literary historical en-tr'acte to his treatment of Faulkner, the civil rights witness.

Having established, as the central metaphor of his southern literary his-tory, the posture of ambivalent contortion — the *contrapposto* he mentions repeatedly from Tate's "double focus" description of the modern southern writer ("*The Fugitive, 1922–1925: A Personal Recollection Twenty Years af-ter*") — Rubin deploys it retrospectively in search of precedents. Cable, for example, had it in a limited supply ("Politics and the Novel: George W. Ca-ble and the Genteel Tradition" [1970]). William Elliott, in the Old South, had it not at all because he was too invested in the ideological treasury of his society ("Second Thoughts"). Clemens, though, had a surplus. In his editor-ial introduction to the postbellum period in *Southern Writing: 1585–1920*, which he edited with Richard Beale Davis and C. Hugh Holman, Rubin places Clemens at the head of the congregation of writers of that period. His Clemens is the ambivalent South-hater of *Life on the Mississippi*, in love with the Edenic place but ready to dynamite the false front built by Walter Scott imitators. Unlike any other southern writer before Faulkner, Rubin claims in "'The Begum of Bengal': Mark Twain and the South" (1975), Clemens brought "critical scrutiny" to bear upon the sacred "pieties" of southern life and cul-tural experience, but he did so from within the passionate community of the South (58–59). In that way he (Clemens) anticipated the great twentieth-century icon of southern dividedness, Quentin Compson, who said quite a lot about his deep moral turbulence but did little except to kill himself when faced with the necessity of living in a world of history. One could also pro-pose that "discovering" the "tradition" of internal, passionate, conflicted love-hate also creates space for Rubin himself, as the literary historian of the South in the South. Not surprisingly, one of the warmest and fuzziest of mod-ern fictional southerners, Atticus Finch, takes the same passionately con-flicted position.

In "Notes on a Rear-Guard Action," the critic uses Faulkner directly, not through Quentin or another of his character-surrogates, to enact southern literature's conflicted attitude toward its own historical circumstances. For Rubin, Faulkner had marked the trail with *Light in August*. The powerful ambiguity of Joe Christmas gives the requisite flesh and blood (the realistic mimesis) to the issue of race and to the attitude of the southern critic: split between honor for the stable and time-hallowed community and the moral imperative of equality, the southerner (critic or writer) identifies with Joe Christmas for whom race is doom even though, with finesse, it might have been avoided. In this novel Rubin could show that "the way that the book is written and what it shows" are coincident ("Notes" 139). Shifting to the collective pronoun, Rubin also shifts from the descriptive to the prescriptive. *Light in August* traces a pattern all genuine southerners should recognize and follow: "Both the right and the difficulty of doing right were very sharp realities, and we could not ignore their existence. So we worked out, as all human beings would naturally do, some very elaborate compromises with our integrity, and we persuaded ourselves that these would suffice" ("Notes" 145). On one side of the fine line is allegiance to the "we," the community that provides the guaranteeing mimetic reference for all meaning. On the other side is a kind of apostasy or estrangement, an alienation from "time and place," that mean death for the artist. Faulkner is the way out of the dilemma, for from the novel Rubin shifts to a resurrected Faulkner who "would have put on his coat and tie and hat and gone over to the campus, and stood quietly alongside of James Meredith," not at all unlike Atticus facing down his underclass neighbors at the Maycomb jailhouse ("Notes" 149). What we know of Faulkner from biographies and his letters (and, as long as we are choosing a team from his characters, from Gavin Stevens and Chick Mallison) strongly suggests that the man William Faulkner probably would not have desired involvement in the desegregation of Ole Miss. But the pull of his literary gravity makes his imaginary attendance necessary; no other personification of the community will do.

The election of Jimmy Carter as U.S. president in 1976 did much to change (or to mark a change in) the meanings of southern community and southern history. Rubin responded to the change in *The American South: Portrait of a Culture* (1980), a collection of essays by several authors commemorating the admission of the South to the American mainstream — propaganda, of a sort, originally assembled for the United States Information Agency, proclaiming a South triumphant over the worst crimes of its apartheid. Whereas the part of race was a cause of dispute in earlier works, in *The American South* there is no whiff of reaction. Several African-American authors contribute essays on African-American writing, and Rubin devotes most of his introduction to a reweaving of race, literature, and history.

His pattern tends to decentralize race and to substitute community—to move history aside for myth. Rubin regrets the expense of so much antebellum southern intellectual energy on politics and oratory devoted to the defense of slavery. Not that John C. Calhoun, the major offender, was morally wrong: he was simply ignorant of the historical limitations on slavery. Expansion out of the South "could not possibly be made economically feasible" in Rubin's historical view, so all of Calhoun's proslavery treatise writing amounts to a waste of his energies and the community's attention (*American South* 4). He was not evil, just a windbag; and the social views he espoused must be junked because there was, in Rubin's view, no way they could have been implemented.

The core of the community's "self-definition" was so strong that it survived Calhoun and the rest. It survived civil war too. "If southern sectional identity were dependent on slavery, then the loss of the war and the end of slavery should have destroyed that identity," Rubin proposes. "It did not" (*American South* 4). Reasoning retrospectively from his idea of the community of palpable force, Rubin reinforces the southern myth by removing, or demoting, slavery from the list of reasons the Confederacy as a nation went to war. For the instant, slavery replaces racism as foundational to southern social relations and community imagining. End slavery and you end the reality of racism, which is not thought to migrate into other social formations of power.

Nor has the southern community held onto itself as an aristocratic remnant in a modern democracy, Rubin asserts. Whereas other conservative political-cultural movements of the twentieth century (for example, T.S. Eliot's views as summarized in *Notes toward a Definition of Culture*, the Action Français) were avowedly elitist, the Agrarian movement in the South, "by virtue of its roots in the southern community," was neither aristocratic nor snobbish. Furthermore: "Its community assumptions saved it from intellectual hatred. It had no role for antisemitism or any other sort of xenophobia, either in its principles or its dynamics. . . . At heart it was not even pro- (or anti-) segregation, though the expected fealty was paid to that staple of white southern enterprise, for race relations were tangential to its concern, which was an assertion of the value of the humane community in protest and rebuke to dehumanization and materialistic, acquisitive society" (*American South* 12). The southern Agrarians, Rubin argues, were closer soul brothers to another antebellum American writer, Henry David Thoreau, than to Calhoun. Both, I think, would have been surprised at the seating arrangement. As for the assertion that the southern community was neither pro- nor antisegregation — what sort of reading of the texts, and events, can lead to such an interpretation? How does one "see" and rebuke "dehumanization and materialistic, acquisitive society" on the one hand and not, on the other, see and rebuke the dehumanization of black human beings during slavery and under Jim Crow?

Rubin's sanguine, nostalgic revision of the Agrarian movement seems at least partially undermined by one of the essays in *The American South*. Blyden Jackson's personal memoir "Growing Up Black in the Old South and the New: or, Mr. Wheat Goes with the Wind," exposes the elaborate network of southern conventions and rituals that kept the African-American as effectively subordinate after emancipation as before. Jackson's experience of growing up black in the American South is closer to the one described by Ellison in *Invisible Man* than it is to the image of the impartial southern community praised in Rubin's peroration.

Rubin's more recent work seems to continue in the vein of nostalgic detoxification of the southern image. Was slavery the cornerstone to southern identity, materially or psychologically? No. Was the Agrarian ideology elitist (as some contemporary revisionists have claimed) or even fascist (as more extreme critics alleged in the 1930s)? No, and no. Was southern public resistance to desegregation in the 1950s and 1960s a deep and determined sign of the majority's will to resist change? No.

In *The Edge of the Swamp: A Study of the Literature and Society of the Old South* (1989) Rubin goes so far as to recant Quentin's famous rejoinder to his roommate: "You cant understand it [the South]. You would have to be born there." Ostensibly a reading of Simms, Poe, and Henry Timrod, *The Edge of the Swamp* is also continuous with Rubin's decades-long attempt to weave literary and historical modes of expressing and knowing the South. Prominent among the items on his agenda in this book is an argument against Lewis Simpson on the one hand (whose work on southern literature and history Rubin finds insufficiently grounded in the particulars of time and place) and Eugene Genovese on the other, whose early work proposes a South altogether too capitalistic (17ff., 26). Rubin prefers the sacred but accessible middle ground, which for him supports a South consistent with "historical common sense and human nature" (41).

What this position effectively means is that the community definition of the South becomes ensconced as the one and only "natural" path to the South itself. Mind naturally apprehends the South this way, Rubin argues, and therefore is not stampeded by, to use two examples, the hypothesis of the South as an aristocratic enclave or the prominence of racial guilt at the core of the southern self. The plantation, Rubin asserts, was in essence and in fact, a middle-class operation that Americans North and South would have recognized as such (39). "Historical common sense" tells us that it was the antebellum equivalent of the big house in the suburbs. And the antebellum southern slave owner was no seething cauldron of racial guilt and hate; he was no different from a present-day tobacco grower, who would plow his crop under if there were another way to make a living (43–44).

Rubin's reaction to the poles of southern discourse, as he sees them, seems perhaps ill-considered. To reduce history to such a low common denominator as common sense risks sapping it of its potential to illuminate the present. If the past was the present except for accessories, why be curious about it? Even though the dilution of history-as-difference enhances Rubin's concept of community, by leading to the claim that southerners of whatever century would recognize each other as brethren, his assertion of the commonality of past and present in fact reduces the South to banality: slaves are equivalent to sticks of tobacco; the quarters, the urban ghetto. There is the real amnesia.

IV

SOUTHERN LITERATURE ANTHOLOGIES AND THE INVENTION OF THE SOUTH

Historical sense and poetic sense should not, in the end, be contradictory.
ROBERT PENN WARREN, *Brother to Dragons*

In his introduction to *The Invention of Tradition* (1983), Eric Hobsbawm classifies "invented traditions of the period since the industrial revolution" according to "three overlapping types": "(a) those establishing or symbolizing social cohesion or the membership of groups, real or artificial communities, (b) those establishing or legitimizing institutions, status or relations of authority, and (c) those whose main purpose was socialization, the inculcation of beliefs, value systems, and conventions of behaviour" (9). Anyone who has ever taught "the literature of X" using an anthology will recognize herself somewhere in Hobsbawm's categories. Some anthologies establish communities where none had been perceived; others nourish underfed constituencies. All foster the impression that the voices housed in any given anthology consciously talk to one another. More traditional American literature anthologies establish "relations with authority" between the New England canon and social/political traditions and other regional U.S. writing.

Anthologies of southern literature have, of course, fulfilled each of the functions Hobsbawm delineates. At the beginning of this century, for example, *The Library of Southern Literature* had as its main purpose the "establishing or symbolizing [of] social cohesion or the membership of groups, real or artificial communities" in and through the positioning of its phalanx of editors and academic sponsors over the writers themselves and by its devaluing of such members-in-shaky-standing as George Washington Cable. More recently, Forkner and

Samway's *A Modern Southern Reader* notably *relegitimizes* southern literature by connecting it to a quasi-religious belief system (see below, pp. 72–73). Hobsbawm's third category, though, has consistently identified the agendas of all the southern literature anthologies to have reached print.

As much as a critic of Louis Rubin's stature influences the construction of southern literature, he cannot be in every classroom every day. Classrooms are to the literary canon what seismic disturbance is to a volcano. There are periods of dormancy during which the population lives comfortably on the slopes of Vesuvius; then comes an eruption and we are hip-deep (or worse) in the lava of controversy. Many, understandably upset, blame teachers and literary theorists, whom they suspect of being arrogant and underemployed, for unleashing storms of "political correctness" that ignore "literature itself," and for changing the rules in the middle of the game.

No literature anthology, southern included, is innocent of political games-manship. Recent controversies over standards for the teaching of American history, and for the compilation of "books of virtues" (such as William Bennett's by that very title), only make this point clearer. Perhaps nowhere in literary study is a political agenda so near the surface as in an anthology. Reviewing *The Heath Anthology of American Literature* (first edition, 1990), for example, Richard Ruland cuts through the usual hue and cry over the apparently sudden discovery of political "correctness": ". . . for this [the *Heath*] is a book about power, about who has had it and used it to shape American society and who has not. It is also about power in the academy, a reaction to the political and economic success enjoyed by aesthetic formalists since T. S. Eliot concluded that 'it is never what a poem *says* that matters, but what it *is*' . . . and the theoretical formalists and their heirs continue to hold most of the best jobs" (339; emphasis in original).

Teachers and students of southern literature should take notice of these ripples of controversy for several reasons. As Gerald Graff has argued, in *Professing Literature: An Institutional History* (1987), "Rather than try to insulate the curriculum from political conflicts, a more realistic strategy would be to recognize the existence of such conflicts and try to foreground whatever may be instructive in them within the curriculum itself" (251–52). Indeed, teachers and students of southern literature have a world to gain from foregrounding the "conflicts," for the entire history of southern literature is abbreviated in the history of its anthologies.

The *Heath* editors, for instance, expelled much of the literature of the Old South from the first edition of their anthology on the grounds that the politics in such works as Kennedy's *Swallow Barn* (1852) and the vast expanses of Simms disqualify them from the American literature canon because, as Paul Lauter, author of the section introducing "Early Nineteenth Century: 1800–1865," explains, they "consistently display gross racial stereotypes and long-discredited apologies for the slave system" (1: 1194). Lauter is adamant on this point: "But for an anthology of primarily written texts, the compositions of the Old South fade into relative obscurity. One need only compare the shrill and sentimental efforts to answer *Uncle Tom's Cabin* with the original to see why" (1: 1194). Yet in the second edition (1994) the editorial embargo is relaxed, although the admission of George Fitzhugh carries a warning label: reading Fitzhugh might prove "painful," the editors warn, and such excerpts are presented only because they represent what "most Americans" no longer believe (1: 1241–42). How Richard Weaver would have relished this battle!

A critique of the anthologization of southern literature ought not, however, snipe at the victory parade as it goes by. As Lauter wryly remarks of his own cause: "The victors, it is said, write history; perhaps, too, they establish the terms on which culture continues" (1: 1194). Perhaps victory also induces amnesia as much as defeat does; a victor's reading of *Uncle Tom's Cabin* might understandably miss the "gross racial [and gender] stereotypes" in Stowe's novel. And what cultural good is served, for example, when the *Heath* editors include "The Battle Hymn of the Republic" and exclude "Dixie"? Do they think "most Americans" will forget how to whistle it? Brooks, Warren, and Lewis, mentioned briefly above as editors of *American Literature: The Makers and the Making* (1973), had a saner solution: they printed both songs, but under the heading "Folk Songs of the White People."

The history of southern literature as a separate field of professional academic study must be seen as an offshoot of the bigger struggle to establish American literature in the American university curriculum. The academic campaign for American literature, as Kermit Vanderbilt describes it in *American Literature and the Academy* (1986), opened in the Roaring Twenties when a cadre of American literature critics and scholars, chafing under the elderly and condescending hand of the *Cambridge History of American Literature* (1917–21), decided to push their own political agenda: the privileging of Americanness over literaryness, as the *Cambridge History* had defined those terms, and the creation of professional status for a new American literature group within the Modern Language Association (MLA). The journal *American Literature* (established 1929) and the American literature group of MLA were successful power plays, signs that the academy would have to shift to accommodate American literature *and* its professionals. The breaking away of the American Literature Association from the MLA, more than fifty years later, indicates that politics continues, the ever-present rhythm of conflict and consensus in human political life.

Southern literature had not been invisible before the academic uprisings of the 1920s, however, nor were its interests ignored in that movement. *The Library of Southern Literature* (Alderman et al., 1908–13), musty with turn-of-the-century, nationalist reassurances that the South and its writing were loyal adherents to the Union, still occupies several linear feet on library shelves (usually exiled to an annex) but hardly seems the sort of anthology one would haul to class three days a week. The mastodon is not forgotten: very recently Edward Ayers and Bradley Mittendorf acknowledge it as a distant precursor to their *The Oxford Book of the American South* (1997). Anthologies by Montrose Moses, with its long-winded explanatory apparatus (1910), William Malone Baskervill (1903), and Simms biographer William Peterfield Trent (1905) were available for consultation. But by whom? American literature, much less southern, was seldom taught in U.S. universities.

One of the rebel founders of the American literature movement, Jay B. Hubbell, had probably done more than the pre–World War I anthologists to keep alive the literature of the South and fold it into the emerging mainstream of American Literature: his two-volume *American Life in Literature* (1936), one of the first American literature teaching anthologies, carries substantial selections by William Gilmore Simms, Thomas Holley Chivers, Henry Timrod, Paul Hamilton Hayne, as well as letters by Robert E. Lee — most of which would be banished from "American" literature anthologies these days as relics of what "most Americans" no longer believe.

The consolidating achievement of this founding generation of American literature scholars is, of course, *The Literary History of the United States* (1948), now on the distant side of its midlife crisis, a work that no longer speaks ex cathedra but is itself an object of study. No one now doubts the political nature of the *Literary History*. Published in the midst of the cold war, bracketed by the communist threat to Greece and the Berlin blockade, the *Literary History* and its champions proposed their work as proof positive that American culture was indeed a mature world culture, destined for world cultural leadership. Robert Spiller's *The Cycle of American Literature* (1955), a condensation of the ideological views supporting the *Literary History*, serves as a brief in favor of this American cultural preparedness. In Spiller's "objective" view,

American literary history taught Americans, and the world, the cultural values that would lead them all to victory in the struggle against Soviet communism. American nationalism plainly rose to the surface in "our" literary history. Even Vernon Parrington's declaration of independence from British literary patriarchy in the 1920s, according to Spiller, was not strong enough to meet the renewed national purpose: "The literary historian of this school [Parrington] owed his ultimate debt to Taine, Hegel, and Marx, but as an American and a democrat he recognized the social philosophies of none of these masters, taking from them only the method of relating literary expression directly and simply to the life which it expressed" (viii). The American mind would not be mortgaged to an ideology, for ideology was a disturbingly European way of thinking about history. American thinking was direct and empirical, do-it-yourself democracy in Whitman's sense, spawned in the unmediated encounter between the "I" and the world. A study of American "literary expression" would demonstrate the superiority of the simple over the sophisticated, and, Spiller was confident, the emergence of American "cultural maturity" after its protracted minority to British and European seniors would appear as a "certified" reality (vii).

As Ruland reminds us, an anthology "describes the practice [of literary selection and grading] at a specific historical moment" (357) — and the particular moment for southern literature was shared with the America Spiller and his comrades had entered in the Western cultural sweepstakes. Cold War emergencies had reduced the number of contestants for world cultural hegemony to two — East and West, slave and free. American literature scholars had made a strong case for leadership of the West; English literature would no longer lead the way. In addition to the *Literary History* and numerous anthologies, critical books such as F. O. Matthiessen's *American Renaissance* (1941) and Richard Chase's *The American Novel and Its Tradition* (1957) caught the spirit of the contest by arguing for a long and unified tradition and mature culture. Matthiessen's editors supplied his title. The term *renaissance* enhanced American cultural longevity by linking it to the recently invented tradition of thinking of the cultural achievements of classical Greece and Western Europe in terms of stand-alone eras with major figures (Sophocles, Michelangelo, Shakespeare) to personify value systems. Chase topped off his argument for a single, unified tradition in the American novel with approval of William Faulkner as a major figure. Rescued from suspicion of pathological dissent from the American consensus ("The School of Cruelty" albatross hung around his neck by Henry Seidel Canby), Faulkner brought the region and its literature into the sunlight.

Southern literature called for separate attention at this moment and also appropriated the term *renaissance* (sometimes rendered in its Latin version *renascence*, preferred by Tate) as the sign of its claim to cultural unity, longevity, and maturity. Louis D. Rubin, Jr., and Robert Jacobs's *Southern Renascence* (1953) claimed the privilege of being "the first book that dealt with modern Southern literature in any kind of overall and coherent fashion" (152). Fred Hobson has recently reiterated the claim that *Southern Renascence* "define[d] and open[ed] up a field of study, the literature of the post-1920 South, as distinct from the southern writing that had gone before" (743). The Rubin-Jacobs book was a symposium, though, not an anthology. Its usefulness on the front lines of the classroom must have been, and still is, limited.

An anthology appeared on the scene at almost the same moment, attempting a more comprehensive construction of southern literature and its history than any symposium could. The first—and in many ways still very useful—teaching anthology in the renaissance is *The Literature of the South* (1952; rev. 1968), edited by Richmond Croom Beatty, Floyd C. Watkins, and Thomas Daniel Young. The general editor and author of the foreword was Randall Stewart, who was not shy about the (literary) politics of *The Literature of the South*. The anthology's purpose was manifold but explicit. It would showcase the achievement of the moderns (Part 4, "The Modern Renaissance," consumes nearly one-half of the entire anthology to cover only thirty-four years [1918–52] of literary history), thus arguing for the rebirth of the Western cultural community in the American South of the mid–twentieth century (xvii): a lesson learned, perhaps, from Mattheissen's book. The anthology was also compiled "to show the continuity of Southern letters" (xvii), for continuity rather than rupture and conflict was needed in a time when American cultural mores were under stress in a world-ideological battle and southern mores in particular were under political and cultural siege at home.

On the more specialized literary front, Stewart's anthology set out to valorize the neo-Agrarian invention of southern cultural meaning. His foreword specifically echoes, and condenses, the cultural blueprint of the South as it was promulgated in *I'll Take My Stand*. Stewart affirms, for example, that southern literature had always demonstrated the greater value of ethics over science, of "ancient virtues" over "modern gains" (xix, xxi). In shorthand, this is Ransom and Tate's argument, as refined by Weaver. As a permanent cultural monu-

ment, Stewart argued, southern literature merited genuine and favorable comparison with the ages of Dante and Shakespeare (xvi). "The New England
Legacy," for which Stewart sheds a perfunctory tear, had given way to its successor—the modern South; so the South can seize the title "renaissance"
from New England as its symbolic trophy in the cultural sweepstakes.

The trio of editors under Stewart followed a southern studies, as opposed
to a southern literary, plan: "An effort has been made to supply the reader
with enough editorial comment to indicate important tendencies and to suggest the correlation of the literature with its changing political and social
background" (Foreword xxii). Their choices in the material are revealing, especially when compared with subsequent anthologies (and with their own
revised edition of 1968) in which the canon and its "political and social background" undergo change and modification.

The introduction to Part 1, "The Early South to 1815," hews closely to
the myth of a cultivated aristocracy as the founding order of southern culture.
Eugene Genovese, in recent arguments discussed elsewhere in this book, continues this line of internal southern cultural debate and self-fashioning. Richmond Croom Beatty, who edited this section of *The Literature of the South*,
dwells upon the opulence and leisure, the learning and refinement of the
Virginian club. Patrick Henry, the only man from outside the closed circle of
learned agriculturalists, merits just a cameo appearance, and we are told in
no uncertain terms that his famous speech was pieced together posthumously
by William Wirt, Esq. Lurking in the background is the dour Puritan staking
claim to the wellsprings of American mind and culture, but his challenge is
never acknowledged. The "patterns of life" southern land-owning white men
soon established would feed directly into the twentieth-century Agrarian emphasis on the enmity between agrarianism and urban industrialism but would
have no appreciable impact on southern (and American) patterns of racism.
Slavery, scarcely mentioned, is relegated to the general historical background
along with such impersonal factors as changes in world economic circumstances. A strong southern consensus for agrarianism and a natural social
stability founded on "natural aristocracy" (9) are the important lessons of the
colonial and revolutionary periods.

This political construction of southern history and society continues from
the period introduction into the selections. William Byrd II is here, of course,
but laundered. We read only of a dalliance with a white barmaid afflicted with
scabs; the racier record of "The Secret History" is withheld. (Not surprisingly,
the *Heath* carries a good deal of it [1: 541–60]). George Washington is repre-

sented by his "Last Will and Testament," in which we learn of his intention to free his [actually mostly Martha's] slaves upon his wife's death. John Taylor is represented by a chapter from *Arator* (1818) analyzing the competing claims of agriculture and manufacturing as economic bases for a society; not surprisingly, Taylor is seen as an Agrarian precursor to *I'll Take My Stand*. Taylor's ideas on the acceptability of slavery as an institution and his deep fear of slave insurrections, prominent in *Arator,* are not presented. Consensus among the Virginian Fathers is preserved by omitting Taylor's response to Jefferson's concern about "boisterous passion" sparked by the continued exposure of white youth to the everyday physical, psychological, and sexual abuse of slaves. Taylor thought that such worries as those Jefferson voiced in "Query XVIII" only made insurrection more likely. The effect of such editorial choices is to present the early south as conforming to the myth of genteel political consensus and clear moral conscience about slavery. To that ideological end the "natural *aristoi*" of the early South are shown to be quite sure of their natural rank — both Jefferson's and Taylor's comments on natural aristocracy are included — and equally convinced that a hierarchy erected mainly on money acquired in trade is an unnatural social structure that can only end in miscarriage of the national/natural cultural ideal.

To construct the "first South" in this particular way requires an agenda of selection as well as editorial explanation and interpretation. What seems clear in Stewart's anthology is that the value given the twentieth-century, Agrarian interpretation of southern history and culture projects its shaping influence into the past: the past becomes an adumbration of a certain southern present. That southern present is marked by cultural maturity, consistency, and moral probity. Such fundamentals would be enjoyed by any people at any time; they are especially needed for a culture on the threshold, in the early 1950s, of years of pressure to change its most "natural" ways of life to those decreed by a liberal, bourgeois democracy.

Construction of southern myth and history continues in the second section, "The Rise of the Confederate South." As in the previous section, slavery is subordinated to a defense of agrarianism as the central cultural interest of the South (9, 104). Calhoun's political, social, and economic writings tend to dominate this section. Political science and proslavery writings outweigh the literature. The editors take John Pendleton Kennedy lightly; *Swallow Barn* does not satisfy their craving for realism and direct political address. Simms is "versatile" and "facile," left-handed compliments bequeathed to Simms's reputation by Trent's biography and filtered through an early New

Critical aesthetic. Although Poe is "not fundamentally a Southerner," he gets almost fifty pages of the text, and his critical project, however doomed by his own confessions of histrionics and his hysterical jealousy of Longfellow, is linked with the enterprise of New Criticism to pull him into the southern fold and to bolster the claim of continuity in communal aesthetic outlook over time. A certain obtuseness about African-American culture can be seen in the judgment that slave spirituals carry power only in the decibel level numbers of voices can generate. Civil War songs and ballads, on the other hand, are "lofty" "sophisticated songs" of "high polish" (114–15). The surviving editors of the 1968 revision of *The Literature of the South* avoid this brier patch by omitting both spirituals and Civil War songs.

"The New South," turned to in the book's third section, is a political battlefield in Stewart's anthology—a lesson to us that the issues of the 1880s and 1890s were not dead in the 1950s. Radical Republicans Charles Sumner and Thaddeus Stevens are demonized in the introduction (437), and the Klan is presented as an honorable citizenry's only response to "corruption" under occupation regimes. If Thomas Dixon is not listed in the table of contents, his ghost haunts this introduction. Parenthetically, we are reminded that even though the conservative-agrarian stream of southern thought seems to have lost out after Appomattox, it was to fight back successfully against the progress and industrialization that had infected New South thinking (438). Sidney Lanier is well represented. Perhaps this is the late high-water mark of the reputation of Lanier, the Keats of the South and a favorite poet of Edwin Mims, whose help and support are acknowledged in the preface (xxiii). Local color is frankly identified as made-to-order for a magazine market that had swelled after the Civil War. It is interesting to see that Thomas Nelson Page outranks Cable in this anthology (444), perhaps the last time Page would stand so tall, and that selections from his work range beyond the ubiquitous "Marse Chan." Selections from other authors are familiar. Booker T. Washington is the first African-American; W. E. B. Du Bois is absent.

The section on "The Modern Renaissance" is clearly the Mt. Sinai of the volume. Here the major thematic tablets for the understanding of southern literature as an entity are delivered: a preference for agrarianism over progressivism, as more classically humanistic, is the distinguishing southern mark, as it has been since the eighteenth century. By the standards of subsequent anthology editors, this is a stripped-down hermeneutic; but its simplicity is (as Weaver had seen) its power. Such a classic humanistic spirit had appeared in the history of culture before, in Periclean Athens and Elizabethan England

(Stewart 613). Surprising in this presentation is that the editors acknowledge a competing intellectual movement (the New Humanism of Babbitt, Paul Elmer More, and others) against which Agrarian conservatism defined itself. Usually the Agrarian ideology is presented *sui generis*, as is the case in Ben Forkner and Patrick Samway's "modern" reader (5, 237).

The representative men of the southern renaissance are...white men. Stark Young, Thomas Wolfe, William Faulkner, and Robert Penn Warren receive separate subsections in the introduction and hefty selections. But there is a rich context for them: a full-length play by, not Williams, not Hellman, but Paul Green; Frank Owsley on sectionalism and the yeoman; an incongruous section on folktales and folk songs (omitted from the revised edition); and a diverse selection of other writers who were then living.

The Literature of the South, for all its early 1950s southern chauvinism, is still a teachable anthology. Its major useful feature is that, like the modern architecture of its milieu, its load-bearing piers and beams are clearly visible: form is function. You can read the ideology that holds the volume up with hardly a footnote. Its South and southernness are made to order for its moment; Thomas Jefferson, for example, is presented as a "strict-constructionist" (35) who, by implication, would not have interfered—judicially or otherwise—with the internal matters of a state that preferred "separate but equal." For a region facing the volcanic changes to be triggered by *Brown v. Board of Education*, this ideological purpose is clear: by emphasizing the continuity of agrarian humanism over industrial depersonalization in southern hearts and minds from the eighteenth century on, this anthology argues for cultural maturity in the South, for coherence, for direct links with the mainstream of classical Christian culture, and for even more direct links to the founders of the government that was then leaning so heavily on the South to change. Even if, by the standards of revisionism today, Stewart's anthology is decidedly politically incorrect, it is frankly what it is. It is unfortunate that it passed out of print in the mid-1980s.

Southern Writing, 1585–1920, published in 1970 with Richard Beale Davis, C. Hugh Holman, and Louis D. Rubin, Jr., as editors, competed briefly with the revised edition of the Stewart anthology until the former went out of print in 1976 when the publisher, Odyssey Press, sold the book—ironically—to Scott Foresman, publishers of *The Literature of the South*. *Southern Writing* also strives to present "Southern literature and culture" (v). Its main "improvements" over the revised Stewart anthology are increased attention to African-American writers in the South and interpretive sections that give pride of place to southern insurgents—individuals and classes who do not comfortably fit the genteel consensus.

Davis's introduction to and selection of materials for the early period (1585–1800), weakens the hegemonic hold on southern cultural expression for the same period established by *The Literature of the South*. Davis acknowledges the presence of literate communities besides the plantation aristocracy who had voices in the invention of the South. He mentions merchant-adventurer pamphleteers and Anglican divines as two groups whose contributions to southern writing (he stops short of calling what they wrote "literature") were quite different from the stately works of the leisured aristocrats. Politics, oratory, satire in verse and prose, and religious writing by Maryland Jesuits and small communities of Quakers break up the monolithic impression of a plantation patriarchy thoughtfully perusing Catullus and filling their ample leisure with erudite treatises on agronomy and social philosophy. Davis is also more tolerant of the practical concerns of the southern population; to him the folk in the shadow of the gentry tended to be as curious about natural history and practical agronomy as they were about the principles of government and the organization of society. His selections create the impression of a diverse and fluid literate population (shoulder to shoulder with an even larger illiterate one) out of which we—through our cultural experts—have inherited Jefferson and Madison, and other colleagues, as the only signifying remnant. By its selections, an anthology can passively give the impression that only what is between its covers actually existed. Although Davis does not stress the point, he gives us some raw material from which to refine alternatives to the master themes of agrarian versus industrial, natural aristocrat versus untouchable. There were, his selections imply, other ideas and other ways of looking at the southern experience.

Not so with Holman's brief introduction to 1800–65. The Agrarian master theme is invoked (310), and very little reordering is undertaken. Under Holman's scrutiny William Gilmore Simms does begin his comeback trail—by virtue of his range of observation and eye for historical detail. The selection of his writing is diverse and substantial (312). Poe is still odd-man-out in the southern canon, but necessary nevertheless (312). The gradual acknowledgment of African-American southern writers can be seen in the debut of Frederick Douglass with chapter four of the *Narrative of the Life of Frederick Douglass*, which recounts the betrayal of his escape plan. It is perhaps significant that, although Douglass maintains his position in later American and southern anthologies, he most often does so with a different chapter: the one in which he fights Covey the slave breaker for his freedom and self-respect. This selection is, for example, the choice of Ayers and Mittendorf in *The Oxford Book of the American South* (37–45). And of course the difference between a thwarted rebel and a triumphant one is vast. George Moses Horton is also new, the first professional African-American poet in the South — perhaps an answer to Phyllis Wheatly of Boston, who hold the title of first African-American poet in most American literature anthologies. William Wells Brown is represented with several chapters from *Clotelle*. But Holman is not so insightful in his appraisals of antebellum women writers, observing that "neither Mrs. Wilson [Augusta Jane Evans] nor Mrs. Hentz [Caroline Lee] merits serious attention today" (387) Feminist scholars in southern literature and history have invested serious attention in these writers and are publishing important dividends that belies Holman's dismissal. Timrod closes Holman's section with a few poems and the welcomed appearance of his 1859 essay "Literature in the South," an essay holding important clues to the problems in the relationship between the southern writer and his/her community.

Rubin heartily embraces his section, 1865–1920. Local color, he explains, was (and still is) a genre not far removed from the commercial demands of its time and place. Ideological reconstruction was under way during the postwar period, and the local color story, the reconciliation romance, and nostalgia for the Lost Cause were formulas that editors, writers, and readers knew well and demanded often.

Rubin is more interested in the dissenters — writers with attitude problems — than he is with the established rankings as they appear in Stewart's *The Literature of the South*. Because Rubin was, in his early engagements with the powers of southern literary study, something of a misfit himself, his critical sympathies seem to go out to similar misfits in, as Hobsbawm might say, the work of inculcating beliefs, value systems, and conventions of behavior. Clemens comes first in Rubin's section and esteem: selections from *Life on the Mississippi*, including the rambunctious tirade against southern infatuation with Walter Scott, anchor the Clemens section. Lanier is retained, but he is reduced in stature; his achievement is demoted to "vague" and "fuzzy" (644). Cable conclusively surpasses Page in the standings; such genteel writers as Page carry reduced prestige with Rubin. Women writers — Grace King, Kate Chopin, Mary Noailles Murphree — achieve enhanced status.

Inclusion of Charles Chesnutt and James Weldon Johnson represent a rethinking of the southern canon from an African-American perspective, and Harris's Uncle Remus stories are suspected of being more subtle than Disneyesque transcriptions of folktales in phonetically rendered dialect. Irwin Russell's "Christmas-Night in the Quarter," the most popular dialect poem of the nineteenth century, is retained as a sort of museum piece. Booker T. Washington, of course, is represented, but his antagonist DuBois, acknowledged in 1996 as the author of one of "The Books of the Century" by the New York Public Library, still awaits the call. The section closes with Mencken's "The Sahara of the Bozart," a blustery harangue that works very well as the jumping off point into the renaissance of modern southern writing. One can well imagine the next classroom move: "O.K., class, if you were a young poet in Nashville in the 1920s and you felt the sting of Mencken's essay, what would you do?" You would start *The Fugitive* and write "Ode to the Confederate Dead" and *The Tall Men* and create the southern renaissance.

Rubin's section presents a clear curriculum of "beliefs, value systems, and conventions of behaviour" in transition from the conservative consensus represented by the Stewart anthology. The thematic imperatives of the Agrarian critics are felt even though their own works are not. Rubin tries to preserve some of the cultural longevity and coherence of the South while squeezing in the African-American voices and explaining the appearance of certain kinds of writing in terms of its historical circumstances. And yet his attention to "historical realism" runs head-on into the Agrarian myth of southern mind and culture. His reading of southern literature in the 1865–1920 period teaches us that the southern attitude toward life was "basically religious in nature" (a view stressed by Ransom and Tate in the Agrarian manifesto and repeated by Weaver and others) and that southern culture as a whole was "unable to view social conditions as the primary determinant of human conduct" (643), a conclusion based on Agrarian aversion to sociological thinking rather than on the postbellum literature. Much of Glasgow and Cabell, for example, disputes the former point, and such strong southern genres as the plantation romance and southwestern humor rely foursquare on social class and conditions as "determinant[s] of human conduct." *Southern Writing, 1585–1920* is an anthology distinctly torn, in some sections, between the beliefs of its editors and the words of its selections.

At the close of the decade of the 1970s, Rubin returned in a solo anthology, *The Literary South,* in which he casts off the social and cultural contexts of southern literary study: "The majority of teachers now approach Southern literature not so much as an historical artifice, paralleling the political and social history of the region, as they do critically and imaginatively, in order to show it as embodying the concerns and attitudes of the historical community. In other words, historical emphasis is now thematic and topical, not documentary. I have therefore included very few of the old 'standard' historical documents.... There is little about the South and its people in these documents that may not be appropriately developed through literary analysis of fiction and poetry" (v). This editorial position seems appropriate to the era of Jimmy Carter, the putting-to-rest of the long national nightmare of Watergate, the slow settling-in of the guilt of Vietnam, and the striding into what has turned out to be the false dawn of rehabilitated racial relations. Historical documents, as perhaps the Pentagon Papers symbolized, had no good news to tell.

Literary and aesthetic modes of study and thinking, we were reminded, kept politics and social action in their proper places. The shift in orientation away from southern literature in a social and cultural context — the original concept for the southern literature anthology — to a reliance on literature alone as the only "appropriate" subject matter and "literary analysis" as the only approved method of critical thinking on that subject matter reflects the establishing of a generation of teachers trained in New Critical modes of literary study.

The Literary South seems designed for this sort of market on both sides of the teacher's desk. It begins with a section of roughly sixty pages on the colonial South. Gone are most of the promotional writings — what Richard Beale Davis in *Southern Writing, 1585–1920* had wryly called "come-hither" pamphlets (11). Replacing them is the editor's claim that until the South begins to think of itself *as the South* under the pressure of emergent sectionalism there is not much point in studying its writing. With what remains Rubin attempts some literary analysis of a fairly bold nature — moving, for example, from John Cotton's poems on Nathaniel Bacon's rebellion on a beeline to Poe and thence "straight on to the assertions of the twentieth-century Southern critics that poems must be used as objective entities in language, not as extensions of the poet's biography, statements of intellectual history, or for their ideological content" (6). This critical triple-jump over three centuries seems risky; the headnotes to Cotton's work in the earlier *Southern Writing* suggest that Cotton's wife might have been the author of some or all that has come out under his name (Davis, Holman, Rubin 69). And the fact that much is skewed or lost by Rubin's preference for an exclusive formalism is obvious; even Rubin, almost in spite of himself, returns to Poe in *The Edge of the Swamp,* and uses biography and intellectual history for a compelling reading of Poe as a southern poet.

In *The Literary South,* however, Rubin remains unmoved by the ideology apparent in his own editorial choices. Jefferson, for example, is seen as a pseudoliberal rather than the Agrarian conservative of earlier interpretations. His concerns about the psychosocial effects of slavery in "Query XVIII" are still here, but his sentiments about "natural aristocracy" are gone. Rubin tries to balance on a thin wire over the problems of Jefferson and the history of the South represented in him, and in the attempt he exposes all of the dangers of forsaking context for "pure" literary study.

Part Two, "Literature in the Old South," steps up the ideological temperature. Here we are told that the primary structural element and design for the South is community, the opposite of which is alienation, the pattern of the North: "These [antebellum Southern] authors were very much involved in the civic life and concerns of their community and there was very little of the kind of intellectual and emotional detachment and alienation from society that one finds in New England writers" (70). Were Cooper, Irving, Emerson, Thoreau, Fuller, Melville intellectually and emotionally detached from "the civic life and concerns of their community," from the conditions of manufacturing "operatives" and mill workers, from prevailing theological debates, from the war for Texas and the Fugitive Slave Law, from the interests of women in social equality? Even Emerson came out of the transparent eyeball once in a while. In such passages we see cultural invention working overtime.

In *The Literary South* Rubin has shifted his investment from context to text. For that reason (and for others perhaps more practical) his arrangement is distinctive. Simms remains, but in truncated proportions: a few poems and the story "Grayling." His letters to James Henry Hammond, which show a few degrees of alienation from the ruling elite of his community, are omitted; and "Grayling" invites a strong interpretation that pits the community-focused mentalities of the grandmother and grandson against the rational and alienated mentality of the intervening alienated generation, the son/father. Moreover, what are we to make of the complaints of Timrod in "Literature in the South," retained in *The Literary South,* that the southern writer is a neglected stranger in his own community?

Other controversial statements sidle into the editorial sections. Poe, we are told, was a kind of realist: "The here and now, not a future perfection, is where the truth lies" in Poe's vision (71). Can the here and now be the turf of the author of "Ligeia," "The Fall of the House of Usher," *Eureka*? Rubin is compelled to go out on such literary limbs because, perhaps, he needs to make Poe, the major antebellum figure of southern writing, different from

Emerson or Hawthorne, competing major figures in the other region. Rubin yearns to make Poe incapable of the symbolic structure of the scaffold scene in *The Scarlet Letter*. But the ground shifts: the plans for the house of Usher and the house of Pynchon were drawn by partners in the same firm.

Whereas previous anthologies had been relatively frank about their ideological agendas, *The Literary South* seems intended to leave the impression that it operates without one. In an age sensitized to ideology, though, it is difficult not to feel it in this anthology. Often one feels steered toward a certain end with language that is powerful but indefinite. Consider the generalized statement on the antebellum writer and his language: "The Antebellum Southern writer faced a dilemma. In order to capture the highest human values and aspirations, it was necessary to write in a language that left out the flesh and blood actuality of daily life, as well as a broad spectrum of human nature" (75–76). What are "the highest human values and aspirations"? What were they in the Old South? What, more precisely, is meant by "daily life" and "a broad spectrum of human nature"? Is this statement a version of the slavery bind: to write about "a broad spectrum of human nature" the antebellum writer would have been obliged to deal with slavery and race; to do that would have alienated him from his community; alienation would have disqualified him as a southerner?

On the more immediate level of creating continuity and plot in the anthology, though, the editorial intent is plainer. Who can reunite the two opposites, language and actuality, highest values and flesh-and-blood? The answer seems clear, for the literary reputation of Samuel Clemens rests on these very pillars: the vernacular and the universal, common reality transformed into high art. He is the major figure between Poe and Faulkner.

"After the War," the third section of *The Literary South*, parallels in abbreviated form his essay in *Southern Writing*, with a few modifications. Clemens is still first, but his tirades against the Scott-saturated southern mentality are gone. Instead Clemens is reborn as Quentin Compson, the writer who is eternally pulled toward and repulsed by the South (289). This development is not surprising. As Faulkner gained in reputation and prestige, his themes and characters became — in the terms of literary analysis — the fulfillment toward which earlier southern writing aspired; if you wrote before Faulkner and could not show some contribution that he had absorbed your standing in the canon was suspect. Cable is reduced to one short story; "The Freedman's Case in Equity" is gone, perhaps in the hope that the nadir in southern race relations had been passed. Lanier is brought back from "fuzzy" and "vague" exile to the ambiguous status of being "interesting." By and large the literary selections for this historical period are the same that can be found in previous anthologies.

The section "The Southern Literary Renascence" is the keystone to *The Literary South*: here are the operative definitions that, projected backward in time and forward to "After the Renascence," the last section of the anthology, create the illusion of continuity and coherence. Following the familiar roll call of the names of those who made the renaissance comes the definition, the kernel of the anthology that defines its own character as a document in and of its historical moment:

> All [these authors] tended to ground their writings in their regional experience. However much they differed as individual, original artists, their works seemed to have many characteristics, including some that were largely lacking in other American writers of the period: a sense of the past, an uninhibited reliance upon the full resources of language and the old-fashioned moral absolutes that lay behind such language, an attitude toward evil as being present not only in economic and social forces but integral to the "fallen state" of humankind, a rich surface texture of description that would not be confined to the dull hues of the naturalistic novel, an ability to get at the full complexity of a situation rather than seeking to reduce it to its simplified essentials, a suspicion of abstractions, a bias in favor of the individual, the concrete, the unique, even the exaggerated and outlandish in human portraiture. (411–12)

Like all definitions, this one is flawed. We are asked to accept certain terms without elaboration: "old-fashioned moral absolutes" and the "full resources of language." Like all definitions this one forgets a host of examples that fit its specifics but lie outside its field of attention: Howells, Dreiser, and Dos Passos could not achieve a "rich surface texture of description"? It blinks at the danger of its own circularity: how much do the stories of O'Connor, McCullers, Capote, Welty and others actually create "a bias in favor of the individual, the concrete, the unique, even the exaggerated in human portraiture" that then becomes the standard by which their work is judged? Repeated often enough, like a southern *mantra,* the definition achieves the status of datum.

Such is the case with *A Modern Southern Reader* (1986), edited by Ben Forkner and Patrick Samway, S.J., both of whom have graduate degrees from Chapel Hill. Their introduction assumes as fact that the "great age of Southern letters" is the post-Mencken twentieth century. How much did anthologies themselves contribute to this perception? For Forkner and Samway, however, there is an even more severe corridor of definition. The Agrarian group, we are told, was (is) "the single intellectual movement in modern Southern letters" (5) and it follows, then, that if your writing cannot somehow be reconciled with that message, it does not belong under the heading "southern."

Forkner and Samway also push the authority of earlier canonical ideas into new territory. The community, which in Rubin's earlier work still had some threads of historical connection (for example, with the New Deal in the 1930s and 1940s or civil rights in the 1960s), becomes in *A Modern Southern Reader* a kind of mystical body—shared faith rather than shared historical experience. The editors' version of the Agrarian gospel is just that, a gospel that pushes "philosophy," "values," "stewardship," "the incarnational theology of the Bible," and "a spiritual dimension" (5, 462) as the significant tropes in southern literature. The editors go one step further to suggest that the proper way to find the South in their *Reader* is to probe for myth, to read for the inspiration: "We know, however, from our own collective experience of contemporary situations that Southern history, of events as distant from us as the battle of Bull Run and the surrender at Appomattox, even when studied chronologically [read: historically], have both an inner and an outer dimension, and these have to be properly aligned so that our vision of them [read: myth] has perspective, depth, and vital meaning. Historians must go beyond an analysis of the properties of the events they are investigating to the point whereby they can appreciate the thought expressed in these events" (459). This is a prescription for reading the South as a divinely inspired text, a prescription written for literary interpretation by Richard Weaver and others who continue to see the South as a community of fundamental "religiousness."

The same editorial team has recently added *A New Reader of the Old South* (1991) to their earlier reader. Editorial comment is limited to a thirty-four page introduction in which Forkner and Samway explain the origins of this second reader in their attempt to account for the predicament of the modern southern writer in unresolved conflict with the southern past. It might be unfair, they argue, to devalue Old South writers for being "unable or unwilling to penetrate the deeper life of southern character, white and black, male and female" (xii). The horizons of the knowable change over time. But even allowing for the strong Forkner-Samway leaning to the modern, their Old South reader is welcome. Its introduction can serve the user well as a research guide and bibliography; many works are mentioned in it that are not included among the selections in the actual text. And the contents themselves, in addition to some short stories and poems familiar from previous anthologies, include excerpts from slave narratives and popular songs that have lead relatively invisible lives in the history of southern literature.

A more diverse reading of the south (old and modern) is Paul D. Escott's and David R. Goldfield's two-volume *Major Problems in the History of the South* (1990); the first volume covers the Old South with the break at Reconstruction, and the second ends with the phenomenon of Sun-Belting. The editors have assembled "documents and essays," the former contemporary with the historical period under study, the latter representative of "the existing scholarship...published during the last decade" (vii). They promise to avoid taking sides in ideological battles, preferring rather to present both sides. They are as good as their pledge except, perhaps, for the period of the 1950s on to the present; here they neglect the small but vocal southern conservative voices, neo-Confederates like Richard Weaver and M. E. Bradford.

Escott and Goldfield's two volumes could turn the literary South back to the historical and cultural studies model of forty years ago—and now in fashion again. Volume I gives surprising visibility to native American peoples in the proto-South; even the destabilized hegemony of Davis in *Southern Writing. 1585–1920* proves conservative by comparison. The "back country" population, heretofore seen darkly in Byrd's "Dividing Line," takes on more human dimensions in the writings of the various itinerant ministers who toiled in those raunchy vineyards. Johnson Jones Hooper, by the way, turns out not to have exaggerated Simon Suggs very much. The edifice of the Old South aristocracy of myth—leisured, conversant with the classics, and benignly paternal to their dependents—is cracked. Landon Carter was constantly fretting over pilfered goods, blinked not at having suspected slaves whipped, and feared collusion and conspiracy in the Quarters. Place this next to the oft-anthologized chapter from *Swallow Barn* in which Frank Meriweather guides us through his happy slave quarters. Juxtapose, also, the turbulence in Georgia over slavery (outlawed in 1735 and reinstated, 1750) next to Washington's, Jackson's, Lee's instructions to free their slaves, and you understand the enormous complexity thinly covered by such good intentions. Jefferson was not the only hypocrite. Read Marcia Cummings Lamar's letters as she awaits death from a problem pregnancy, and you will realize that one neglected aspect to the southern woman-on-the-pedestal was her suspicion of a conspiracy to hide the scary facts of childbirth from men and women alike.

It is not, however, that *Major Problems* aims to batter the consensus of southern literary study to rubble. What the selections in the two volumes abundantly illustrate is that tissues connecting literary work and historical experience are shot through with intricate design — never simply mimetic, never wholly conscious, never wholly symbolic, never wholly one single thing. The section in Volume II on the southern renaissance, for example, includes traditional "essays" by Woodward and Tindall validating the "movement," an essay by Richard King shedding rare light on its unconscious dynamics, and "documents" by Odum, Mencken, and Gerald Johnson outnumbering Ransom (the sole Agrarian voice). In such a context, the student sees that Agrarianism was not "the single intellectual movement in modern Southern letters," as Forkner and Samway, speaking for the myth, claim.

What is to be done? The history of southern literary study, traced along the path of anthologies, is a history clearly adumbrated in Hobsbawm's anatomy of invented traditions. It is a record of the fabricating and wielding of southern social power, of reactions to changes in the meaning of "socialization" to the group, and — of course — of shifting relations of power among African-American writers, women writers, and the white males who have traditionally held the power. As a more diverse community demands its narrative of identity, anthologies respond. And grow: Ayers-Mittendorf's *The Oxford Book of The American South: Testimony, Memory, Fiction* (1997) runs to nearly six-hundred pages, includes more than sixty authors, and covers a historical arc from William Bartram in the late eighteenth century to Dennis Covington. While Ayers and Mittendorf are economical in their period introductions, they are strong in their implicit argument that something deeply personal and autochthonous distinguishes southern identity. Regardless of genre, regardless of historical moment, the I of the southerner stands out as exceptional in American history.

If there is presently an authentic crisis in/of southern traditions, as Eugene Genovese suggests and as I have debated elsewhere in this book, then major publishers have decided (as Rhett Butler did) that there is money to be made in the wreck of a civilization. In addition to Oxford, W. W. Norton promises a "Southern Reader" in the fall of 1997. What charges this complex brew of historical/cultural interests? Don't we all know the South well enough by now? Or is "the South" a process rather than a finished product, a process of cultural definition otherwise unavailable to several American "publics"? In the next two chapters I explore survival and resistance tactics in two groups using the South as a process of definition: black southern writers and southern women writers.

V

AFRICAN-AMERICAN WRITERS AND SOUTHERN LITERARY HISTORY

We are witnessing a cultural and political atrocity—an increasingly successful campaign by the media and an academic elite to strip young white southerners, and arguably black southerners as well, of their heritage, and therefore, their identity.

EUGENE GENOVESE, *The Southern Tradition*

What case could be made linking the cultural identities and political interests of black and white southerners within a common heritage, or narrative of identity? The answer lies deep in the chasm of the word "arguably" in Eugene Genovese's assertion. The history of the reception of African-American writing by southern literary gatekeepers has, until recently, inspired little hope that one identity fits both, that in the compound of African-American–southern, the latter subsumes the former. As the previous chapter on southern literary anthologies demonstrates, the sanctuary had been barred to all but the most accommodating (not only on the matter of race) for decades. Early anthologies (those compiled in the 1940s and 1950s) generally upheld separate but equal literatures for the races.

Recently, however, two senior southern literary critics have suggested that rethinking is under way—but a problematic rethinking in which black southern writers can be "redeemed" for literary history if their "heritage" can be argued into congruence with that of white southerners. Fred Hobson, in *The Southern Writer in the Postmodern World* (1991), and Lewis P. Simpson, in *The Fable of the Southern Writer* (1994), have separately affirmed that the black southern literary heritage is thriving within the southern tradition, and that, moreover, the former might rescue the host tradition from postmodern doldrums.

Transplanting C. Vann Woodward's claim from the early 1970s that the black southerner is the "quintessential Southerner," Hobson, in the final pages of *The Southern Writer in the Postmodern World,* advances the argument that the southern, male African-American writer "might be seen as the quintessential southern *writer* — with his emphasis on family and community, his essentially concrete vision, his feeling for place, *his* legacy of failure, poverty, defeat, and those other well-known qualities of the southern experience" (101; emphasis in original). The mantra is familiar. Simpson seconds Hobson's motion, in his preface to *The Fable of the Southern Writer,* and characteristically adds a nuance of his own. "A further fulfillment of the literary promise of the South" may be in the offing, he writes. "This will occur when the African-American quest for identity turns from the self-conscious rejection of the South toward participation in the southern self-interpretation" (xvii). Evidence of the turn, Simpson predicts, will be found when "the 'intertextuality' of white and black writing" in the South is fully acknowledged and explored (xviii). Admitting that he is "very conscious of the fact that [he is] dealing with the white writers of the South," Simpson does not offer a demonstration of the proposed intertextuality (xvii). Hobson does. His chief witness is Ernest Gaines, whose fiction "realizes . . . most of those qualities I have mentioned that were long assumed to be the domain of the white southern writer" (94).

Both Hobson and Simpson have underestimated the difficulties in accomplishing cultural crossover from African-American to southern literary heritage and history. First, attempting to transpose Hobson's orthodox, Agrarian-patented paradigm to works by male, southern African-American writers (his consistent and emphasized usage of the male pronoun effectively excludes female writers and jeopardizes his argument) runs into difficulty almost from the start. Family and community, sense of place, the legacy of failure-poverty-defeat emit significantly different meanings in works by African-American southern men. The issue of "concrete vision" — always a less-than-concrete concept — is even more at-risk with younger African-American writers. The works of Raymond Andrews (1934–91), for example (discussed below), make "concrete vision" one of many strategies, not the baseline.

Second, Simpson's implicit call for a halt to projects that imagine African-American identity in acts of rejection of the South and a transferral of this literary and cultural effort to "the Southern self-interpretation" is much more difficult to imagine, and to argue. What interest could exist that might persuade a black southern writer that his identity is to be found in an ideology so consistently exclusionary and prejudicial to him and to images of him?

In the next chapter I shall argue that the interests of a self-conscious community of southern women writers prompts them to imagine their traditions and identity aslant to (or quite separate from) the officially imagined South. How much more acute this degree of separation must be for a community of black, male, southern writers whose heritage and the power to name it have been denied by the same narrative they are now urged to affirm? From Richard Wright and Ralph Ellison, who saw the situation clearly, to more contemporary writers Raymond Andrews and Ernest Gaines, the answer to this question has never been wholly affirmative.

For all they did to found southern literary study, the Agrarian Fathers and their disciples in the 1940s and 1950s made the inclusion of black writers and their heritage difficult. Except for Warren, who in the 1950s was willing to see the desegregation crisis from both black and white perspectives, other brethren kept to a hard line of exclusion. Even the feared "progressive" W. T. Couch, who had functioned as the enemy for *I'll Take My Stand*, was something less than moderate when push inevitably came to shove. In the publisher's introduction to *What the Negro Wants* (1944), Couch, after explaining the volume's ground rules, under which the editor could choose those contributors he wanted but would be bound to "caution them against going to extremes they could not justify" (ix), Couch made sure he got on the record against changing "customs and practices and discriminations of the South" overnight (xx). Writing confidently from a white perspective, Couch was sure that the result of the "complete elimination of segregation" by legislative action would be as disastrous for the black population of the South as for the white (xx). By this deft and surreptitious move, advocating legislated desegregation became an unjustifiable "extreme." It was ideological control like this that positioned the black southern writer in a hall of mirrors and brought forth literary responses significantly more complex than the entrenched formula repeated, above, by Hobson and others.

A good starting point is Richard Wright, whose mantra of race-race-race was as unreadable by the conventional southern literary establishment as their place-past-community was to him. Well into the 1950s Wright's work was still officially labeled "propaganda." What the conventional formula lists as enabling parameters of meaning for the "quintessential southern writer," Wright saw as a political and social straitjacket. From *Uncle Tom's Children* (1938–40) to *The Long Dream* (1958), white and black family and community are presented, to put it mildly, as dysfunctional. Wright's "feeling for place" is anything but reverent. And "failure-poverty-defeat" are simply what they are, not the enforced failure of southern culture under Reconstruction, not poverty inflicted on a prostrate population by occupying regimes, not defeat in the Civil War.

In "The Ethics of Living Jim Crow," prefacing the 1940 edition of *Uncle Tom's Children*, Wright makes it stunningly clear that the utopia proposed in southern-renaissance theorizing is a dystopia for the victims of southern apartheid. Wright's South is not a lush, pastoral Eden but rather a valley of cinders where the "soil" does not nourish but literally wounds those confined to a struggle for mere subsistence (2). The plantation as social system, symbolized in white southern cultural iconography by the big white house* is a venue to be feared and hated in Wright's world (5). Wright's literary crime was not so much that he pushed themes that called for political action but that he revealed the "official" language of what Lillian Smith called "signs without words" (big white house, church on Main St.) as a language of oppression. His exposure of literary oppression should not have surprised anyone; Tate, by no means rare among his fellow white southerners, was on record in 1934 as favoring the continuation of "the white rule" and against a legislative ban on lynching.

The language recommended by his white peers, and the identification retroactively urged, simply will not suffice for southern writer Richard Wright. "Big Boy Leaves Home," often presented as one of the most powerful denunciations of lynching in literature, is also a denunciation of the literary tradition and protocol a black southern writer was constrained to recognize and use if he wanted to be accepted as something other than a propagandist. What, for instance, could be more traditional, in the literary sense, than the pastoral world in which Wright's story begins? Big Boy, Bobo, and their friends are Spenserian shepherds. Their race does not signify until/unless the bower in which they disport themselves is reclaimed as the private domain of milady and her hero, The Man. Except for the repeated train whistle motif, which means North and flight, there is every reason to believe that God's in His heaven, all's right with the world. The idyll continues as the boys, following Whitman's advice, become "undisguised and naked," swim, and lounge on the shore of the forbidden pond soaking up sun and warmth, making body noises, "laughing easily" (17).

---

*Charles S. Johnson gives an excellent digest of symbol and meaning in *Shadow of the Plantation* (1–3).

The serpent in Wright's inverted Eden is, ironically, Eve, the white Lady, traditional literary-cultural symbol of "The South." Wright's demolition of the icon in "Big Boy Leaves Home" is deliberately subversive of southern cultural semiotics. The woman on the pedestal, usually the object of venera- tion and worship, is the fuse for fear and panic. The "rape fantasy" overturns the pastoral—both seen as conventions. Big Boy and his pals immediately scramble, for they know they face a fate worse than death for even seeming to "eyeball" the White Lady.

Another symbolic figure now enters—the chivalrous white male. Wright, of course, knows this figure from the underside—as Faulkner had in making Percy Grimm for *Light in August*. Both writers know that in an instant the cultural hero can become deranged psychopath when the reservoir of racial/ sexual feeling is breached. Wright exacts a kind of textual justice by having Big Boy kill the white paladin with his own gun. The gun metamorphoses into the pen, and Big Boy, into the black author (Wright): Wright was "telling" the jury of orthodox literary eminence that he had no interest in furthering the cause of southern identity when the means disfranchised his own voice and experience.

Wright's work might have eventually drowned in a sea of propaganda and Freudian symbolism, but not because he could not swim in "literature." What could the southern renaissance have taught him that he needed to learn? The "literary qualities" and "ideological context" of writing by black south- ern men mark a battleground that has defied an easy truce, at least since DuBois directed attention to the writing of the color line at the beginning of this century.

Whatever else Wright accomplished in his writing—social change, jere- miad, social role modeling—he made a point that continues to mark an ide- ological chasm for many readers and critics, especially those who identify their field as southern literature. Wright simply and repeatedly insisted that life and art could not be separated, that those who did so at best deluded themselves into thinking they knew something about either, at worst engaged in precisely the kind of amnesia-producing propaganda they professed to ab- hor. *Native Son* (1940) makes this point before it gets to the extended "soci- ological or philosophical disposition" that saps some of its narrative (Menand 82). As the first subdivision of the novel, "Fear," makes plain, the black man's life (Big Boy is now Bigger) is fouled (if not doomed) from the start by the majority culture's control of his imagination. There are no images for com- munication and thought (save violent ones) except for those of the white master class. As Bigger gazes into the sky at an airplane that cruises like a dream of his unimpeded imagination, he knows that white boys get all the privileges (19). When he thinks he is escaping, in the cinema, he is only looped back into the ideological noose of the patriarchal master through Hollywood images of what he must be and cannot touch, of what he is simultaneously lured and forbidden to desire: the white woman (33ff.). Art forms within art forms create, for Bigger and for the black male artist generally, a discourse that is inevitably political. Just as the literary establishment of the South, like the entrenched political one, was naming all protest "extreme," Wright was learning that extremism was the condition of his experience.

When the young southern literary establishment confronted the issue of race in/of southern writing in the person and work of Richard Wright in the 1940s and early 1950s, the odds were good that although Wright might be lauded for his "power" he would be taxed for his lack of "literariness." The public climate was thick with the politics of race; one would have had to live under a bell jar not to know it. *Uncle Tom's Children* (reissued in 1940), *Native Son* (1940), and *Black Boy* (1945), the latter two Book-of-the-Month Club selections, handed the decade over to Richard Wright. And, with *Native Son* having since been designated a "Landmark of Modern Literature" by the New York Public Library, it would seem that Wright has held his own without the help of the renaissance.

Nor was he alone. Other black male writers—with far less luck in the New York Public Library's "Books of the Century" rankings—kept the focus on the intertwining of race, region, and literature. Like Rayford Logan's *What the Negro Wants* (1944), Bucklin Moon's *Primer for White Folks* (1945), an anthology of essays, editorials, and short fiction by black and white, male and female American writers, "was conceived, not as a book for the expert in race relations, but rather for the average American who is disturbed by the rising racial tension which he feels around him and by the paradox of white and Negro relationships in a democracy waging a war of liberation and equality" (xi). The answer to the paradox, Moon indicates, lay in unpacking "misconceptions," "stereotypes," and "legend" concocted by whites for the purpose of understanding the Negro (xi). Reading and writing were, therefore, necessarily intertextual, but the aim was political: to subvert or negate white southern reality.

Moon's novel, *Without Magnolias* (1949), makes the same point in editorializing fiction set in a southern milieu strongly foreshadowing Ellison's *Invisible Man* (1952). *Without Magnolias*, in other words, serves as a transition text from the so-called propaganda fiction of Wright to the so-called modern literature of Ellison. Ellison, indeed, knew Moon's novel and used it as an example in ongoing controversies he waged with Stanley Edgar Hyman and Irving Howe on the nature and meaning of African-American experience and literature. The purport of Ellison's two-front debate with Howe and Hyman, like the diptych of *Without Magnolias* and *Invisible Man,* is that a theory of literature and identity that claims to have black and white under the awning of "southern" merely draws a curtain over the problem of race and literature.

Moon's novel is set in a small Florida town, near enough to Jacksonville and Daytona so that some of the characters can visit the beach. The town is the location of a small, black liberal arts college with a founder-president not unlike Booker T. Washington. The parallels with *Invisible Man* are clear. Moon's fictional college president, Ezekial Rogers, follows a Washingtonian strategy of smiling cooperation with the local white power structure and financiers who annually decide on the college's funding. One of these white men is a liberal editor with good intentions but failed nerves; he writes editorials counseling "gradualism" in the black movement for equal rights. Another is a local broker who made a fortune in soft drink stock and whose idea of being liberal is to correct his vocabulary from "nigger" to "nigrah." The third is a faceless follower of the other two.

The parallels with *Invisible Man* continue. On the faculty is a young sociology professor, Eric Gardner, who has come south after growing up among the black, color-conscious middle class of Washington, D.C. He has written a book on the sociology of race to which many other characters in the novel allude. No one, however, says much about the book other than that it has made waves. Gardner calls the president "Kingfish" and, in general, pushes the theme of his playing the minstrel stereotype over genuine identity. Gardner is about as out of place in the South, with his progressive ideas and collection of jazz records, as President Rogers is in Harlem when he goes to New York on college business and attends a cocktail party for the "Talented Tenth."

Gardner eventually marries Rogers's secretary, whose name, Bessie, and whose jealous relationship with her more beautiful sister Alberta, echo the relationship of Bessie and Nonnie Anderson in Lillian Smith's *Strange Fruit* (1944). In fact, Alberta disappears from the novel for a time into a submissive affair with a married white man in New York; Moon explains the affair in racial and psychological terms that apply as well to the relationship of Nonnie and Tracy Deen in Smith's novel.

The important characters in the large cast of *Without Magnolias* include Rogers's wife, Ethel, a socially and color-conscious woman with more fear than life force; Esther, the mother of Bessie and Alberta, a more "traditional" (that is, folk-modeled) black woman; Luther, Esther's only son, a cooperative and hard-working black man; Eulia, his wife; and George Rogers, son of the college president, who is away in the South Pacific during most of the novel but whose return home maimed (he has lost an arm — readers of Cable's novel *The Grandissimes* will recognize the Bras Coupé figure) brings the racial, generational, and political themes to closure. George Rogers, Eric, and Bessie close the novel by "fleeing" to the North after Eric's public comments about the racism inherent in dropping The Bomb on Japan rather than Germany lead to his dismissal and threats of bodily harm: his convertible is badly vandalized while he and Bessie are watching a movie in a segregated cinema.

Plot summary, as is evident from this truncated program of characters and action, is a tedious substitute for the novel itself. Unlike *Invisible Man, Without Magnolias* does not follow its race protagonist through as many permutations of black identity. Yet, the novel's field is packed with variations on black identity, male and female, individual and social. The black women, regardless of age, talent, or beauty, are, for instance, limited by their ultimate reliance on sexual fulfillment with a man for "meaning" in their lives. Two of the women, Eulia and Alberta, seem satisfied only by white men. The black men are classified according to whether they respond to Washington's "compromise" behavior (Rogers, Luther) or Du Bois's "talented tenth" (George, Eric).

Without Magnolias is not particularly successful as a novel; it actually bears a stronger resemblance to Moon's *Primer* than to a comparable work of fiction — say, Elizabeth Spencer's *The Voice at the Back Door* (1952). But it is not negligible, for it surveys the field for African-American fiction and explicitly argues that politics is inevitable. Its title comes from a section midway through the novel when Alberta Matthews broods upon her decision to come home to Citrus City from New York, where her white lover lives: "That was what home was — the South. Not the gallant South of the magnolia and the julep, or the handsome white man and his beautiful wife, the lost cause that the movies were so fond of portraying, but the real South in back of the stage-set big house — niggertown across the tracks, circled by a harsh and frightened ring of poor whites whose only justification for being alive was that those above them had decreed that they would always, no matter how low they might sink, be better than a Negro. Home, Sweet Home, she thought, and it tasted bitter to her mouth" (138). There can be no black southern writing, Moon says in apparent agreement with Wright, without the oppressor's images and language, and therefore no black southern writing without protest against an enforced intertextuality that serves as a kind of symbolic bondage. The language of signs and symbols, then, must be deconstructed before — if ever — it can be used.

Where Wright bludgeoned southern textuality-as-identity (as it was controlled by white custodians), and Moon diagrammed it, Ellison eschewed outright protest by deploying what he called "'the American Negro tradition' that abhors trading on one's anguish and teaches strategies of survival instead" (Pinckney 56). Unlike Wright's frontal attack, Ellison's "strategies of survival" are sufficiently subtle as to entice critics committed to admitting a nonabrasive black writer to the southern canon to read him as affirming that project. Those with a need to find a black southern writer to bolster the southern canon accepted *Invisible Man* more or less oblivious to Ellison's restless position on African-American identity in its southern context.

Ellison is a prickly cultural negotiator; his terms for entering any literary tradition other than the Modernist, as is evident in his collected essays on the topic in *Shadow and Act* (1964), are stern. In "Richard Wright's Blues" (written in 1945), Ellison holds Wright less accountable for the "protest" in his fiction than the whites (southern and otherwise) who had burdened the black writer and the experience he portrayed with "certain psychological attitudes": "The first is the attitude which compels whites to impute to Negroes sentiments, attitudes, and insights which, as a group living under certain definite social conditions, Negroes could not humanly possess" (86). Black identity, and the narrative that invents it, have for so long been the property of whites, Ellison argues, that losing this fabrication might be a necessary first step in arriving at a genuine self. He might not adopt Wright's means for jettisoning the burden, but he understands the need to do so.

"The second attitude," Ellison continues apropos of Wright, "is that which leads whites to misjudge Negro passion, looking upon it as they do out of the turgidity of their own frustrated yearning for emotional warmth, their capacity for sensation having been constricted by the impersonal mechanized relationships typical of bourgeois society" (86). The Negro is idealized as a "symbol of sensation, of unhampered social and sexual relationships" (86) because white identity has tabooed these things. Whereas Wright could be said to have seen black identity in a hall of mirrors maintained by the white master class, Ellison saw the black image behind a mask *and* in a mirror. Creative duplicity was a stance that bridged Uncle Remus and *The Waste Land*; Ellison credited his reading of Eliot's modernist landmark as his turning point (Pinckney 53).

Nothing thereafter would be simplistic, and the search for simplicity itself would be suspect. Tropes of camouflage, visibility and invisibility enter Ellison's discourse several years before *Invisible Man* becomes a public text. The "defensive character of a Negro life," he observes from inside and outside that life at the same time, "so distorts these forms [of expression, such as the blues, the novel] as to render their recognition as difficult as finding a wounded quail against the brown and yellow leaves of a Mississippi thicket—even the spilled blood blends with the background" (93).

In 1945 Ellison saw Wright and the politics in his work more or less separately. But he also saw that whites who read Wright could not make a similar distinction. In "Beating That Boy," Ellison sees the politics *of* Negro literature as an issue to be differentiated from politics *in* Negro writing. "There is, nevertheless, an inescapable connection between the writer and the beliefs and attitudes current in his culture, and it is here exactly that the 'Negro problem' begins to exact a powerful uncalculated influence" (99). This distinction is one Ellison would insist upon throughout his career. Chastising Irving Howe, whose muted praise of *Invisible Man* he wanted to amend, Ellison asserted: "The protest is there, not because I was helpless before my racial condition, but because I *put* it there" (137; emphasis in original).

Shadow and act, visibility and invisibility, become potent tropes because they carry, for Ellison and for the reception of black writing he attempted to analyze, an amphibious, intertextual nature. Act is the object of intention, what I (as author or critic) "put there" in the work. Shadow is that "inescapable connection" between myself and my historical, cultural, social connection: not what I think I know but the surreptitious conditions determining my knowing anything at all. As the act has an overt politics, the shadow is characterized by a politics as well. There can be no segregation of the one from the other. As Ellison succinctly declares in "Twentieth-Century Fiction and the Black Mask of Humanity," written in 1946, published in 1953, "Art by its nature *is* social" (*Shadow* 38; emphasis in original). One might as easily assume that a tomato plant could bear fruit with its roots suspended in midair as we might that *Adventures of Huckleberry Finn* (Ellison's choice) owns its meanings solely in an airless formalism.

Ellison wanted art both ways because he believed it actually was ambidextrous: form and politics, politics in and politics of. He knew that most readers, especially most white readers reading black texts, would see only one part of the complex whole — the part that served the ideology of status quo. This is the gist of his complaints against Stanley Edgar Hyman in "Change the Joke and Slip the Yoke" (1958) and against Irving Howe in "The World and the Jug" (1963–64). The critics of the fledgling southern literary canon, in roughly the same years, made the same error: so intent on excluding the politics in Richard Wright, they missed the politics of Ralph Ellison.

"Twentieth-Century Fiction and the Black Mask of Humanity" is crucial in this context, for in it Ellison seems to want to give us (whites) clues to his camouflage. The issue of race for the southern artist (no less for the critic) is fraught with traps. "The early Faulkner," Ellison casually notes, "distorted Negro humanity to fit his personal versions of Southern myth" (25). So did Samuel Clemens. So do we all. "Indeed, so rigidly had the recognition of Negro humanity been tabooed that the white Southerner is apt to associate any form of personal rebellion with the Negro. So that for the Southern artist the Negro becomes a symbol of his personal rebellion, his guilt and his repression of it" (42). Not only the early Faulkner but the late too: no more incisive two-sentence comment on *Intruder in the Dust* (1948) has been written.

When we replace "the Negro" as symbol in individual literary works with the African-American writer and the issue of his admission to the southern canon, do we not reenact the kind of takeover of identity about which Ellison complains? Is black literature in the South really about the South in such ways that we can view the interests of both as coincident?

Invisible Man touches on most of these problems. Whereas Wright (earning Howe's praise and James Baldwin's pity) saw a political agenda as a way out of the blacks' plight in the twentieth-century United States, Ellison sets up the invisible man to see protest as yet another co-optation into white-determined identity. Advancing into the modern world from "the shadow of the plantation" is both positive and negative. When, in *Native Son*, Wright chose heavy snow to blanket Chicago during Bigger's attempt to flee as the symbol of white suffocation of options and possibilities, he imagined that repressive force as acting from above and outside. Ellison saw the control as having infiltrated black identity, as at least partially indicated in each act of thought. The black sharecropper Trueblood might be trotted out for a demonstration of the spiritual as a folk art form, but he is a deep embarrassment when telling his incest dream ceases to be metaphorical (*Invisible Man* 46;

58ff.). Cultural identity is a narrative the invisible man has not quite fully anticipated. The vet, a wise fool, knows that advancing into the modern world would turn black youth into the walking dead, for modern means white: "'Behold! a walking zombie! Already he's learned to repress not only his emotions but his humanity. He's invisible, a walking personification of the Negative, the most perfect achievement of your dreams, sir! The mechanical man!'" (92). The vet's warning goes unheeded; the youth takes Mr. Norton's advice and reads Ralph Waldo Emerson (106). One race's "transparent eyeball" is the other's "invisible man"—an intertextuality of appropriately double-edged subtlety.

Ellison seems to be as anti-industrial in *Invisible Man* as the Twelve Southerners were in *I'll Take My Stand*. The Puritan/Emersonian tradition is the bête noire for both. Whereas the southern Agrarians promulgated a program for disavowing modernity—denying history in favor of "tradition"—Ellison's protagonist, like Ellison himself, knows that his identity is made up of what he would like to disavow, as Ellison's own name, Ralph Waldo, links him with an ideology he would like to jettison. Invisibility, then, is not retreat from history, Ellison was quick to point out in his response to Howe. One was always in history, and the African-American was always in a specific history. The invisible man's donning overalls and his impassioned, effective speech at the eviction of elderly blacks from their tenement illustrate an investiture in historicizing identity. The dispossessed tenants are eighty-seven years old, which would put their birth dates in 1865, the year the Old South ended and the new order of modern history began. What does "the black" have to show for "emancipation"? Only the litter in the snowy Harlem street. Even the invisible man's effective rhetoric is ambivalent of outcome. Rhetoric gets him noticed by the Brotherhood, and notice is his entree into a "radical chic," where masks are donned and discarded as often as Kleenex and real social injustice is ignored. The invisible man learns that it is not history he has entered but a gallery of masks or representations. Booker T. Washington, Rinehart, sharecropper, Invisible Man—he can inhabit them all. On one side Tod Clifton lives up to the suggestion of his name; he plunges into his death having been consumed by the mass of the black American's history of oppression and shame. On another side, Ras lives up to his name, plunging into an inconsequential racial apotheosis.

Ellison wanted readers like Irving Howe to grant legitimacy to his invisible status: between history and race there was another stand. Howe seemed disinclined to accept a third alternative. Critics assembling the southern literary canon at the time were more willing listeners. Louis D. Rubin wrote that Ellison, at last, was a "Negro novelist" unimpeded (as Wright had been) by "social purpose" (*South* 19).

Ellison desired—even specified—status as a literary artist that has proven easy for most white literary critics, southerners especially, to imagine. Insofar as he wished to be taken as a literary modernist—an Eliot or Joyce to Wright's Dreiser—acceptance was easy. As Howe noted offhandedly, "the esthetic distance urged by the critics of the fifties" (11) created a kind of cushion for *Invisible Man*. A vocabulary of literary criticism as "craft, skill, and technique" (Pinckney 53) kept the political and social text of *Invisible Man* in the middle distance, and suited the author and his southern critics. Ellison himself had few compliments for critics who tried (or expected him to be) a spokesman for his race: "Thus when we approach contemporary writing from the perspective of segregation, as is commonly done by sociologically-minded thinkers, we automatically limit ourselves to one external aspect of a complex whole, which leaves one little to say concerning its personal, internal elements" (*Shadow* 17; n. 1). And yet he wanted social-cultural grounding for the "personal, internal elements"; he wanted blues to be a form and a tradition, *his* tradition as a black artist—as the terza rima of Dante could be Eliot's or *Ulysses* could be Joyce's. As Trueblood's blues passage in *Invisible Man* clearly shows, the content that came with the form argued as forcefully that one's art was racially and ethnically "determined" (*Shadow* xvi) as the artist himself insisted that he "put" the form and content in the work by conscious fashioning.

In the reception and evaluation of literary works by black southern men, the issues raised by the Ellison-Wright standoff have proven as stubborn (if not as overt) as the divide separating DuBois and Washington. Is the folk expression *literary* art? Stanley Edgar Hyman was not the first critic to suggest as much. Ellison acknowledged Hyman's attention but was wary of being classified with the folk. In rebuttal he wrote that "novelists in our time are more likely to be inspired by reading novels than by their acquaintance with any folk tradition" (*Shadow* 58). If the African-American artist were to draw consciously on his folk tradition, would he not also draw upon the experience of oppression that Howe, for one, saw as inevitable?

Answers become no clearer in the works of African-American (and southern) writers who have come in the wake of Ellison. Two examples: Raymond Andrews, whose work corroborates Ellison's point that novelists are influenced by novels at least as deeply as by folk traditions, and Ernest Gaines, whose work has risen to canonical status, show that claiming one's tradition(s) — modernist, African-American, Faulknerian-southern — is always a political as well as an aesthetic act.

The work of Georgian Raymond Andrews is persuasive argument that the path from African-American southern writer to "a further fulfillment" of southern literature is not smooth. As a male African-American writer drawing upon southern subject matter and maturing as a writer chronologically so as to pick up traditions from Wright and Ellison, Andrews helps us to understand the tangle of literary politics and history with which Ellison wrestled. Andrews's novel *Appalachee Red* (1978) presents a highly wrought, highly ironic Ellisonian work that drops its late-modernist erudition when the reality to be represented is the suffering of African-Americans under the heel of white southern oppression. *Appalachee Red*'s congruence with the tenets of renaissance literary identity is clear, yet the relevance of that identity is subverted as a matter of the novel's plan.

Appalachee Red is a "yoknapatawphian" novel in that its boundaries are quasi-geographical. Andrews's "postage stamp of native soil" is Muskogeon County, in the red clay northeast of Atlanta. There are crackers and aristocrats in the white population; among the blacks are town-dwelling bourgeoisie, farmworkers, churchwomen, semimythical baseball players, an effeminate gay man, a gentle giant — the full roster. The historical action of the novel spans the time from Armistice Day, 1919, to November 22, 1963 — conceding "history" to the white calendar yet tagging to those official dates significance from the unofficial history of the African-Americans of Appalachee.

Red is the son of John Morgan, the white aristocrat of the county. Little Bit Thompson, Red's mother, is a black woman who works in Morgan's parents' house. Little Bit is also married to a kingly black man, Big Man Thompson, who is shut up on a prison farm when Morgan returns from World War I without (like F. Scott Fitzgerald and Faulkner, and Faulkner's Percy Grimm) getting into combat. Out of frustration, Morgan makes Little Bit his mistress, and she gives birth to Red. After Big Man returns from prison and Little Bit leaves Morgan's "service," she gives birth to a second son, Blue. In the climax of Part One of *Appalachee Red,* Little Bit is beaten almost to death, and her husband is shot to death, by the town sheriff, Boots White. Before the violent death of his father and the maiming of his mother, Red had been sent away, like Moses. Years later, on Thanksgiving Day (November 22), 1945, Red returns to the town after deserting military service.

Red proceeds to seize power over the blacks in town from both Boots White and the existing black commercial and social structure. His power base is a juke joint and gambling den, ironically called the White House and located on Wall Street in Appalachee. Red also serves the best barbecue in that part of Georgia—cooked by a gay black man named Darling Pullman. It is important for the reader to register (and Andrews is anything but sparing with hints) that two simultaneous but not mutually exclusive sign systems are functioning: one is white, official, rendered as the ideological system that represses the blacks of Muskogeon County; the other is black, underground, subversive of the official power. Darling Pullman, for example, subverts the image of Mammy as food provider and maternal bosom.

In the second part of the novel, Red consolidates his power over the black population and eventually succeeds in establishing a kind of separate but equal regime in which he holds the social and economic reins on the black side of town. There is a black middle class in Appalachee, proud of their light skin and straight hair, but Andrews gives them short shrift. Eventually Red's half-brother, Blue, whom he had sent north for a college education, returns to lead a campaign of sit-ins and civil disobedience. Blue's redefinition of black power and his rejection of "accommodationist" relations with the whites of Appalachee eventually displace Red. He leaves town with Roxanne, John Morgan's daughter and his own white half-sister, on November 22, 1963— the day of John F. Kennedy's assassination and the burial of his own mother.

No synopsis can do justice to a novel teeming with incident, character, allusion, symbol, and literary gamesmanship. What Andrews has done in *Appalachee Red* is to notify readers that the "essentially concrete vision" of southern experience in southern fiction (an identifying trademark of the southern imagination in Hobson's case) can no longer be taken for granted. Ellison's modernist claim that other books influence the books of African-American writers is linked with Wright's frontal protest in *Appalachee Red*. Andrews strikes a tense equilibrium between affirming the folk and dismissing the (white) modern, and vice versa. Whereas Wright's race feeling is visceral, Andrews vacillates between head and gut. Whereas Ellison defends a border between protest and literature, Andrews writes in a liminal zone where literary systems are the means (and one of the ends) of protest.

How far will the formula of the southern renaissance explain what Andrews has made? By most accounts the renaissance was as dead as the proverbial doornail by the time Andrews began to write in the 1970s. White southern writers like Walker Percy were doing shadow theater with the exiting cast and scenery. Faulkner had been dead for a decade and more. The new New South of Jimmy Carter and Atlanta seemed to have rebuffed the old clichés. Protest seemed uncalled-for after the dark nights of Vietnam and Watergate. Perhaps it was time for all of us (finally) to say good-bye to moonlight and magnolias? Andrews is wary of any definitive answer.

Very early in *Appalachee Red* Little Bit Thompson is ushered into the domestic and sexual service of the presumptive white patriarch of Appalachee, John Morgan. An earlier Georgia novelist, Lillian Smith, had seen such an event as sexually criminal and racially tragic in *Strange Fruit.* Andrews sees it as just "another white-man-black-woman love affair, a then-prevalent southern pastime" (7). Andrews's cool handling of hot subject matter hints that what had been seen as first-order realism must now be thought of as trope. The adroit manipulation of literature-affect rather than the powerful presentation of "life," signals that Andrews has set his course for postmodernism by way of parody.

The reach of parody is an issue in *Appalachee Red* when Red shames Boots White by rigging his election as sheriff, then making him a gift of a white horse and an all-white cowboy costume. Boots cannot resist wearing the costume all over town; he makes himself such a parody of race and repression that even his white constituents are embarrassed. Parody is also an issue when Andrews turns it on the folk. In his repetition of the type-scene of self-creation through violence (for example, the fight between Frederick Douglass and Covey the slave breaker in Douglass's autobiographies or the birth of Big Boy in his killing of the dog in Wright's "Big Boy Leaves Home"), Andrews sees a place for parodic self-subversion. The scene in which Red expels Bird and Snake, his rivals for dominance in Appalachee, from his speakeasy, is a case in point. The two black men from the country — going by folk names — wield knives, but Red counters with a big pistol saved from his army days. The Bird, staring down the barrel of a .45 automatic, can only think to himself: "*a white man's thing. . . . a white man's thing*" (128), relieving readers of making the phallic interpretation and glossing retroactively the killing scene at the pond in "Big Boy Leaves Home." Not all the violence in *Appalachee Red*, however, is diluted by symbol. Earlier, when Boots fires several bullets into the body of Big Man and nearly stomps Little Bit to death with his jackboots, no discernible symbolic overlay softens the impact.

Andrews's characters exist not only in a mythic South where they represent another renaissance's story but also in a sophisticated literary-historical condition in which they can construe their own symbolism for us. This swing between simplicity and reflexivity occurs many times in *Appalachee Red*, most notably perhaps in the virtuoso ending of the novel in which the burial of Little Bit is the occasion for African-American religious and social aria — like the Easter Sunday sermon of Reverend Shegog in *The Sound and the Fury* (1929), the equally famous rewrite of it at the conclusion of Styron's *Lie Down in Darkness* (1951), or Chapter V of *The Shadow of the Plantation,* in which sociologist Charles Johnson explains the black church by evoking actual services. How far and in what particular ways can we take Andrews's novel as a transcript of what goes on in the South? Is it about the South? Or about white and black ways of imagining the South?

Does *Appalachee Red,* so full of southern matter, have as much to do with the imagined community of the South as it has to do with an imagined African-American community? Red is chronologically parallel to Malcolm X and even bears his pre–Nation of Islam nickname. His takeover of community power from Big Man mimes a changeover from folk identification to accommodation in (white) history for the black folk. The inevitable encounter between the half-brothers Red and Blue — White (Boots) having been banished to irrelevance by parody — signifies a symbolic ground of action upon which strategies of invention take precedence over organic processes. Red and Blue have the same mother but different fathers. Red knows the genealogy, but his brother does not. Red finances Blue's education at the University of Michigan (whose sports cheer is "Go Blue") with the agreement that should Blue ever come back to Appalachee he (Red) will exact full payment. After dead-end jobs in the North and Freedom Rides in the South, Blue (a variation of the Invisible Man) returns to Appalachee just as his mother dies. The brothers meet in the local jail where Blue has been incarcerated after trying single-handedly to integrate the dining room of the Appalachee country club. The confrontation between the two brothers, not accidentally reminiscent of an imagined meeting between Malcolm X and Martin Luther King in the Birmingham jail, is climactic. It is clear that Blue and his new model of racial power and justice (based on taking power from the white man rather than cutting a deal for separate but equal, as Red would do) will be the new paradigm.

The conclusion of *Appalachee Red* is literally loaded with cross-referenced semiotics. Little Bit is buried on November 22, 1963. Red had made his ominous return to Appalachee on the same date in 1945 while everyone was at the Thanksgiving Day high school football game. Red also makes his exit on the day of his mother's funeral, leaving his black mistress Baby Sweets be-

hind and taking with him in his mythic black Cadillac his half-sister, Roxanne Morgan, who dissolves in a prolonged fit of sexual desire and denial as
she surrenders to her obsession with Red, whom she calls Hawk. Appropriat-
ing Faulkner's radioactive climax in *Absalom, Absalom!* (*"I'm the nigger that's
going to marry your sister"*), Andrews turns the system of meanings inside out.
In *Appalachee Red* there is nothing but invented (southern) meaning.

Appalachee Red makes manifold literary historical points: that rejection of
the southern (white) narrative of identity is in itself a culturally and aesthet-
ically mature act; that there is a tradition of such acts readable back to slave
narratives and perhaps further; and that there is a tradition of white readers
being a bit slow to acknowledge each and all of the above. At his remove
from the heyday of the southern renaissance and the reign of its ideology,
Raymond Andrews responds to another agenda, another tradition with internal necessities that may prove eventually to have little or nothing to do
with "a further fulfillment" of a southern literary culture that had been so in-
hospitable in the past.

Ernest J. Gaines (b. 1933), one year older than Raymond Andrews, en-
joys a significantly better rapport with "southern literary tradition." Whereas
Andrews anticipates postmodernism by self-conscious manipulation of signs
and tropes, Gaines sticks to the rules of the well-made modern novel, one of
which is the separation of aesthetics and protest.

Gaines moved from the South to Vallejo, California, for high school and
then studied literature and creative writing at San Francisco State College
and at Stanford University (in Wallace Stegner's creative writing program)
in the late 1950s. Gaines is, by his own temperament and admission, a New
Critical writer: "I think art is order. I think art must be order, no matter
what you do with it. I don't care what Picasso did with twisted faces and
bodies—all of that sort of thing—I think there has to be a form of order
there, or it's not art" (Gaudet 16–17).

Gaines's talk suggests that his literary heritage—as he sees it—is not in
any significant way racially determined. He repeatedly mentions such classic
modernist figures as Hemingway, Faulkner, Twain, Conrad, and Joyce as models he meant/means to emulate. As for connection to the African-American
literary tradition in the United States, he is clear on not feeling a part of it:
"No black writer has influenced me. I went to California when I was fifteen
years old. Of course, I had not read any books here in Louisiana.... All of
my reading—even if I wanted to read about peasant life—turned out to be

by white writers. . . . When I went to college, I studied white writers. We are talking about the early fifties. Richard Wright was probably the most well-known black writer at that time, but his work *Native Son* was not taught. . . . You did not read *Invisible Man* as a part of American literature at that time" (Gaudet 33). Ellison had his "anxiety of influence" with Wright ("'I simply stepped around him'" [quoted in Pinckney 58]); Gaines knows of no trace of Wright or Ellison in his formation. If there could be a raceless African-American novelist, one who kept propaganda and aesthetics absolutely separate, it might be Ernest Gaines.

That possibility may, in fact, be the reason Gaines is now mentioned as the savior of a southern renaissance thought to be moribund. Fred Hobson "returns" to the work of Gaines after finding "dismal" conditions in the southern communities of Alice Walker and Richard Wright. "For it is Gaines more than any other black Southerner," Hobson concludes, "who realizes in his fiction most of those qualities I have mentioned that were long assumed to be the domain of the white Southern writer": community and place (94). When Gaines writes about racial conflict, "we find no editorializing, no special pleading. The story, the individual drama, is all" (94). Rubin's judgment in the cases of Ellison and Wright is echoed here.

But so also is the blinkered reading. Gaines's works do not so unambiguously refloat southern literature on the pontoons of classic "qualities." Ellison, in his rejoinders to Hyman and Howe, had warned against white critics, especially southern critics, who would assess the meaning and significance of black writing by standards brought to the writing, not by those derived from the work. It would be wise to consider Gaines in light of this caveat.

The Faulknerian presence in Gaines's work is strong. Whether it is the target of satire or parody is another question. Hobson marks Faulknerian sightings as further assurance of Gaines's traditional southernness (95). Such is the case, for example, in *Bloodline*. In Gaines's retelling of *Absalom, Absalom!*, Christian Laurent, aka Copper, the mulatto son of Walter Laurent and nephew of Frank Laurent, returns to the Louisiana sugar plantation where he was born to claim his patrimony — just as Charles Bon returns to haunt the design of Thomas Sutpen and as Red returns to Appalachee. But the Laurent plantation is not as prosperous as Sutpen's Hundred, and Frank Laurent is no mythical vessel for multiple meanings. To the black narrator, Frank Laurent is nearly powerless: "He was dressed in his purple silk robe. He looked awful sick and weak that morning. Frank was in his late sixties. He had suffered a heart attack about five years ago, and the doctor told him that he had to hire a' overseer or give the plantation over to his niece to operate" (163–64).

More Horace Giddens than Thomas Sutpen, Frank Laurent is the symbol of a dying order. Gaines neither excuses the old order nor lights a bomb to explode it. Rapacious, predatory, white male sexuality, denial of civil rights, and denial of social life to blacks were its evils. But the black community of retainers who have survived see as many evils in Copper's return as they see in the status quo. Copper is as arrogant in ordering the black servants as his white father had been in begetting him (204). His exposure to the world threatens the older blacks as much as — perhaps more than — it does the Laurents. Frank Laurent knows he will be dead sooner rather than later; rules can change after he is buried (216). Waiting suits Gaines's blacks, too, for they seem unprepared for Copper's Nat Turner-like call to be "men" by rebelling (208). Copper's Faulknerian catalogue of outrage and suffering — lynching, castration, violation, all under the auspices of "law" (209) — has little impact on the blacks except to make them opt for a kind of conservative inaction. They actually support Frank Laurent's view that until the law is changed to compel him to grant civil rights to the blacks, he will continue to withhold those rights (216). Faulkner's version of this confrontation in *Absalom, Absalom!* was punctuated by a series of climaxes — fratricide, murder, arson. But Gaines concludes *Bloodline* on an anticlimactic note. Copper, faced with his uncle's refusal to recognize his demands, merely goes away promising to return.

In *Bloodline*, "well-known" southern qualities seem not very positive. The sense of community and tradition among southern whites personified by Frank Laurent is anemic. The unity in the communal spirit of the blacks lies in suspicion of Copper, the militant liberator. Legacies of failure, poverty, and defeat seem confused; that is, the experience of some blacks — like Copper — is rejected by others.

This confusion can be seen more clearly in Gaines's *In My Father's House*, for the plot of this novel parallels that of *Bloodline* and, for added comparison, that of *Appalachee Red*. Etienne, a denied son, returns to claim his birthright, or at least his father (Phillip Martin, a black minister and civil rights leader in Gaines's "postage stamp" St. Raphael Parish) believes that is why he has come back. The son returns, as Copper and Red and Blue did, with outside ideas and a new name: Robert X. The blacks of the town of St. Adrienne who greet him know the instant he utters his name that he means trouble, and they shun him (8). Phillip Martin is, on the other side of the cultural coin, a black leader in the mold of Martin Luther King. Even though there is a conflict in the novel between blacks and whites over issues of social equity and legal justice, the resonant conflict occurs within the character of Phillip Martin and in the thematic arena of traditions of black manhood and community leadership: X (urban, new) versus King (rural, old).

Early in his manhood Martin had been sexually "predatory," picking up and discarding black women, fathering children whose names he could not recall. He changes when he accepts religion, communal-racial responsibility, and (most importantly) conjugal responsibility to his wife Alma. Not until he goes to her for more than sex—for intimacy in conversation, companionship, and confession of self-doubt—can he (and the author) call himself a man.

In My Father's House, although set in the South, is not primarily about the South. It is about the problems of black male identity vis-à-vis black women, white men, the community, and the continuing history of the Washington-DuBois divide. Martin has reached a truce with his white counterpart, St. Adrienne's Sheriff Nolan: "The two men had no love for each other, still there was no running hatred for each other either. Each felt the other was doing his work the best way he knew how, and both accepted the fact that there would be conflicts between them" (84). There is no such truce, however, between Martin and the rivals for his leadership and identity. Through his son Martin is forced to confront the searing experience of the rape of his daughter and his son's imprisonment for killing the rapist. X's alter ego in the novel, Billy, a Vietnam vet whom Martin meets, doubles the message inherent in the racial-familial situation brought to light by Martin's son: "This country here is the last cultural crutch for Western Civilization—what *they* call civilization.... Burn it down, you destroy Western Civilization. You put the world back right—let it start all over again. Somebody's got to pay for it, that's all" (162; emphasis in original).

Martin opposes Billy's apocalyptic view, as he must, by claiming that if one were to destroy everything there would be nothing left to fix. In the confrontation between Martin and Billy/X there is the clear allegory of a conflict in African-American leadership and male social roles. Andrews had mapped it out using parodic coordinates; Gaines is more realistic. It is not difficult to conclude which side he approves of in *In My Father's House*. "If I had been sent to Watts," Gaines explained to an interviewer, "where you had a total black ghetto, maybe the other thing [radicalization?] could have happened to me. If I had gone to Harlem, it could have happened. If I had gone to the South Side of Chicago, it could have happened. But I was lucky" (Gaudet 36).

Martin's growth survives the challenge of Billy/X. When X commits suicide, Martin is freed to lead a protest he had had to suspend to get his son out of Nolan's jail. And the search for any public acknowledgment of his son (and of his past self) enables him to pass from a "paralysis" that lay upon black manhood since slavery to a kind of salvation when, at the close of the novel, he goes to his wife for counsel and shared grief rather than for, in her terms, "the bed."

To make Gaines a redeeming southern writer is to delete much of this interpretation of his work. His "place"—pardon the problematic echoes of prior racist confinement of the African-American male—seems to be in another tradition. His most recent novel, A Lesson before Dying (1993) bolsters this conclusion. Set in St. Raphael immediately after World War II but before Brown v. Board of Education, A Lesson before Dying concerns the growth of Grant Wiggins, a school teacher, from alienation from his racial community to a redemptive reconnection. The saving means is the unlawful execution of a black youth to whom Wiggins ministers as a secular priest, but Wiggins's reconciliation with the community is also measured by the degree of rapprochement he achieves with the female community in the process.

Wiggins's predecessor in the classroom, a mulatto named Matthew Antoine, had bequeathed the nihilist credo "nothing matters" (66) on his deathbed, and the falsely accused and condemned young man Jefferson echoes it when he tells Wiggins, "Nothing don't matter" (73). It is precisely this nihilism—absence of manhood, as Wiggins's godmother puts it—that she charges him to teach Jefferson to outgrow.

The plot, then, follows a series of visits by Wiggins to the parish jail where Jefferson awaits execution. Jefferson had taken deep offense at a slur demeaning him as "boy" and had killed the insulter. Wiggins must test the viability of his own human (black, male) nature in trying to talk Jefferson into adapting to the original slur and to the "justice" system that will take his life for protesting it. The salvation of all concerned (including one white "centurion" who witnesses the execution) is at stake.

First, Wiggins must work through a refinement of his relationship with Vivian, a woman with two children separated from her husband. Wiggins's love for Vivian seems genuinely intimate (not the simple "bed" of Phillip Martin's early years). But as Jefferson's execution draws nearer, and as Wiggins's relationship with the condemned man deepens, he realizes that there are dark reservoirs of gendered self-awareness in himself that he refuses to explore. He gives Vivian a speech very similar to one Phillip Martin gives to his son (*House* 102) and similar as well to one Copper delivers in "Bloodline" (224): "We black men have failed to protect our women since the time of slavery. We stay here in the South and are broken, or we run away and leave them alone to look after the children and themselves. So each time a male child is born, they [the women] hope he will be the one to change the vicious circle—which he never does" (166–67). Grant does succeed in becoming John the Baptist to Jefferson's Jesus. He breaks through Jefferson's nearly inarticulate nihilism, teaches him to acknowledge the love of his godmother, introduces him to his membership in the black community, and makes him a kind of stream-of-consciousness evangelist whose notebook the white deputy gives to Wiggins after Jefferson's execution. That *A Lesson before Dying* ends in rather full-dress Easter symbolism diverts one of its main channels of development: Wiggins's reintegration into a racial community from which (through experience, education, and gender) he had been alienated. At the conclusion of *A Lesson before Dying* what is affirmed is not southern literary or social mores but rather the black man's membership in a traditional black community—if not necessarily at its head—and not very obliquely the Western, Christian world order Billy wanted to destroy in *In My Father's House*.

Nominating Ernest Gaines to redeem southern literary history may have some validity. But such an assignment should be made cautiously. What is the context? What are the interests served or ignored in such a choice? Are the criteria brought to the work, mined from it, or both? What has been elided in the criticism? The "place" of the black male writer in the orthodox construction of southern literature is mined with more perils to interpretation and literary-historical politics than we (white male) writers can comfortably acknowledge. Surveying the writing of black men since Richard Wright shows us that other issues, other meanings, other forms of power are at stake. The southernness of the black male writer seems peripheral to the fiction many of them have written. The hope for literary renaissance tells us more about ourselves than it does about the literature we comb for good tidings. It might serve well to translate Adolph Reed, Jr.'s, chastising of the white political Left into literary terms: "The key problem is that whites on the Left don't want to confront complexity, tension, and ambivalence in black politics. In general, they simply do not see political differences among black people. They do not see that blacks are linked to social, political, and economic institutions in a variety of different ways, and that those different links, and the networks that flow from them, shape interests and ideological perception no less, and no less subtly, than among whites" (18).

If the links and networks connecting, or distancing, the black southern writer from the official traditions of meaning and form in southern literature are open to reinterpretation, how much more so are those of white southern women writers? For so long thought to be only the *object* of writing, southern women have developed interests and modes of ideological perception and protest that are not necessarily congruent with those of the southern literary establishment. Over time this complex negotiation of recognition and meaning has gone through many phases. With the promotion of Faulkner's Quentin Compson to the status of universally acknowledged spokesperson for the southern psyche, a critique of that negotiation seems possible — possible, because Quentin is the target.

VI

SOUTHERN WOMEN WRITERS AND THE QUENTIN THESIS

For, in general, the study of Southern Literature has largely involved a community of scholars and gentlemen who are friends and fellow workers, and it has been a privilege to be part of this activity.

LOUIS D. RUBIN, JR.

In the same paragraph with the sentence above, Louis Rubin lists the names of those "students of the South and its literature" to whom he was indebted in the making of *The Literary South* (1979), his anthology of southern literature. Twenty-two names are called out for thanks: all male. Of more than fifty individually named contributors to *The History of Southern Literature* (1985), eleven are women. The name of one woman appears on the title page of the latter book, accompanied by the names of six men. There are no women among the Twelve Southerners of *I'll Take My Stand*, and only Laura Riding has made her way into the expanded group of Fugitive Poets.

Counting beans does not, in the end, necessarily prove the existence of anything other than the beans themselves. More particularly, listing the names of the participants in a scholarly project does not prove that those not named were in fact deliberately excluded. But, the overwhelming predominance of "gentlemen" in so many southern literary projects gives them a gendered character which must be taken into account.

Anne Goodwyn Jones, in *Tomorrow Is Another Day: The Woman Writer in the South, 1859–1936* (1981), explores the exclusion of the southern woman writer from her literary history and suggests what different character that history might have if she were admitted: "the southern lady is at the core of a region's self-definition; the identity of the South is contingent in part upon the persistence of its tradition of the lady" (4). As the honoree of thousands of toasts and tributes, the southern woman embodied the South but she was not permitted to formulate the toasts themselves, nor has she been wholly admitted to the imagined "community of scholars and gentlemen" who have for so long enforced the cultural program of southern literature. When the southern woman wrote, took up the work of cultural self-definition of which she herself was "diadem," Jones explains, those traditions of writing and of self-definition were shaken. Speaking for herself was not compatible with being spoken for or about.

The second half of the nineteenth century in the literary history of the United States and of the South furnishes abundant examples of the conflicted relationship between the image of the woman writer in the South and her actual cultural work. Bertram Wyatt-Brown's history of the Percy clan from the eighteenth century to the present, *The House of Percy: Honor, Melancholy, and Imagination in a Southern Family* (1994), furnishes a telling example. Sarah Anne Ellis Dorsey (1829–79) was a descendant of patriarch Charles Percy of Natchez (1740–94). Walker Percy, the most famous literary member of the large family, was a later descendant in the male line. If his posture toward the role of southern gentleman and writer was ironic and oblique, Sarah Dorsey's was sincere, direct, and material. In her last will and testament, Sarah Dorsey put her money where her mouth had always been: she bequeathed Beauvoir, her house on the Gulf Coast, to Jefferson Davis so that he would have a room of his own in which to write his memoirs.

Dorsey was born Sarah Anne Ellis in 1829 to Thomas George Percy Ellis and his wife, fifteen-year-old Mary Malvina Routh. Sarah, Wyatt-Brown states, idolized her father, especially after his early and mysterious death in 1838. She distanced herself from her young and vivacious mother, with whom she had little in common, and the distance only increased with the widow's remarriage.

Sarah's stepfather was generous with his substantial wealth, and spent generously on his stepdaughter's education. She was trained in the traditional female embellishments (art, music, dance) at a Philadelphia academy. And she extended her education into languages (French, Italian, Spanish, and German), as well as law and bookkeeping (Wyatt-Brown 124). Influenced by the intellectual societies and literary salons in the Northeast, Sarah tried to bring such social and intellectual gatherings into being in her native Natchez, with only marginal success.

Plain by contemporary standards of female beauty and unable to bear children, Sarah married Samuel Dorsey, a wealthy man the same age as her stepfather (twenty-eight years her senior). Wyatt-Brown sees her choice as a symptom of her suspicion of romantic love. She replaced that facet of traditional feminine character with large doses of male hero-worship. Dorsey venerated her biological father's memory, and when the Civil War began she extended that veneration to include Confederate warrior-priests. Bishop/General Leonidas Polk was high in her pantheon (Wyatt-Brown 131).

When federal troops advanced on a family plantation in Louisiana, and eventually torched it, Dorsey and a caravan of more than one hundred slaves and retainers trekked west to Texas where, combining Scarlett's stamina and Melanie's sense of sacrifice for The Cause, Dorsey served as a nurse in a Confederate hospital. Her war work, Wyatt-Brown concludes, was not an accessory to her life but central to her commitment to the ideal of the South: "Always working within the framework of Southern Convention, she was a firm believer in the code of honor in all its noblest manifestations, as she deemed them. By such means she and other Southerners — rich and poor alike — justified their rejection of Northern, especially abolitionist, indignities, and asserted their claims to independence" (Wyatt-Brown 132). As part of her credentials as a "believer in the code of honor in all its noblest manifestations," Dorsey "knew thoroughly" the *Meditations of Marcus Aurelius*, handbook of southern stoic honor and something of a holy scripture for as-yet unborn Percys: William Alexander and Walker.

Dorsey lived within "the Southern Convention" more completely than, for example, her fictional sister Edna Earle, the legendary heroine of Augusta Jane Evans's *St. Elmo* (1866), who strove, ultimately to nervous exhaustion, to become a writer *in* the South. Dorsey was a woman writer of the South who exposed but did not contest the constriction of that role. In fiction, biography, and her patronage of Davis, she affirmed the role and function of the southern woman writer of her time; she served the myth by serving the chief makers of it.

Her first novel, *Agnes Graham* (serialized 1862–63), was followed in 1866 by her biography of Henry Watkins Allen, Civil War governor of Louisiana, who was quickly assumed into the heroic male pantheon Dorsey maintained. Wyatt-Brown theorizes that Dorsey used the Allen biography not only to shore up the Lost Cause but also to "work out her understanding of a southern woman's role in a male world and even the status of women as writers and thinkers in general" (134). To bolster his conclusion, Wyatt-Brown quotes Dorsey herself: the feminine mind, she wrote, is "entirely too *subjective,* to attempt in any way the writing of *history*" (qtd in Wyatt-Brown 134). A woman violates natural law when she thinks historically, Dorsey maintained. Edna Earle finds the same taboo in her literary career, but the "natural law" that stops her usually inhabits a male body.

Dorsey wrote several novels before her death from breast cancer in 1879, but her most lasting impact on the South's literary culture is probably her recruiting of Jefferson Davis, upon his return from European exile in 1876, to write his memoir, *The Rise and Fall of the Confederate Government* (1881). She made the ex-hero's work easier by willing to him her Gulf Coast home, Beauvoir. In unmistakably material ways, Sarah Dorsey was, as Wyatt-Brown claims, "the mother of the Lost Cause" (135).

As the model of the southern woman of letters existing comfortably within cultural "convention," Sarah Dorsey affirms the ideological divide between thinking history and thinking myth. The latter was the only fitting work for a woman of "'delicacy or propriety'," Dorsey wrote (qtd. in Wyatt-Brown 156). The woman writer in the South was to affirm her culture's myth. About the only thing for which Dorsey faulted the Greeks, for example, was their choice of a woman for the muse of history (Wyatt-Brown 155). Women, as writers, wives, or participants with men in a common culture were never, in Dorsey's estimation, worth as much as men (Wyatt-Brown 144–45).

Paradigmatic quarantining of woman apart from history and from any cultural work, especially writing, that might impinge upon male preserves, continued into the twentieth century. In an earlier book, *Figures of the Hero in Southern Narrative* (1987), I explored Ellen Glasgow's "dismantling" of this reserved cultural power. Glasgow exposed the fallacy of the "natural" separation of historical thinking from the female mind by locating it in sexual bastions guarded by men. Her fiction, especially the "southern" novels published before the 1920s, exposes cultural phallocentrism by arguing that official history is not the only or even the fullest record of what happened to southern civilization, and further that the "heroes" have not summed up all that was meaningful in the myth. It is not surprising to discover that even after Glasgow dismantled male possession of the South, the same ideology rolled on for decades in professional study of the South.

It is not difficult to catch gendered ideology at work. Glasgow encountered resistance to the situation of the woman writing before anyone (male) had read the content of her work. She made use of this frustration in the character of Susan Treadwell in *Virginia* (1911). Glasgow fought through it; in *Virginia* she leaves the fighting to the daughters.

Another line of resistance is established, on the critical front, by the repetition of ingrained habits of interpretation that *seem* neutral to gendered issues but in effect are not. Consider, for example, Lewis P. Simpson's reading
of Elizabeth Madox Roberts's novels, especially *The Time of Man* (1926). In
"History and the Will of the Artist: Elizabeth Madox Roberts," Simpson fits
Roberts into a paradigm that negates her gender by appearing to transcend
it. According to Simpson, Roberts, like Faulkner, built lived experience in
local time and place into a statement addressing the large claims of history,
will, and art. Roberts's choice of rural Kentucky, like Faulkner's of north
Mississippi, "was dictated by the discovery that her imaginative reaction to
life in her native state defined the encompassing experience of the modern
literary artist: the experience of a constant tension between the self and history" (*Fable* 54). That the self in the case of Ellen Chesser, the protagonist of
The Time of Man, is female does not register in Simpson's calculations.

His identification of Roberts as "artist" accommodates his over-arching
thesis, set forth in an earlier book, *The Brazen Face of History* (1980): modern southern writers are to be construed as exploring and dramatizing modern estrangement from the natural caused by the conflation of self and mind.
Thomas Jefferson made a very early step in this troubled direction, and insofar as Simpson sees the southern imaginary flowing from Monticello (ade-
quately symbolizing in architecture and siting the confrontation of Mind and
Nature), Jefferson's mode of imagining southern experience becomes the central one.

For Simpson, then, the narrative of Ellen Chesser's life in *The Time of Man*
"confirms her immanence in history, her innocence or ignorance being only
the reverse of the conscious awareness of history" (*Fable* 60). And Roberts's
interests in this imagined life confirm Simpson's thesis about the southern
writer. Even the (hetero)sexuality that plays a part in *The Time of Man* is
subsumed to Simpson's thesis. That is, Ellen's sexual nature is not historical.
For Simpson, divisions of human sexuality do not entail allocations of power,
only divisions of biological function. Simpson's Roberts, being post-Freud,
understands the sexuality of her characters — as does Simpson himself — as
having been displaced from the "external" controls of an "elaborate, transcendent symbolism derived from an amalgam of classical and Hebraic-
Christian myths" to the imperative of self. The "mind's search for the meaning of sexual behavior encloses the self in history with finality" (*Fable* 61).
That is, for Ellen Chesser to think of herself as sexed subject (or for readers
to think thus about her) spreads the modern malaise.

Simpson's reading of Roberts is arresting for what it leaves out. Simpson takes the "man" of Roberts' title to be universal for humankind when it might just as plausibly refer to the succession of all-too-flawed males that shape the possibilities of Ellen Chesser's life from her father, under whose will she wanders from tenant farm to tenant farm at the opening of the novel, to her husband, under whose will she is doing the same at the close. Ellen's father, Henry Chesser, is an semicompetent tenant farmer who uproots his family when his failures collide with his pride. Her first love, Jonas Prather, discloses his bastard child with his proposal of marriage. He takes Ellen's pledge of betrothal, then marries another woman, leaving Ellen to find out from a third party. One of Ellen's formative experiences in the passage from girl to woman is her discovery of the body of a neighbor woman (a suicide by hanging) whose husband had deserted her for a younger lover. And Ellen's own husband, Jasper Kent, moves the ever-growing family at his whim, carries on an affair while Ellen is pregnant with their fifth child, and then rages at her simply because another man admires her politely from a distance. Paraphrasing *The Time of Man* in this (admittedly selective) way suggests that human "will" is indeed gendered and further suggests that Ellen is at least as much a woman as alternative to modern Mind.

Saying these things is not to argue that readers of such a novel as *The Time of Man* must choose one position or another. It is, however, to argue that in the record of interpreted literary meanings, choices have been made. And it is to argue further that when the choosers of meanings are predominantly "a community of scholars and gentlemen," even lofty intentions leave interesting lacunae in the record.

One particularly ubiquitous lacuna goes by the name Quentin Compson. It is next to impossible to avoid Faulkner's character in any study of southernness. Quentin is the major life-support system in southern cultural discourse. As the agonized voice of its center, his remarks about the South echo in books and essays, introductions and epigraphs. Although I agree with Michael O'Brien that Quentin's usefulness has been exhausted, and that he and his words "should be sealed up in concrete and deposited in the Tombigbee River" (O'Brien 163–64), I want to postpone the moratorium just long enough to use Quentin against himself.

Flannery O'Connor, whose views on the intersection of gender and southern literature have been generally overlooked because we have been taught not to think of her as sexed, observed acidly of a "Southern Young Man of

Parts" who came to visit her in Milledgeville that he "is busy building him-self up to be Quentin [Compson]. I think they all want to go to Harvard or Princeton so they can sit in a window and say I hate it I hate it but I have to go back. Or maybe they only learn to say it after they get up there" (*Habit* 63–64). O'Connor's razor-sharp irony does in a few lines what several of Glas-gow's novels accomplished by pulverizing the erstwhile heroic figure: the heroism and cultural eminence of Quentin and his clones is learned behav-ior, style rather than substance.

Even when he is not named, Quentin's "experience" of the South and southern history is authorization for a "familiar [southern] eschatology" (O'Brien 163). C. Vann Woodward is as responsible for the proliferation of the Quentin stratagem as any literary critic: "The experience of evil and the experience of tragedy are parts of the southern heritage that are as difficult to reconcile with the American legend of innocence and social felicity as the experience of poverty and defeat are to reconcile with the legends of abundance and success" (*Burden* 21). Briefer than most, Woodward's formu-lation is no different from definitions by Rubin or Brooks or Tate or any of the legion of white males who have assumed responsibility for inventing a style for thinking of the South.

Feminist critics are not unanimous on an alternative to the Quentin thesis. Some, like Carol S. Manning, might be called moderates: Manning points out the defects in the Quentin position but wants to preserve the status quo long enough to modify it for the admission of southern women's fiction (Man-ning 1–12). A little to the left are critics like Susan V. Donaldson and Anne Goodwyn Jones, who would like to modify the meaning of "history" in the prevailing southern formula (usually along lines of Foucaultien "genealogy") and, thus, run southern women's history into the mainstream at an angle (Donaldson 177ff).

More extreme is the position of southern lesbian critic Mab Segrest, who would have community admit neither men nor their history: "For there have always been Southern women who knew that they did not want to join the white men in Mississippi for anything; who have known that WE did not lose the war" (Segrest 29–30; emphasis in original). Segrest's view represents the most radical denial of the Quentin thesis, and it is not merely a matter of polemic. Her reading of the figure of the spinster (like Jones's reading of the southern-woman-as-author, but more radically) breaks the hold of the consensus in thematic literary readings: "The other terrible absence in male-dominated fictions is the absence of female community, or even its possibility. In all the stories I described [*Absalom, Absalom!*, "A Rose for Emily," "The Ballad of the Sad Cafe," and "Good Country People"], the spinster was alone, set apart from both men and married women. The small-town communities within the fictions showed complete lack of support for female self-identification. Without either respect for female solitude or the presence of female community, of course spinsters were seen as freaks (Segrest 35).

Segrest's critique fractures the ideal of community by alleging that representations of it have been unreflectingly male. As I have argued just above, Simpson's reading of Roberts could fall under this indictment. If Segrest's image of community is as narrow from the feminist side as any might be from the male, it is nevertheless provocative. In her "fable" of becoming a southern writer, exclusion from "the community" is double. She dates her initiation to the moment when she spied, from a distance, the black children who were integrating her school in the Alabama of George Wallace: "I have a tremendous flash of empathy, of identification, with their vulnerability and their aloneness inside that circle of force [the white males of the Alabama Highway Patrol]. Their separation is mine" (Segrest, 20). Segrest, establishing another ideological center, uses the vocabulary of the former center — race and community identification — to make herself a southern (woman) writer. Extending and "outing" Lillian Smith's deconstruction of the southern imaginary, Segrest links southern women writers in shared consciousness of exclusion from a constructed center.

When the center of a discourse begins to lose its hold, key terms reveal their ideological shop marks. Formerly reliable formulas do not account for all the variables. As feminist critics of southern literary culture and discourse have pointed out, familiar terms sport inconclusive meanings. As Donaldson, drawing upon Foucault, points out, history is only one record of what happened; there are also other "memories of struggles and 'illegitimate' forms of knowledge arrayed against 'the claims of a unitary body of theory which would filter, hierarchise and order them'[87]" (Donaldson 177).* What kind of narrative these "silenced and muted voices lying in the margin" (186) might tell is there for us to learn.

Elizabeth Jane Harrison reads the "other" narrative as a version of the more familiar pastoral. Her reading of recent fiction by southern women,

---

*Quoting Michel Foucault, "Two Lectures," in *Power/Knowledge: Selected Interviews and Other Writings*, 1972–77. Ed. Colin Gordon. Trans. Colin Gordon et al. New York: Pantheon, 1980.

black and white, arrives at a kind of utopian community: "Despite difficulties in overcoming the barriers to sex and race equality, female friendship and cooperative communities become an important part of the new southern garden for these women authors" (Harrison 14–15). Harrison's guide is Nina Auerbach's *Communities of Women: An Idea in Fiction* (1978), a work that is both about utopian communities of women in fiction and the product of the author's own personal experience of "a model community of women [the Radcliff Institute and its Fellows] who gave a local habitation to the Utopias I read about" ("Acknowledgments," n.p.). Female textual utopias exist, for Auerbach, in a ghostly relationship with the male, public community of history: "The communities of women which have haunted our literary imagination from the beginning are emblems of female self-sufficiency which create their own corporate reality, evoking both wishes and fears" (5). These wishes and fears are sexual, political, social, and historical; they are "voiced" in a "code" that, unlike the male code, is "a whispered and a fleeting thing, more a buried language than a rallying cry" (9). For a lesbian critic like Segrest, burial is deep and the code sexually complex. For critics like Donaldson, Manning, and Jones the "silenced" voices are still audible in the Quentinian din.

As Segrest suggests in her memory of identifying with the black children who integrated her school, experiences of racial exclusion may serve as metaphors of sexual exclusion. The historical trajectory of African-American women's writing, from the slave narratives of the nineteenth century to their "recovery" by Zora Neale Hurston and Alice Walker, suggests a common cause. The household, sexual politics of slavery produced in the community of women, across racial boundaries, a lively code, open to many and sometimes contradictory meanings. As Harriet Beecher Stowe would have it in *Uncle Tom's Cabin,* black and white women — though unequal — communicated in the channel of domestic management and sentiment. Chloe and her mistress bond against Mr. Shelby's purely economic decision to sell Tom and Eliza and her son. Eliza Harris and Mrs. Bird openly conspire to circumvent the public code — the Fugitive Slave Law thematically presented as a male language. In texts by African-American women who were slaves, Harriet Jacobs being the most prominent example, conversation within sexual territory but across the racial barrier is more subtle. Sometimes, in Jacobs's narrative, the lines hold, and sometimes they break down.

Solid or breakable, conversation in overlapping racial and sexual channels is vital to an understanding of the African-American woman's image of community as well as to the white southern woman's imagined community. The classic of the first half of this century, Hurston's *Their Eyes Were Watching God* (1937), is almost universally acknowledged as an encoded text on the formation of an African-American woman's community evolving from heterosexual, social dependence on black men into a very strong community of women that, according to Marjorie Pryse, "recreates the tradition of female friendship and shared understanding and heals the lingering impact of separation imposed by slavery and sexism" (15). Rather than attempt to occupy the discourse of history, from which black American women have been excluded even more thoroughly than white women, African-American women writers (with Hurston as the twentieth-century leader) have unearthed the buried languages of African-American folk traditions and community (2–4). The result, for us late in the century, is that in African-American women's writing, history is nearly abolished. Alice Walker's *The Color Purple* (1982) is the most famous text in which "black history becomes firmly rooted in the network of female friendship" (Pryse 20) and, thereby is removed from male control.

Not, however, without complications. As Barbara Christian, and others, have pointed out, the fiction of African-American women writers of the latter half of this century (especially of the last twenty years) disturbs the sexual politics of the African-American community. "[Alice] Walker," Christian asserts, "sees the possibility of empowerment for black women if they create a community of sisters which can alter the present-day unnatural definitions of man and woman" (Christian 243). African-American women's writing, through the power of *The Color Purple*, seems poised to abolish not only public history in favor of "a community of sisters" but also to abolish black men, in their current identity, as "unnatural" pests to this community. African-American male writers, lead by Ishmael Reed, have objected to the abolition (Reed 145–60). Writers less pugnacious than Reed, as I tried to show in the previous chapter, acknowledge the friction.

The themes of African-American women's writing and Reed's objections will have to be part of another discussion. Here, I would like to stay entangled in the codes of white southern women's writing by investigating a few examples by southern women writing in the latter half of this century. Pervasive in this critical discourse is recent work by feminist critics and scholars, both black and white, lesbian and undeclared. Christian frames the terms of the discussion, "One question which these novels [by black women of the 1970s and 1980s] leave unanswered is whether the bond between women might be so strong that it might transcend the racial and class divisions among women in America, and make possible a powerful women's community that might effect significant change" (247).

Something has to give: one definition of southern community, enabling participation in its discourse, requires a "Quentissential" experience of race and history; another claims to "transcend the racial and class divisions among women in America," creating an entirely new discourse in many ways not southern at all. Transcending race leaves the Quentin thesis seriously damaged. In Chapter III I argued that orthodox narratives of southern literary history have been grafted to Faulknerian stock. If the stock is simply left untended, what will happen to the fruit?

The configuration of race, tragedy, moral turbulence, blood violence, and guilt and expiation (the Faulkner-Quentin model), apparently so unquestionably appropriate — even natural — to southern rites of community, produced, to the skeptical mind, the result of voiding the need for cultural change or social action and was therefore seen as an evasion strategy. Heritage was seen as organic; tampering would be death. In times dominated by *Brown v. Board of Education*, the Quentin thesis could be used to obscure certain aspects of southern history and experience.

Louis Rubin was not deaf to this problem. In "Second Thoughts on the Old Gray Mare," an important essay from the 1960s, he takes up the question of the continuity of the literary traditions he had done so much to identify and to promulgate. Is their continuing force healthy for the South in an era when change seems unstoppable? The aim of "Second Thoughts" is to "prove" that continuity is not resistance; Rubin argues that "change in one of the South's most traditional attitudes" (the place of the Negro in the segregated South) will *not* mean an end to the southern renaissance or a destructive revision in our understanding of southern literature as founded on the tragically opposed communal attitudes of racial separation and regional-historical identity. Reading Styron's *The Confessions of Nat Turner*, Rubin convinces himself that fundamental change can occur without hampering the continuity of southern literature as a living body of work distinct from any others in the history of literature in the United States. He concludes that because the nature of the southern community is religious rather than historical, the South can and will negate race as a fundamentally reshaping force. "[W]hat is really happening," Rubin claims, "is that the Negro is being brought *into* the community. The essential community is still there" (Gray 266; emphasis in original).

As in the past, the significance of the essential community is verified in the tragic component of Faulkner's work:

> The South has been caught up in a process of transition which has been marked by considerable turmoil and ugliness. Its literature has been one of the happier products of this process. Not merely along with but indeed *directly out of* the turmoil and even the violence of the changing South, there have come novels and poems which have fixed the image of the South in art and have given to it the imaginative dignity of tragedy and comedy. In particular William Faulkner has created high tragedy out of the southern experience. Not only does this afford southerners the occasion for much understandable pride, but it also constitutes assurances that what has been going on in the region during Faulkner's lifetime and our own is not simply ugly, but also highly meaningful, so that the confused positions we have occupied add up finally to a drama of definition, with the contending forces representing not merely sordid self-interest but profoundly important human needs and aspirations. (Gray 256; emphasis in original)

Rubin's critical voice is authoritative. He declares that southern self-definition is a process of turmoil and violence, that the novel is the literary form in which the authentic cultural image of the South will be found, and that Faulkner has pressed his character upon the entire project.

The gendered subtext in the debate over self-definition was "outed" by Fred Hobson in his Lamar Lectures, *The Southern Writer in the Postmodern World* (1991). Hobson assumes what Sarah Dorsey had assumed in the 1870s, that history is a male preserve, that southern women are to be "Dixie's diadem," not its historians. Southern women writers, Hobson argues, had failed to supply us with the "big work," one with the Faulknerian "sweep of history": "Whether this is because the male, particularly in southern society, was usually conditioned to think more ambitiously, that is, to ponder history and politics in which *he,* after all, could more easily participate—or whether it is because the vision of the male writer has tended for other reasons to be more abstract, less attentive to everyday truths and concrete details than that of most women writers—is debatable" (Hobson 78; emphasis in original).

The question of how a southern woman's writing would or would not bolster the consensus as the Quentin thesis defines it is not a new question. Anne Goodwyn Jones, Drew Gilpin Faust, and Elizabeth Fox-Genovese are among several critics who have sought, from various points on the ideological compass, a southern woman's literary and cultural presence in the nineteenth century that they might then trace forward into collision or conflu-

ence with the apparently genderless southern identity of the twentieth. Whatever the course of the transmission may be, it is evident that fiction by modern southern women is highly conscious of its implication in cross-currents
of traditions that do not share objectives or modes of operation. If their works
share identifying traits, they are the traits of writers united in the complicated enterprise of getting out from under one burden of cultural assumption
(Faulknerian/southern) and trying out the viability of another (feminist/
utopian).

It is not as if we have not seen evidence of this contest of traditions before. *Delta Wedding* (1946), Eudora Welty's first novel, suggests that tragedy
and violence keyed to gender and race are not universally meaningful in
imagining the South. In one scene, Shelley Fairchild — the oldest daughter
of the Fairchild clan but not the one to be wed — stumbles into an encounter
between her future brother-in-law, the overseer on the Fairchild plantation,
and a black field hand. Troy Flavin, the overseer, shoots a finger and a knife
out of the hand of the black worker. Troy, Welty tells us, is not a Delta man
but a son of the hill country to the east — perhaps from the precincts of Yoknapatawpha — where violence is a social habit. Shelley, having jumped over
the bloody doorsill to flee the overseer's office, runs back to the maternal
house thinking: "Suppose the behavior of all *men* were actually no more than
this — imitation of other men. . . . Then all men could not know any too well
what they were doing" (Welty 196; emphasis in original). If the men, merely
imitating the practice of the men they have seen (or read about, as O'Connor might suggest) control the cultural text, what becomes of the argument
from "essential community?" And what of the community that the maimed
black man, repeating Cable's Bras Coupé and the wounded returning veteran of *Without Magnolias*, might have written with the finger the white man
obliterated? *Delta Wedding* adroitly undermines one "southern" community,
that of white males on the public stage, while it reserves point of view and
narrative voice for the women. Consciousness, reflection, memory are reserved to the Fairchild women in the novel. Subtly Welty drives a wedge between the two traditions, suggesting in her technical choice of the women
for points of view that they are the genuine tellers and crafters of cultural
definition and continuity.

Southern women writers who acknowledge Welty among their precursors
have widened and deepened her critique. Their work is characterized not so
much by the stereotypically feminine pre-occupations that Hobson and fellow readers seem to assume, as it is by a complex textual and cultural politics

that attempts to accommodate wrangling claims of aesthetic form, cultural self-definition, and gender loyalties.

This observation is not to assert, on blind behalf of such writers as Lee Smith, Josephine Humphreys, and Jill McCorkle (each of whom published with popular and critical notice in the 1980s), an overt revisionist agenda. I have chosen novels by these three women because their work strikingly represents the "situation" of the southern woman writer balancing the claims of region and gender.

Lee Smith's novel *Oral History* (1983) is an ironic inquiry into the question of the "natural" continuity of southern community in an age when the satellite dish can supply more virtual community than one person can absorb. What is the connection, Smith's novel asks, between lived (southern) experience, contemporary or historical, and varieties available for replication? Is the Quentin thesis the most effective — or indeed the only — means of recovering meaning out of contingency?

The major structural and chronological elements of *Oral History* are mapped, in Faulknerian order, by a genealogical pattern that gradually becomes denser, more fully articulated with names and unions and relationships. In the orthodox Faulknerian recipe, however, the various strands knot and apotheosize in a single male: Isaac McCaslin, Chick Mallison, Quentin himself. But is *Oral History*'s Jennifer a Quentin Compson? Does the meaning of the South, the meaning of history itself, hinge on her findings? Is she dancing on the railing of the bridge over the Charles River? Or, like Isaac McCaslin, is she on the threshold of a genealogical discovery that will "unman" her, unfit her for history? Smith's strategy, in *Oral History*, is to summon these literary ghosts and then to dose them with irony. For Jennifer the past is dead as a mackerel. And her historical community seems far less concerned with conjuring a mythic past from a few minutes before two o'clock on July 3, 1863, than with cruising into the future of mall and theme park.

"Historical time" might elapse in the course of *Oral History*, but communal time (in Foucault's sense, filtered through Donaldson) is different, cyclical rather than linear. The Hoot Owl Holler maps printed on the book's inside front and back covers suggest as much. The reader is reminded once again of Faulkner's use of maps for his apocryphal Yoknapatawpha. A fully drawn genealogy, however, is never dramatically supplied in the novel, even though *Oral History* covers the years from immediately after the Civil War, when Almarine Cantrell (I)'s father Van returns from battle and dies, to the

1980s with the bubba apotheosis of Almarine (II), flush with Amway dollars and successful developer of the homeplace into Ghostland, "the prettiest theme park east of Opryland itself" (Smith 285). The transformation of Quentin's native ground from southern birthright to golf course ate away financially and psychologically at the Compson scion; in *Oral History* no one seems to care very much. Under the control of the men, community is deauthenticated, turned into a commodity, a replica of itself and, after lapsing into Baudrillardian simulacrum, seems to engage no one.

The truly authentic "events" in *Oral History* are almost exclusively those of a muted, female sphere: marriages, births, breakings of unions, deaths, and burials. Only rarely does Quentinian, tragic history make an appearance in the novel, and always by violence: the death of Almarine (I) in a family feud; Richard Burlage's encounter with a union sympathizer during his second visit to Hoot Owl Holler (when the man shoots out the rearview mirror of his car).

Community in the "old" or essential sense (as a shared, conscious and unconscious set of prompts and gestures and attitudes organized around an image of that community in history) is traced on its way down and out in Smith's novel. The literary and cultural power often cited as the distinguishing mark of the renaissance (for Woodward, Rubin, Simpson, and others) is weakly apparent in Smith's work. Not because, as King's or Hobson's theses would have it (that history is beyond the woman writer's ken either by choice or by aptitude) but ironically because it is well within her ken as a script of learned behaviors diminishing in meaning with each repetition.

Nor is tragedy Smith's genre. Jennifer, like Quentin the receptacle of the voices of the past, escapes his tragic end by possessing the voices via her tape recorder, not in her head. In the latter days of *Oral History* she is quite resistant to tragic haunting. The men in her life are resistant to tragedy as well. Her mentor and future husband, Dr. Bernie Ripman, is an outsider like Shreve who sees the South as a vast entertainment as gripping as *Ben-Hur*; and her grandfather is Richard Burlage — a decadent Richmond aristocrat who went to the mountains to recuperate from terminal self-consciousness. Both men wish to subdue the "wild" or "fantastic" nature of the Holler inside the brackets of an academic discipline or a shallow ego that puffs itself as authoritative.

Jennifer, the unacknowledged granddaughter of Richard Burlage and Dory Cantrell (the golden child of the mountain sanctuary), suffers from anemic cultural blood thinned by too much exposure to imitations of life taught from textbooks by the likes of Bernie Ripman. She can see her kin only through the fatal mediation of academic jargon (not "community" but "extended family situation") and the equally embalmed coldness of the conventions of the picturesque (Smith 6). The most telling sign of her dislocation comes at the close of the book when her uncle Almarine (II) roughly kisses her—an unwanted sexual assault—and she erases the episode with the irrelevant cliché that he and all of his kind just live "so close to the land" (Smith 290) that what actually happened to her in fact did not.

Jennifer comes by her obtuseness genetically as well as culturally. Her grandfather, Richard Burlage, jots down his impressions as he has them; every experience has a secondary aspect almost before the primary. His first sight of Claypool Hill, the rail depot nearest Hoot Owl Holler, reminds him of its simulacrum—a stage or movie set (Smith 106). Having passionate sex with Dory—whom he sees not as a herself but as a portrait by Botticelli—he steps back mentally to muse upon himself in the act of making love (Smith 146). Burlage's affliction approaches the pathetic—not the tragic—when, about a decade after his first encounter, he revisits the mountain coal camp where Dory lives. Not surprisingly he comes as a Works Progress Administration photographer, one whose cultural work is to confront the three-dimensional real and to transform it into the two-dimensional virtual. He sees twin girls, Maggie and Pearl, but does not think to ask if they might be his own daughters. Dory appears, but in such a fading light that her image escapes his mechanical apparatus as well as his personal recognition. Ecstasy forgotten, Burlage departs.

Smith's achievement in *Oral History* is unthinkable without the orthodox thematics and narrative patterns of Quentinian southern literature. *Oral History* seems to eschew the "sweep of history" and the apotheosis of the hero in confrontation with history, not because the author cannot grasp such concepts but because Smith prefers to handle theme and structure with the irony of a postmodern southerner cognizant of her gendered perspective.

Perhaps taking the lesson of *Delta Wedding,* Smith shifts the central focus of community experience from the isolated, tragic male to the community of the female. To Granny Younger, for example, whose record of experience is kept in herbs, poultices, and witches, go the significant acts of expelling Almarine (I) from the site of the miraculous birth of his daughter Dory, and of naming the child herself—that is, rescuing the child and all she symbolically represents from male configuration. Dory is born at the center of a community the male literally cannot register because that community is in its very constitution beyond his "history." Richard Burlage, for example, never sees Dory except as mediated by an image made by Botticelli (Smith 116). He counters Dory's own passion, her calls for Richard to serve her sexually, by his own spectatorial retaliation. Their first time in bed, Richard marvels at Dory as an object: "'Sit up. Sit up for a second,' I said. 'I want to see you,' and she sat up and lifted her blouse to reveal them, two white orbs as round as apples, with the nipples aroused and pointed" (Smith 145). As grateful and amazed a lover as Richard is, he transforms Dory from living woman into still life with apples. On his return to the mountain years later, he fails to capture her image at all.

Oral History signifies on traditional images of the origin and nature of southern community in history, even as it pleads for a redefinition of community in the woman's register. Linda Wagner-Martin has addressed this question by interrogating the traditional relation between place and community as it is thematized in works by southern women writing "now." Her questions are unsettling to the older consensus when we consider how possible answers might reverse or negate crucial assumptions supporting that consensus. Wagner-Martin indirectly tries to hold up the bridge between old and new by attempting to assimilate the model of Isaac McCaslin/Sam Fathers to the female experience. But Oral History anticipates amelioration by suggesting that such a model of initiation into history by ordeal is marginal, a cruel and unusual punishment for the privilege of identity. The initiation of Dory's son Jink through such a bloody ritual re-presents the Faulknerian "original" (Smith 192ff).

Oral History sets the terms for covert revision of the Quentin thesis of southern identity and suggests that white southern women writers working in the last third of this century find that thesis a vehicle for ironic antistrophe rather than affirmative strophe. Memory dissolves over time. Place is replaced with virtual reality. Rites of identification are jolted off-center by the suggestion that their presumption of universality might be vulnerable.

Josephine Humphreys's Rich in Love (1987) carries the critique of historical southern community further by suggesting that the central agonistic rite of belonging — racial conflict — might be more antique than vital. In Humphreys's postmodern South there is no simultaneity of real and replica; in Rich in Love nothing but simulacra are available in the search for meaning. Lucille Odum's narrative shrewdly copes with the faking of place, situating the novelist, as Fred Hobson has pointed out, in the literary company of Walker Percy (Hobson 58–72). Percy's lost gentlemen, however, seek a mooring in a southern history that was, for a former generation, actual. Will Barrett had forebears who knew what to do. Nevertheless, he cannot organize an identity as successfully as Humphreys's Lucille, with no help from history or from the males in her life. The males of *Rich in Love* are clearly prisoners of their expectation that a certain kind of action is called for when, in fact, it is not.

Like Will Barrett or Tom More, Lucille Odum has an eye for the sideshow of reenacted past, the tourist pageant that the modern South has become. Unlike Percy's "heroes," however, she is not paralyzed when she confronts absence of meaning. Her description of one ruined condo development, Osceola Pointe, might seem to fit *Love in the Ruins*: "A fire had since damaged one section, bringing the builders a little more insurance money. The building stood empty, windows out, weeds coming up in the reception court. Hawks nested in a third-floor apartment" (Humphreys 77). Modern ruin has come about as much for moral reasons as for financial shenanigans. The contemporary ethos proceeds—as it had in *Oral History*—along the path from the genuine to the simulacrum driven by blind demands of the market because "good men" have forfeited the power or nerve to distinguish the real from the fake. Humphreys's downtown Charleston scenes, for example, point to trumped-up tourist replicas that Alexandra Ripley's "historical novel" *Scarlett* presents as the real thing back-dated a century. There is a sort of ironic, postmodern propriety in Ripley's having Scarlett, a replica cubed, walk through an "Epcot" setting. Lucille would reverse this fall into fakery, if she could:

> I had an urge to commandeer the [tour] bus and take the tourists on a different kind of tour, run them up Highway 17 to the new Builderama, Osceola Pointe, Palmetto Villas, Rhody's house, Fishbone's. I'd roll down all the windows of the bus and let people hang their heads out and really see something worth seeing, the transformation of the world. "Look what's *happening*," I'd say into the microphone.
>
> I tried to keep my eyes on their faces as they climbed down off the bus, but all the faces had a deadly sameness that made it hard to look one in the eyes. I could tell what the trouble was: they had been to Epcot. After Epcot, Charleston is hardly worth seeing. (Humphreys 186; emphasis in original)

Lucille, though, lives in an enclave of the authentic, Mount Pleasant, the only "remnant" of the real left in the boondoggle of the new (Humphreys 16). No thanks to the men. Lucille's father, Warren Odum, retired demolition genius, understands less and less as he gropes into a future left vacant by the flight of his wife. Even in his heyday, Warren was only good at blowing things up. Billy McQueen, Lucille's brother-in-law, is a struggling graduate student in history (what else?) and a high school teacher. He labors over a facsimile of the past, his dissertation, while he is a failure in most of the present. To induce Rae, Lucille's older sister, to marry him, Billy punctures condoms until she becomes pregnant. He does spot a radiant, suprarational quality about Lucille. Like Dory in *Oral History*, she sports an aura; she is rich in love. Lucille's reciprocal passion, like Dory's, leaves the man bewildered.

Lucille befuddles her brother-in-law and controls her father because she understands that the world in which the men operate is no longer, and probably never was, an essential community endowed with "natural" meaning but rather a semiotic system sustained by unreflective repetition. Like Shelley Fairchild in *Delta Wedding,* and with less acerbic irony than O'Connor meeting her "young man of parts," Humphreys through Lucille maintains that self-definition in the postsouthern world takes place in a hall of mirrors, not in a fixed system.

What makes Humphreys's foray into this "Percy-an" condition striking is the economy of her means and the fullness of the result. It is relatively simple, for example, for Lucille to capture her boyfriend Wayne in the role of Huck Finn. He expects her to be an audience for his drama of identity. But, as Lucille had with Billy, she turns her rich love upon the putative subject, Wayne or Billy, and reverses the defining process, turning performer into watcher. By merging Wayne and *Adventures of Huckleberry Finn*, Humprheys leverages a cultural situation as well as a psychological one.

Twain's "classic" has been used in the American literature canon to disseminate, as universal, a gendered model of human identity and maturation. Huck achieves his moral maturity through brotherly friendship with Jim and success in a string of challenges as the two travel down the River. Quest has traditionally been used for universalizing what is actually a gender-specific cultural process. Twain's novel marginalizes or trivializes the female and her place in the maturation of the individual and the direction of history. Nevertheless, *Adventures of Huckleberry Finn* survives. Moreover, it survives in some schemes as "one of the great novels of the Old South . . . [sought by] modern Southern writers [in] their search through the novels of the Old South for some dramatic insight into their own condition" (Forkner xv). Ben Forkner and Patrick Samway, S.J., in their introduction to *A New Reader of the Old South*, argue that Twain's novel is a coherent and comprehensive literary representation of the civilization of the Old South: for better and worse, all classes, races, castes, places, and genders find a place in the totality. No novel can be perfect in its duty to represent a culture, the editors admit, but Twain's succeeds better than any other southern text of the nineteenth century.

Humphreys's rejoinder is simply to suggest that *Adventures of Huckleberry Finn* and the civilization it is thought to represent are in fact texts. The reality that they are said to signify is irrecoverable in the here and now; their history has no authority but that which we have been schooled to grant it. Billy's profession as history student and high school teacher thus implicates him as part of the problem that history is.

Lucille (her father's daughter after all) deftly demolishes the assumptions of history. She displaces it with a version of the Cixousian "laugh" — a woman's passion. The two instances in which Lucille brings up the comparison of Wayne and Huck frame scenes in which she and Wayne make love under emotional and physical rules Wayne — for all his unkempt sincerity — does not understand:

> "What is going on here. How come all of a sudden you're . . . like this?"
> "I thought that was what you wanted."
> "Yes, but you — you enjoyed it."
> "I'm not supposed to?"
> He sighed and frowned. He was Huck Finn, naive, easy to deceive. (Humphreys 162–63)

Nor is it only sexual politics that will be changed, translated, when the woman asserts subjectivity. Lucille is also engaged in a rethinking of southern cultural politics. The local statue of John C. Calhoun proves to be sterile, as far as Lucille is concerned, as a cultural icon. In her revisionist historical view, Calhoun — the personification of white, male hegemony — is obsolete: "The textbook I had, for example, went into some detail on the subject of John C. Calhoun's theory of nullification, holding that the southern states ought to be allowed to reject any federal law not to their liking. 'A state shall not be bound by any law deemed injurious to the interest of the state . . . ' blah, blah, blah. I knew what *that* was about. As a red herring, it was of some mild interest to me, showing how men can dress greed as philosophy" (Humphreys 46). Once the toga is pulled aside, Calhoun loses his status as icon. Lucille is the dynamiter's daughter; she knows just where to place the charge to bring the whole construction to the ground.

Lucille opts to signify on history with another icon, Osceola, whose statue provides her with an answer to the "blah, blah, blah" of the official version.

Osceola is the victim, rather than the perpetrator, of "greed as philosophy." In his portrait Lucille reads "the gentle serenity of a man who sees fools and traitors all around him" (Humphreys 71). Now his image, cut loose from its history, stands at the entrance to the ruin of Osceola Pointe, appropriated by the descendants of the people who originally dispossessed him, themselves foreclosed. The image of Osceola signifies more than the vanishing native traduced by the greed of the master race. Osceola as image introduces cross-racial meaning systems. In DuBois's *The Souls of Black Folk,* for example, Osceola is "the Indian-Negro chieftain" whose futile stand against the white man in the swamps of south Georgia prefigured the history of black folk and indicts white male hegemony in the century of the color line (DuBois 122).

Osceola's statue carries something still more significant for *Rich in Love.* Lucille has found that, through a hole in the neck, bees have established a hive, and she decides that *her* Osceola is filled with honey rather than Calhoun's coded blather (Humphreys 70). The honeyed center adds the feminine to the figure of Osceola and suggests that Humphreys uses him as a rich emblem for the synthesis of race and gender. Such a complex figure signals a bypassing of the traditional reading of the tragedy of race in the southern narrative and suggests that it might always have been, as Welty's feminine eye had seen in *Delta Wedding,* a learned pattern of male imitation, not an essential tragedy of the community as a living whole.

The honey in the statue of Osceola also functions like the honey Imogene Threadgoode bestows on Ruth in *Fried Green Tomatoes at the Whistle Stop Cafe* (1988): the sign of a passion that cannot — officially — speak its name (in the novel or in the film). Such subversive energy is, however, clearly present, undisclosed, covertly expressed in ironic subversions.

The gradual emergence of gendered female discourse undermines the traditional identification of southernness with the theme of racial tragedy. In *Fried Green Tomatoes,* for example, our attitude toward the Klan is maneuvered away from an exclusive fix on race. Reading the novel or watching the film, we are induced to hate the KKK first because one of its members, Frank Bennett, batters Ruth, his wife, and is probably guilty of other crimes against women as well. Only after this negative is established does race enter the system of our reactions. Lillian Smith, before *Fried Green Tomatoes,* and Dorothy Allison in *Bastard out of Carolina* (1992) since, have used the same coupling of sexual abuse with racial terrorism to stigmatize the male community. Even though Humphreys moves toward a similar realization of a community of women transcending racial barriers, she preserves heterosexual lines. *Rich in Love* is not *The Color Purple* or *Strange Fruit.*

Rich in Love is, however, conversant with Alice Walker's re-visioning of racial politics through the sexual. At Fishbone's, a juke joint where Rae sang with Tick Willis's band before she married Billy, Humphreys collects the narrative for a "tragic" scene. Tick Willis, the black piano player, steps off the bandstand for a moment to talk to Billy about how to handle women (Rae in particular), and Lucille fears that the two males will explode into a fight over the familiar "tragic" pretexts: race and sex (Humphreys 115ff). But no fight takes place in Humphreys's version. Rae sings, and her performance, like honey poured on sparks, muffles the racial confrontation by submerging it in a "utopian" female community (Rhody, Evelyn, Lucille, Rae herself) that inundates the macho antics of Billy and Tick. Race, as both a social fixture and a determining literary thematic, is marginalized by the newly centered female community.

One additional case-in-point to conclude: Jill McCorkle's *Tending to Virginia* (1987). Linda Wagner-Martin points out the coincidence of title and theme between McCorkle's novel and Ellen Glasgow's *Virginia*; both, she argues, are significant to southern literature because both assess the relation of woman's narrative of identity to the existing cultural narrative of the South. Wagner-Martin sees this relation as essentially affirmative of the southern literary ideology and of the community that lives in and through it. "Although McCorkle or Smith [Lillian] or Walker [Alice] or Gibbons [Kaye] do not explicitly say it," Wagner-Martin summarizes, "the governing power of women's lives must ultimately come from their finding control, perhaps through some art that allows the redemption of the past (family past, historical past, personal past) in the satisfaction and beauty and work of the present" (31). Novels in Wagner-Martin's conciliatory category do not require the demolition of the image of the past and icons of the southern literary tradition. My reading, perhaps implicitly clear in the readings of *Oral History* and *Rich in Love*, finds less redemption and more ironic subversion.

Doris Betts adds clarity to this distinction in her introduction to *Southern Women Writers: The New Generation* (1990). What gender does not (or cannot) change, Betts alleges, time (history) does. When the central historical referent for southern identity is no longer the Civil War but Vietnam, radical change can be felt in the foundations of southern society and literature.

Women writers in the South, Betts implies, are the first to feel the tremblor because they have known about it all along: "Though Southern women writers are not blind to evil or irrationality, they are also less preoccupied by them than Robert Penn Warren or William Styron. Regional guilt over a morally unjustified war has become, since Vietnam, no longer regional" (Betts 5).

Tending to Virginia seems to bear this out. In McCorkle's novel, as in *Oral History*, a genealogical table serves not only to identify characters and their positions relative to one another in time and in blood; it also moves history away from chronological domination by textbook event and into associational grammar. This move undermines the hold of traditional southern history by diminishing the importance of the past as prologue in a narrative line and by implication demotes the Quentin thesis from its former status as prime narrative determinor. Framing experience as a female "space" rather than a Quentinian line implies the substitution of a different standard of meaning. In a spatially re-formed history, the past tends to fade and a utopian present supplants it. *Tending to Virginia* is "aware" of history in the way Betts has described.

Tending to Virginia covers, roughly, the years from the turn of the century to the 1980s. Historical coordinates are few; male members of the kin group go to war or are killed there, but readers are not told which war is the particular occasion. We can make guesses based on context. When David Turner, Virginia's uncle, is reported killed in a helicopter crash, we reasonably guess Vietnam. The muting of public, chronological history—a common technique and theme in novels from Glasgow and Roberts to our contemporaries—mutes as well the particular history which had, traditionally, contributed a major weight to the tragic sense derived from Quentin. Shifting gears from Civil War to Vietnam in effect mothballs Quentin: the guilt and shame of Vietnam are freely available to everyone in the population, and there is no longer an apotheosis in Pickett's charge.

Historical muting also causes readjustments in the sense of self and sense of place. Without a public arena in which to carry out the quest (and in which to be *seen* carrying out the quest), the traditional male appears as an obsolete image of his former universalized self, and the testing of the solo self against the elements, another man, or the void (the sort of male self-actualization ritual commonly derived from such works as *Adventures of Huckleberry Finn*) is replaced by a seeking of relation with other women that accomplishes mutual identity rather than the enhancement of the one at the cost of the many.

Tending to Virginia assembles this complex cultural system by aiming memory and psychology at a central event: Virginia Suzanne Turner Ballard's pregnancy. In *Oral History* and in *Rich in Love*, for example, pregnancy and birth are shown to be at the center of the process of identity making. Men are irrelevant after impregnation. Granny Younger expels Almarine (I) and usurps the patriarchal prerogative by naming Dory. Rae "forgets" her pregnancy in *Rich in Love*. Virginia vacillates, for her pregnancy is not a simple biological condition; it is the complex system of emotions, memories, and cultural roles that constitute the state of woman's identity over time.

After Virginia is drawn to her grandmother's duplex—along with her mother, Hannah, her great-aunt Lena, her aunt Madge, her cousin Cindy, and even possibly-lesbian neighbor Felicia—the communal doors are shut. Virginia resents her husband's visit and asks him to leave: "He has overstepped his boundaries, invaded her territory, changed everything," she feels (McCorkle 129). As a law student currently consumed by the short-term goal of passing exams, Mark Ballard signifies male, as John C. Calhoun had in *Rich in Love*. Most of the men in *Tending to Virginia* contribute to this unsavory caricature. Cindy's ex-husbands and current boyfriend seem oriented only to the short-term goal of getting Cindy into the sack. And she—obsessed by Jane Fonda workouts and designer labels—is the sexual object the patriarchal market in women has made her. Great-aunt Tessy's marriage to Harv Pearson (she was thirteen, he thirty) opens up the suggestion that marriage is, by its very nature, conducive to abuse and cruelty—or at least to the surrender of the female imaginary to male will. The fate of women characters in Glasgow's *Virginia* and Roberts's *The Time of Man* might be summoned as precursors to *Tending to Virginia*. Tessy's childhood and erotic imagination were all but smothered in her marriage to Harv, a pattern set forth in the earlier novels. The demonic climax of this pattern arrives in the disclosure of the character of Raymond Sinclair, Cindy's father: psychological terrorist, abuser of his daughter, black hole of cynicism whose dead hand is loosened only with Madge's public confession (to the assembly of women kin) that she had obeyed Raymond's order to kill him when his terminal illness became unbearable. With men such as these representing the traditional range of cultural activity—military service, public work outside the home, major consumer decisions, the professions—it is no wonder the women circle inward upon their own sphere: pregnancy and birth, intimacy and love, memory, care.

This emergent community of women is called into being, so the novel hints, by historical circumstances: the traditional community with men at the top of the hierarchy has disappeared because the men themselves have—most of them are dead. But the times have changed too; the traditional foundation of their hegemony has been demolished. There is a Piggly Wiggly where Virginia's grandmother's house had once stood. That house, enclosing the marriage of Emily and her husband, stands for the ideal of the traditional marriage. *Tending to Virginia* reinforces the part of Wagner-Martin's hypothesis claiming that the withdrawal of place from the lexicon of southern cultural identity requires a new grounding for identity. In Wagner-Martin's formulation, the new grounding—a community of women—does not entail the banishing of the male. In its deeper recesses, *Tending to Virginia* might not bear out this part of the hypothesis.

The work of clearing the ground of the old is done by women remembering, talking. In a pivotal scene, funny and resonant at the same time, the assembly of women abolishes the phallic signifier by heaping its names upon it: "that," "pecker," "dick," "peter," "one-eyed trouser snake" (McCorkle 216). The forbidden sanctuary of the phallus is disrupted. It is as if the name of Yahweh had been uttered and the world had not fallen apart. "[I]t ain't much to see," says Madge, whose emotional life had been enslaved to Raymond until well after his death (McCorkle 216). Eudora Welty, again, seems to have ventured forward with the foundation scene: Ginny, Easter, and Nina spying naked Loch Morrison posing like Perseus in "Moon Lake."

The postphallic community of women possesses an alternative instrument of enabling power, a power less destructive and severing (and less prone to wound women) than the Perseid phallus. Like the memory invoked when the related women commune with each other, this power engulfs rather than cuts, merges rather than separates. Simply, it is clitoral rather than phallic.

It reaches its apotheosis in Hannah, Virginia's mother, when (as wife, mother, niece—all layered roles of relation) she receives news of her uncle David's death in a distant war. First, she recasts the dead man in the image of his happiest moment alive, then she takes the resurrected David and conflates him with the other living bodies it is her role to nourish: "And now the warmth of this tiny body pressing and sucking her breast is not enough for her. Now, more than she ever has, she wants Ben [her husband]. She wants to feel his body cover and press against her; she wants to close her eyes and move against him, to feel every motion, and then to open her eyes and see that he is still there" (McCorkle 286). If the demonic male hand of death (Raymond Sinclair's) can reach back into life, the life-giving body of the woman can resurrect the dead in a brave new world of milk and honey.

What is powerful in the fiction of contemporary white southern women is their common, if not concerted, challenge to the Quentin thesis. It is not that the prevailing literary historical and critical apparatus is or must be, in all instances, totally dismembered but rather that it must be seen as man-made, the product not only of a time and a social condition (though that would be bad enough when the assertions are of "transcendent" meaning) but of gender too. Through the heyday of "modern" southern writing, from the 1920s of the renaissance, through various announcements of its end, to the prophecy of a second rebirth by those who look to the African-American male writer as savior rather than propagandist, the canon has been presented as essentially linked to an ideal of southern community conceived in history but transcending the materialism of historical circumstances. The emergence of southern women's writing, however, makes that literary orthodoxy seem partial, at best. What is emerging in southern literature, to confound the critical attempts of traditional defenders to extend the hegemony of renaissance ideology, is a body of work by white women writers that calls up "forgotten" meanings of precursor texts and proposes a new configuration of southern "community." The more defenders try to stretch the Quentin thesis to fit historical/social change, the more the thesis thins at its weakest seams.

VII

SOUTHERN WRITING UNDER THE INFLUENCE OF WILLIAM FAULKNER

What one misses in the fiction of this period, however, is the all-pervasive, dominating presence of William Faulkner.

THOMAS DANIEL YOUNG

When Dan Young wrote his lament for the departed William Faulkner in *The History of Southern Literature*, he was setting out to explore "A Second Generation of Novelists," southerners writing in "The Recent South, 1951–1982." The southern literary-critical protocols with which Young (and many others) worked had been largely based on Faulkner's works, and the fraternity in charge of enforcing these behaviors were linked by a kind of shared sonship to "Pappy," the name Faulkner cottoned to in his latter years "in the University." Faulkner's importance to southern literature can scarcely be overstated. He was, like Michelangelo to an earlier renaissance, heaven-sent. God, Giorgio Vasari revealed, "chose to have Michelangelo born a Florentine" so that "everyone might admire and follow him as their perfect examplar in life, work, and behaviour" (323). Young's comment suggests a pattern: when the "perfect exemplar" returns to his Maker, erstwhile *vasarii* feel themselves adrift.

As Vasari's *Lives of the Artists* (1568) demonstrates, movements require the services of major figures in order to become sites of preeminent explanations for cultural and aesthetic contingencies. The Major Figure, by virtues set forth in "life, work, and behaviour," sets the standard by which the age and each of its fated participants shall be identified and judged. If the Major Figure establishes legitimacy, he/ she also casts a pall. Evaluating the Sistine ceiling, Vasari put the fear of God's Florentine genius into each and every aspirant then working or to come: "Indeed, painters no longer need to seek new inventions, moral attitudes, clothed figures, fresh ways of expression, different arrangements, or sublime subjects, for this work contains every perfection possible under those headings" (355). Just contemplating Michelangelo's work would, Vasari warned—almost gleefully—throw other artists into confusion (383). But no such confusion would stifle the critic. The perfection that might be the bane of creativity would be the strong framework of analysis and judgment. So, Young, like Vasari, rejoices in Faulkner the Major Figure, the Dominator, and finds in all other work not actually what is there but only the Faulknerian and the not-Faulknerian.

William Faulkner unwittingly left to southern literary history and criticism a "perfect exemplar" that goes by the same name as the writer but is not the actual person: "Faulkner" rather than William Cuthbert Fa(u)lkner (1897–1962). To a few authors, as a part of the "greatness" we thrust upon them, we grant such out-of-biography sovereignty. Their work, despite majestic peaks and regrettable valleys, is conflated with the name of the maker. Whatever Michelangelo Buonarotti (1475–1564) made becomes simply "Michelangelo," the one-size-fits-all name Eliot's chatting women drop in "The Lovesong of J. Alfred Prufrock." The works of William Faulkner become simply "Faulkner." Inside the quotation marks differences succumb to an orderly achievement, "the all-pervasive, dominating presence" that rolls the rough places flat and paves the way smooth for the critical project. If the "South" is a cultural entity, then "Faulkner" is its official language.

An elision in which the biographical author is expunged might actually have pleased William Faulkner, famous for his fierce desire for privacy and anonymity. He once wrote to Malcolm Cowley (who was trying at the time to fix "Faulkner" in public discourse with *The Portable Faulkner*) that he wanted to "blue pencil everything which even intimates that something breathing and moving sat behind the typewriter which produced the books" (*Letters* 282). He never got his wish. Publicity foreclosed anonymity all his life. The looming of "Faulkner," as if in the corner of the room much of the writer's life but surely unignorable after the Nobel Prize in 1950, made anonymity impossible and the life of the cultural sovereign more public than Faulkner could, with very few exceptions, tolerate. Before his life was over or all of his work finished, William Faulkner lived side-by-side with "Faulkner," a fragile and none-too-happy ego partnered with an international icon. If we trace in the author's life a growing sense of alter ego, we can see more clearly the flaws in invoking "Faulkner" as the godfather of southernness in literature.

The domination of "Faulkner" in southern literature leaves a mark on everything made under its influence. In *Karate Is a Thing of the Spirit* (1972), for example, Harry Crews's wandering protagonist wears out a tee-shirt emblazoned with a shroud-of-Turin image of "Faulkner." Does Crews mean "Faulkner" to partake of the ambivalent power of the holy shroud, both potent and bogus? In response to direct questions, most southern writers have sidestepped direct denunciation of the power of "Faulkner." Eudora Welty calmly insists, "When I thought of Faulkner it was what I *read*" (*Conversations* 85; emphasis in original). Faulkner was a majestic presence, Welty remembers, something like a mountain, but, she adds, "it wasn't a helping or hindering presence, [just] something remote in my own working life" (80). Flannery O'Connor had the most effective response to the mountainous presence of "Faulkner." In "Some Aspects of the Grotesque in Southern Fiction" (1960), O'Connor made her famous remark: "The presence alone of Faulkner in our midst makes a great difference in what the writer can and cannot permit himself to do. Nobody wants his mule and wagon stalled on the same track the Dixie Limited is roaring down" (45). What is interesting about O'Connor's remark is how often it is misquoted. Louis D. Rubin, Jr., in "William Faulkner and the Southern Literary Renascence," remembers O'Connor saying that "nobody likes to get caught on the tracks when the Dixie Special comes through" (40–41). "Special"/"Limited"—a small difference—but O'Connor was careful with small differences. She chose "limited" to shoulder some room in the southern literary space dominated by "Faulkner" and by critics who had named him the Major Figure, legitimizing a cultural sovereignty, southern literature, over which they (the critics) claimed ministerial status.

Most cultural/literary histories do not anticipate the simultaneity of the icon and the living human being. We tend to credit the model of Walter Jackson Bate or Harold Bloom's redesign: the precursor who triggers the anxiety of influence is long dead before the ephebe takes up pen. With few exceptions, the same is the case in "Faulkner" studies. Gary Lee Stonum's *Faulkner's Career: An Internal Literary History* (1979) suggests a different view. Stonum distinguishes between "two subjectivities implicated in a writing career" (18). "Author" is the name he gives to the subject produced by the writing; "writer" denotes the subject who produces the writing. "Both are," Stonum reminds us, "abstractions from the historical personage William Faulkner"

(18). Stonum carefully constructs his paradigm: a literary career is chosen, obliges ongoing responsibility for its coherence, and achieves in its full trajectory a "completeness" that can be read retrospectively in the "patterns" embedded in single texts. Completeness and coherence are not easily won. Four restrictions impinge upon the discipline of a literary career: "restrictions imposed by the nature of language, by the preexisting literary tradition, and by the writer's social and historical environment" (23). The fourth, in Stonum's estimation subservient to the other three, is the writer's relationship to his or her career (23). From 1929 to the end of his career and life, Stonum claims, William Faulkner the writer was equal to the escalating demands of "Faulkner" the author; the career has an intrinsic unity analogous to the unity of an individual text.

Stonum undervalues the intrusive power of the fourth "restriction" on William Faulkner's career. By the time the writer reached what we customarily refer to now as his "late period" (the years and works stretching backward from *The Reivers* to the Nobel Prize), William Faulkner was living side-by-side with his objectified career: Faulkner. The needy causes of southern literature, the Department of State, and other official cultural interests loaded the author with claims of "Faulknerian" wisdom that the writer often found beyond his desire or inclination to fulfill. So far beyond William Faulkner's desire was the company of the public self that he undertook to terminate the latter, in the end consuming his own life as well. John T. Irwin has provided a useful preview of this process:

> He [Quentin] evokes as well Faulkner's apparent sense of the act of writing as a progressive dismemberment of the self in which parts of the living subject are cut off to become objectified in language, to become (from the writer's point of view) detached and deadened, drained, in that specific embodiment, of their obsessive emotional content. In this process of piecemeal self-destruction, the author, the living subject, is gradually transformed into the detached object — his books. And this process of literary self-dismemberment is the author's response to the threat of death; it is a using up, a consuming of the self in the act of writing in order to escape from that annihilation of the self that is the inevitable outcome of physical generation. (158–59)

Whereas Stonum sees the call of the career holding Faulkner together in the late years, Irwin leads us to suspect a progressive self-erasure, willed on an unconscious level, and inextricably linked to the act of writing.

Geared for retrospective coherence to "career," an overview like Stonum's forgets that there was a William Faulkner before there was Faulkner. We divided Faulkner's corpus into early and late, greater and lesser, while the writer's heart was still beating. We assembled a set of standards for "American," for "author," for "southern" (derived selectively from his "greater" works) and launched our construction upon the world with symposia and conferences and interviews (in many of which Faulkner himself participated) and reviews and essays and speeches and books. We created, as Lawrence Schwartz has shown, a certain kind of literary reputation for a certain menu of cultural, political, and literary uses that seemed to us (and sometimes to William Faulkner himself) urgent and legitimate at the time.

Because of when and where we levied these claims on William Faulkner, we invested Faulkner with authority on many subjects: race relations, the history of the native people of the Old Southwest, the viability of the American Way versus totalitarian "ideology," the future of democracy and of the human race under the cloud of the atomic bomb, the meaning of Christianity, the role of the artist in society. William Faulkner had few or partially formed ideas and judgments on many of these issues, and he was normally reluctant to divulge, and never willing to debate, most of them. The fabrication "Faulkner" was a necessity. Beginning around the time of *The Portable Faulkner* (1946) and the Nobel Prize (1949–50) and ending only with his death in 1962, William Faulkner lived with an additional burden not often considered: himself as institutionalized cultural force. William Faulkner had to live at least the last decade of his life in the crowded company of representations, projections, avatars, ghosts of himself—many of which he had summoned to put off would-be *vasarii* of all causes.

To paraphrase Bate, we created for Faulkner's late career a "second temple" in which a genius dwelled. Retroactively haloed by the Nobel fame of 1950 and the rhetoric of the Stockholm speech, Faulkner's earlier record of trade failure becomes a sublimely rich classic period. To this literary precursor, William Faulkner fell under an anxiety of influence. Thanks to our public worship, he artistically suffered what he had privately dreaded all his life: "the intimidating legacy of the past . . . the greatest single problem that modern art (art, that is to say, since the later seventeenth century) has had to face" (4). He could not simply be an artist—"like some of the Elizabethans" he fantasized, who did not sign their books and so were left serene and markless (Faulkner, *Letters* 285)—he had to act the role(s) of artist historically in his time. The modern artist, Bate proposes (eerily echoing Vasari), faces the "nagging questions, what is there left to write? and how, as craftsmen, do we get not only new subjects but a new idiom?" (6). If you are William Faulkner burdened by the "rich and intimidating legacy" of "Faulkner,"how do you do ample justice to yourself? How do you do so if one of the motives of your life and work has been a sort of passionate doubt as to how you would invent yourself as a modern artist, and then how a modern artist would fit into your family and history and community? "Faulkner" could not be allowed the slightest hesitation in answering affirmatively, for the integration of artist and community was one of the meanings we had placed upon him.

Joel Williamson's *William Faulkner and Southern History* (1993) tries to bring order out of the chaos of the writer's life. "Virtually no one, it seems, ever knew the real Faulkner," Williamson writes. "But they certainly knew his work" (5). Working with a three-part model of the writer's life and career — apprenticeship, genius, decline — Williamson brings us as close as we have come to merging Faulkner and William Faulkner, work and life. The living William Faulkner, for Williamson, the indispensable Quentin, suffering the burden of race (7); the latter is re-visioned as a product of North Mississippi capitalist, petit bourgeois, provincial culture, predominantly town-dwelling white people, with a shadow not apparently as fearsome as the one Melville's Benito Cereno senses but after all more literal, more flesh-and-blood. Williamson cannot prove that William Faulkner knew about his mulatto cousins; he need not as long as it is very clear that Faulkner did know and wrote about them all in his books. The fictional record stands in for the absent historical.

For all of Williamson's careful biographical reconstruction, there is still the basic question that has always followed William Faulkner: how did this man write these books? Did God go back to the well again and plant a genius in north Mississippi in the first half of the twentieth century, as he had in Tuscany in the fifteenth? The misery of William Faulkner's life seems to rule out the God thesis. In fact, misery seems the condition of his consciousness *except* when he was writing. Neither the books themselves nor the fact of having written them (that is, of being "Faulkner") broke his torment. Indeed, reminders of being "Faulkner" functioned as preludes to withering realizations that William Faulkner must act in history. He did: he traveled, married, fathered children, made speeches, answered questions. During the period of his fame, he undertook national and international public work. But he hated it, and when he could not shield himself as Faulkner, he got drunk.

Rather than accept the later work as positively addressing what he took to be his world's problems, I suggest we see William Faulkner's post–Nobel Prize "phase" as a deeply conflicted, sustained, and eventually hopeless attempt to make "Faulkner" a sufficient diversion to publicity. Noel Polk, writing of *A Fable* and of William Faulkner's "post-Nobel career" in general, prefers the former path:

> His [Faulkner's] public career after the Nobel Prize should not be seen as emerging from a resolution of the tragic vision of his earlier works, but rather as another, a separate, channel for his energies, a channel undertaken for different purposes, aimed at different audiences, and necessarily utilizing different methods of communication; this "public" career does not represent a confusion of his energies, although clearly the amount of time and thought he devoted to this public life necessitated a radical restructuring of those energies. The public career is, simply, an attempt, as a private individual with some public influence, to try to help others deal with many of the insoluble problems that had caused him and his characters such anguish in his fiction. (114–15)

Polk's later "Faulkner" differs from the earlier and tragic one, who seemed (and seems) less concerned with helping others than with making books that demand obsessive aesthetic attention and give him the only consistent pleasure he seems to have known. Polk prefers a stable William Faulkner/ Faulkner transitional duality. The former is capable of "purposes," has aims, is engaged in the problems of others and wills to help them. The latter is a humanitarian, public figure who might be seen to complement its human precursor.

A *Fable* (1954) is the hinge, although William Faulkner's other, later works—*The Town* (1957) and *The Mansion* (1959)—also figure. The positive construction "Faulkner" presumes that William Faulkner consistently intended his work to address the world and to help with solutions to its problems. In Williamson's view, for example, Faulkner directed his efforts toward the southern anxiety about race. But there is no imperative reason in work or life to take this view, and there are many reasons to take another: that William Faulkner was sincere when he said he wanted anonymity, that he resented imprisonment in the role of representative author, that his later work is marked by the desire to unwrite or subvert his public image.

William Faulkner began making and revising a repertoire of roles and personae for camouflage early in his life. Before any of his "masterpieces," before the obligations of career presented their bills, William Faulkner wanted to become a writer to conceal himself in the world. After the "triumph" of the Nobel Prize and post-Nobel "success," the world had found him out. In

Thinking of Home: William Faulkner's Letters to His Mother and Father, 1918–1925 (1992), James Watson collects letters that make the nature and function of "Faulkner"'s repertoire of selves clearer. Faulkner's "apprenticeship" was not just as a novitiate to art but to self as well. Except for the inevitability of subject matter, that art had little to do with the interests of the South. Its conscription into the cause of "the South" abounds with irony.

William Faulkner's youth and apprenticeship have been linked as a topic of critical interest before. If we can lock down the "origins" of the art, the theory goes, we can eliminate certain interpretations and judgments and proclaim others. Cleanth Brooks's indispensable *William Faulkner: The Yoknapatawpha Country* (1962), and subsequent books, sees the young man's turn away from "nature poetry" to the healthy prose of the Yoknapatawpha novels as his and our good fortune. The author was not, Brooks argues, as violent and primitive and impulsive as his characters. We must see the dark side of William Faulkner's work, Brooks insists, as the dark side of "man," not as the working out of tensions in the author himself. Many others have followed the trail. Judith Sensibar finds continuity from the formalism of the early poetry to the formalism of the early prose; her "Faulkner" is on a successful quest for form. Joseph Blotner, Carvel Collins, David Minter, Judith Wittenberg, and others in various ways have tried to reconcile the events of the early life with the outcome of the realized career. The letters in *Thinking of Home* suggest that the channel to Faulkner from William Faulkner was not (to be) without crosscurrents, that being a writer was a painful negotiation for Faulkner all through his life, that the conditions of international fame and his own success as a writer did not so much bring to fruition a self-creation process as long as his life but rather aggravated the conflicts inherent in that life. From this perspective, the risks latent in invocations of "Faulkner" (like Dan Young's, with which this chapter opened) appear increasingly manifest.

In his early twenties William Faulkner was enchanted by self-fashioning. Like most young men and women, he was torn between drawing attention to himself and shunning it. He was narcissistically drawn to (and drew) images of himself, and he made narcissism a prominent image in his early poetry. He was literally invested in manipulating images of himself. His letters to his mother, Maud Butler Falkner, repeatedly suggest his obsession with costume — fashion, cleanliness, fit. From New Haven in the spring of 1918, he instructs his mother (by sketch and word) henceforward to make his shirts with one button at the neck, not two. The local laundry cannot, he complains, press a collar with two buttons (*Home* 54–55). A few years later, back in New York after an abortive career in the Royal Air Force, he reports to his mother on the status of his wardrobe: "I have so far, bought three shirts, three pairs of socks, paid one dollar for laundry, since September (wash most of it myself), paid three dollars to have my shoes resoled and one fifty to have my old blue coat dyed—it was faded so. The pants were unfaithful to me, on both sides. Threw them away, as I couldn't sell 'em at any price" (*Home* 162). In most of the letters to his mother, "Billy" (as he signed himself, aged 21–24) presents himself as a dandy of limited means but scrupulous about the aspect he presents to the world. His youthful letters to his father, by contrast, seem a doomed attempt at typical masculine self-invention (talk of niggers, wops, hardware stores he has seen).

Anxiety in self-invention was not something Faulkner outgrew. He was still concerned with himself in costume nearly forty years later when he was inducted into the Farmington (Virginia) Hunt, and wrote to his brother in Mississippi with instructions to ship his fine riding boots, promising in return to have a picture "struck" of himself in his crimson hunting jacket (*Letters* 450). Jack Cofield's photographs capture the writer looking like anyone but the inspired literary genius.

William Faulkner's penchant for self-presentation reveals another side— self-concealment. In his letters from the R.A.F. (summer-fall, 1918), Cadet Faulkner was clearly more concerned with his tailoring than he was with the causes of World War I and the perils of aerial warfare. History was "out there," operating by its own rules, but the young man—like Conrad's Lord Jim— saw it as a destructive element from which he sought preservation or diversion. One of the new cadet's first promises to his mother is a picture of himself in uniform—if he ever receives the full regalia. The joys of appearing to be a pilot might outdistance the actuality. When the vestments finally arrive, the young man molts: "I have a complete outfit now, and must send all my other stuff home. I'll write you the day I send it, so you can look out for it" (*Home* 77). He is impatient that his mother, now, witness his new identity, lest events rob him of it betimes. Before any photographs in his new duds are taken or sent, he sketches himself in his summer uniform: "Here's the way I look now—trunks and a cork helmet, like a polo helmet, and the eternal stick" (*Home* 79). He is also, apparently, aware of the conventions subsumed in the pose he affects: "As soon as I can, I'll send one [photograph] in my summer clothes, and one standing beside a 'plane, you know, egregious, with one hand resting caressingly and protectively upon its knee cap" (*Home* 89).

Not only is Cadet Faulkner obsessed by the symbolism and fit of his R.A.F. uniform. He is also pleased by his own skill in using clothing to conceal one identity while advertising another. Because of his facility in French — one of his best academic subjects at Ole Miss, and a culture with which he had a long and conflicted relationship (see below) — the young William Faulkner can conceal his Mississippi self. "I have lots of fun with the French Canadians here," he writes to his mother. "They usually think I am French..." (*Home* 115). And, once the armistice has been signed and his aerial adventuring is over, the soon-to-be demobilized William Faulkner "borrowed some civilian clothes and wore them downtown [Toronto]... Had a great time, too. Everyone thought I was a flying officer in mufti" (*Home* 130).

The self that Faulkner takes delight in disguising is not so gregarious as the faux-Frenchman but one he seems to have no trouble describing to his mother. When a package containing food and money and clothes arrives from Mississippi, he reports, "This crowd hangs about like a crowd of vultures, waiting until some one get [*sic*] a box from home. If I were not naturally rather unapproachable, they'd take it away from me" (*Home* 97). Traces of melancholy self-appraisal lurk behind the masks of the young man — cadet, Frenchman, flying officer — traces of his awareness that life without some modes of concealment is crowded with "war, or lightening [*sic*] or marriage or any other unavoidable thing" (*Home* 118). One confronted the "unavoidable" by constructing an alternate self to absorb the buffetings of circumstance.

William Faulkner's affectations — his own self-created "Faulkners" — are well known, but most explanations for them are so far unsatisfying. C. Vann Woodward still finds no adequate explanation for "some eccentricities" among his many "personas" ("South" 42). Ben Wasson remembered meeting one of them, "Count no' Count," in 1916 at Ole Miss — the pre-"u" Falkner aping Edwardian literary bohemianism. After the war, the "Count" wore his R.A.F. uniform around Oxford and made up stories of flying stunts that invented someone for Oxford to know without costing the actual person a grain of his hoarded "unapproachableness." In *The Mississippian*, the Ole Miss campus newspaper (26 November 1919), William Falkner published his first fiction, "Landing in Luck," a short story about an R.A.F. cadet with precious few hours flying time who, by sheer luck, lands a plane sans landing gear. The cadet then begins to construct the myth that he did it all by conscious machismo. The cadet repeats the myth ad nauseam even though his mates know him to be the "biggest liar in the R.A.F." (50).

A few years later, in New Orleans among the *Double Dealer* coterie, similar mythmaking prevailed. "Faulkner" continued to trade on R.A.F. tales and made up bootlegging stories that gulled Sherwood Anderson. His purpose, as always, was to preserve his privacy. He particularly enjoyed a visit to the home of the parents of an Ole Miss fraternity brother because the parents gave him a wide berth: "I have never felt as completely at home. They didn't try to 'talk' to me at all, let me get a book and read too" (*Home* 173). His insistence on privacy could turn cruel when a visit became invasive. Coming out of a writing slump on *May Day* (his working title for *Soldiers' Pay*), he suffered a visit by an agent of the Palmer Institute of Hollywood, California, a commercial outfit that promised to teach its clients to become successful writers. In William Faulkner's version, to his mother, he put on the antic disposition of the ever-cordial southern gent, forced his unwanted guest to down several bourbons, then shut the door on the intruder (*Home* 204–06).

William Faulkner sought an ecstatic private life of writing while he resisted the public life of the writer, sidling into a whiplash he—apparently— did not anticipate. Some of his newspaper sketches of New Orleans had propelled him into the local limelight, and he reported home that he was gaining something of minor celebrity status: visits and invitations, his picture in the *Times-Picayune* and New Orleans *Item*, conversations in which he was expected to utter "wise remarks" (*Home* 180). Before he was "Faulkner" and regularly subjected to interviews he hated, he practiced hiding behind personae. In "Verse, Old and Nascent: A Pilgrimage" (1924) he disingenuously confesses that poetry was part of "a youthful gesture I was then making, of being 'different' in a small town" (*Helen* 163). And, he added, in "Bill," an early autobiographical poem, both literary gift and defensive persona were burdens—perhaps the same burden:

> Son of earth was he, and first and last
> His heart's whole dream was his, had he been wise,
> With space and light to feed it through his eyes,
> But with the gift of tongues he was accursed. (*Helen* 112)

This is the dreaming poet of publicity stills for *A Green Bough*: a faunlike "Faulkner" is swathed in "space and light," reveling in his "gift of tongues," before the curse of being read into the public.

It was this solitary, intense, effaced life of the writer that brought him joy: "Still working on my novel [*Soldiers Pay*']. It is very good. I am about two thirds through—about 50000 words. I kind of hate to finish it. I know I'll never have so much fun with another one. I dream about the people in it. Like folks I know. Awful quiet here now. I spend the mornings working and the afternoons walking (to keep myself down. I am getting fat, I think) and the evenings in visiting people" (*Home* 207). When the novel was finally finished, with a final fourteen-hour burst, Faulkner reported a kind of tristesse: "I fell [*sic*] lost this morning. I riz and washed and et and then by force of habit I ran to my typewriter—and there was nothing to do" (*Home* 208).

So much more intense, then, the inevitable collision between the absolutely private person and the public figure when the Nobel Prize laid his gift of tongues at the world's beck and call. Called upon not only to write for a public audience, or audiences now uncomfortably differentiated in needs and desires, on literary and nonliterary topics (including his own life, about which he therefore invented tales) and to deliver these words himself in person, William Faulkner was rapidly overtaken by "Faulkner." His work after *The Portable Faulkner* (1946), and especially during the writing and after the publication of *A Fable* (1954), often explained as a simple falling-off, is a tortured coming-to-terms with "Faulkner." William Faulkner lived and worked long enough to come under the influence of his own formidable example.

A Fable, then, is a complex fable of self-representation to an audience that had been schooled to expect of "Faulkner" what Irving Howe (and many others) called the "big book," "a summa of vision and experience, a final spelling out of the wisdom of the heart" (268–69). However persuasively critics might argue that *A Fable* is Faulkner's Thomistic statement on the human condition, *A Fable* is thematically confused and ambivalent, a dark summa spelled out in a language doubly coded for the Christ myth and for "Faulkner"'s deliberate undoing. At a time in his life and career when he was routinely asked for the "wise remark," a severe undercurrent of negation in *A Fable* does as much to deny the possibility of wisdom as to affirm it.

At the structural center of *A Fable* is the Christian allegory—a story so familiar to author and audience that William Faulkner suggested to his publisher that the dust jacket show only a crucifix with "A Fable" as subtitle. William Faulkner's attraction to the story of the life of Jesus Christ is discernible throughout his published work: *The Sound and the Fury* (1929) and *Light in August* (1932) have sparked reams of Christian explication. He probably learned the literary use and significance of the gospel from several models; the King James Bible is only one. Joseph Blotner identifies another possible contributor, Emil Ludwig's *The Son of Man* (1928), one of the books in Faulkner's library, a book he apparently acquired from the collection of his father-in-law (Blotner, *Library* 107). *The Son of Man*, a retelling of the life of Jesus Christ, opens, like *A Fable*, with a long-distance scene of a dense urban setting (Jerusalem during Passover) in which humanity is presented as a confused, seething mass. Ludwig's Jesus is a reluctant messiah to this hive, a man who becomes reconciled to his divinity only after much resistance, doubt, and angst. Nikos Kazantzakis's Jesus in *The Last Temptation of Christ* (1960) is a more contemporary version, indicating durability in the genre. A comparison of Ludwig's Christ with Faulkner's corporal, the central figure in the allegory of *A Fable*, must necessarily be limited, but both messiahs show few if any hints that they think they are divine. Ludwig's Jesus is eventually persuaded He is the Son of God and endures the fate prepared for Him. Faulkner's corporal remains, literally, earthbound in ironic suspension. The mud he comes from is the mud he ends up in. *A Fable* provides little literal or figurative ground for the redemptive theme so often attributed to it.

Another book among Faulkner's holdings, André Malraux's *Man's Fate* (1934 Modern Library edition, for which Faulkner declined to write an introduction), furthers speculation on source and model for *A Fable* because it moves the messiah figure and genre from biblical history into revolutionary politics and secular ideology. It might be plausible to suggest that *A Fable* is Faulkner's delayed homage to Malraux's work: both concern failed or miscarried mutinies against entrenched, hierarchical regimes; both report the death(s) of the leaders of these mutinies; both are arranged by calendar and clock (not by conventionally numbered chapters). Perhaps Faulkner's corporal is sometimes difficult to read because he is an amalgam: part biblical Jesus, part revolutionary assassin in the mold of Malraux's Ch'en or Katov, part existential messiah.

Perhaps the corporal is also difficult to read because writing him brought William Faulkner to admit what he did not like about public requirements on his writing: the kind of work Malraux did to complete the construction of his persona as *l'homme engagé*. Malraux's growing obsession with politics and his seeming abandonment of the imperative to "search the soul, which I [Faulkner] think is the writer's first job" (*University* 281–82) was not a fix Faulkner was happy to find himself in when his work became implicated in so many causes other than his own.

The French, after World War II, patented the cultural public relations campaign; the United States' effort that drafted "Faulkner" was late on the field. The French, for example, between whom and William Faulkner there had been a mutual admiration, sponsored a cadre of *les hommes engagés* — Sartre, Camus, Malraux, Beauvoir, and others — politically committed writers and intellectuals who marketed French culture. Camus's trenchcoat and film noir stare, Malraux's uniforms, Sartre's ubiquitous cigarette and horn-rimmed glasses: as effective as the Nike "swoosh" in marketing products to a multinational population.

William Faulkner was never wholly passive in this current as it passed through the United States or the South. He understood, consciously and subliminally, how the game was being played. Someone who had been Count 'no Count surely grasped the concept of self-marketing. He could not resist being an actor in it — being "Faulkner" — although the life of *l'homme engagé* placed him in great self-conflict and must have added to his reasons for drinking himself into periodic oblivion and eventual death.

The temptation to participate, like Ludwig and Malraux, in the transformation of the original Christian story into updated relevance coaxed William Faulkner into the public arena. Captive to pharaoh Jack Warner in 1943, Faulkner was toiling on the script of *Battle Cry* when Howard Hawks, his Hollywood mentor, walked out of the production. Bereft of a project, Faulkner took up a suggestion by director Henry Hathaway and producer William Bacher to write a screen treatment for a story about the return of Jesus Christ during World War I. Faulkner, chronically short of funds, accepted $1,000 from Bacher and undertook the job.

By the following month, September 1943, Faulkner described the work to his agent, Harold Ober, as "a thing. . . . It will be about 10-15 thousand words ["Notes on a Horsethief," eventually incorporated into *A Fable,* is, for comparison, about twice that long]. It is a fable, an indictment of war, perhaps, and for that reason may not be acceptable now. I am writing it out in a sort of synopsis" (Blotner, *Biography* 2: 1152). Something eventually loosened Faulkner's grip on the synopsis; by March 1945 — the war in Europe winding down — he had written 100,000 words, which he cut to 15,000, to produce a work he then told Ober was an "epic poem" about crucifixion and resurrection (1180). In May of the following year he tried to get a series of advances amounting to $6,000 from Robert Haas at Random House for a one- or two-hundred-thousand word book that would be, Faulkner promised, a *War and Peace* that Americans would "really buy" (1217). He was not, it would seem, immune to "big book" talk; and he seems to have sensed that his publishers were not either. He got the money, but also the unavoidable obligation to deliver. In three years the genre had changed from synopsis to epic poem to novel, and the theme had changed from an "indictment of war" that Americans might have found objectionable to an epic they would buy.

The investment by Random House apparently locked the work into the status of "big book." But William Faulkner could not bring the summa to closure in 1946. Several obstacles lay on the tracks. His sense of his audience (as Polk has suggested) changed. "Faulkner" began his intrusion, at first in *The Portable Faulkner,* Cowley's transformation of the writer's separate modernist works into "Faulkner's" significant historical and social saga.

Jean-Paul Sartre was next. Writing in the *Atlantic Monthly* in August 1946 of his encounter with American fiction between 1929 and 1939, he lauded Faulkner as the Prometheus of a new narrative technique for a stultified and abstract French literary tradition. American novelists, Faulkner chief among them, were harbingers of a "revolution in the art of telling a story" (117). Moreover, Sartre reported his confusion and dismay at finding the American reading public all but ignorant of "that old Faulkner," connoisseur of "filth" (115). If William Faulkner took any cognizance of his growing reputation, he would presumably have found it double-edged: an obligation to live up to himself as the technical revolutionary and to surpass his old self with something new for an expanded international audience with, if Sartre was to be believed, sophisticated philosophical and political accents.

The largest interruption in the making of *A Fable* was, of course, the Nobel Prize. After 1949 William Faulkner could no longer pretend to be "unapproachable"; he carried the additional burden of being a recognized, modern, "great writer," whose peers, according to the presentation address at the Swedish Academy, included "all living British and American novelists" ("Nobel" 5). Every work, success or failure, would henceforward be tremendously public. The effaced, joyful, self-absorbed writing of the New Orleans days, or as late as *The Sound and the Fury,* was definitely a memory. No longer could he "just write."

When he returned to *A Fable* after the Prize, according to letters to Joan Williams published in Blotner's *Biography,* the work was just plain hard — no longer a "fine ecstatic rush" like an orgasm (1445). William Faulkner felt increasingly elegiac about his work, as if *A Fable* would be the end of the string (1457), a repeated complaint all through his late phase. In August and September of 1953, the completed manuscript, ten years in the making, cast his whole career into relief simply by putting it all in the past tense: "Damn it," he wrote to his editor Saxe Commins, "I did have genius" (1462). The finished work became, according to the promise made earlier to Haas, "possibly the greatest [book] of our time" (1465) — a blurb to match *The Greatest Story Ever Told* (1949) or its sequel *The Greatest Book Ever Written* (1951).

It could be no less, of course, as the work of the Nobel Laureate retelling the life of Christ. Critics, however, received the great book with muted hosannas. Still, *A Fable* was awarded the National Book Award and the Pulitzer Prize. Ernest Hemingway, who learned of his Nobel Prize about the same time *A Fable* was published, years later made a bad-tempered but apt comment (considering the significance of excrement as imagery in Faulkner's book): it was not pure shit, wrote Hemingway in 1957, just "impure diluted shit" that would make only average fertilizer (Blotner, *Biography* 2: 1644; Baker 676).

It is not surprising that *A Fable* would end up "impure diluted shit" after the meddling of "Faulkner." All of our attempts to extricate from *A Fable*'s wreckage the body of a coherent "meaning" with potential to help its Cold War readers (and ourselves) seem to end in the equivocal, ubiquitous mud so prominent in the text. Its "failure" to become a "big book" may seem less embarrassing if we shift the context of interpretation and evaluation from text to context, from intrinsic qualities to the extrinsic demands that being "Faulkner" made on the "big book."

To think of *A Fable* as, in Faulkner's words, "my epic poem" suggests the possibility that Faulkner saw himself as Dante, someone to voice his civilization's ideals even if he could not make us live up to them. Stanley Kubrick's *Paths of Glory* (1957), a film based on the same historical event as *A Fable*, makes this point positively: the hero, played by Kirk Douglas, gets the chance to shame his hypocritical superiors in the command hierarchy even if he cannot win acquittal of three scapegoat soldiers falsely accused of cowardice. Like many Cold War Hollywood films, *Paths of Glory* shows us injustice in a political hierarchy as well as a way out through the noble bystander. *A Fable* nixes the bystander; all the bystanders in this novel are former incarnations of "Faulkner" and therefore ticketed for denunciation.

General Gragnon, the commander of the division that mutinies in May 1918 rather than make another futile and suicidal attack, is one part of a composite character with his aide who bequeaths him a copy of *Gil Blas* (hopefully abridged) before he (the aide) is blown to smithereens on a quest for the meaning of a "Faulknerian" catalogue of eternal verities: bravery, glory, honor, sacrifice, compassion (59–60). This character is an echo of the Stockholm "Faulkner," who objectified himself as the writer whose obligation was to fend off the consuming question, "When will I be blown up?" ("Nobel" 7) in order to resurrect meaning in "the old universal truths lacking which any story is ephemeral and doomed—love and honor and pity and pride and compassion and sacrifice" (7). Gragnon's unnamed aide is, in this context, the ghost of a "Faulkner"-past, the Swinburnian poet of *Vision in Spring* and *A Green Bough,* and of other poet-selves flushed out of his life's dream when he turned to fiction. The aide had discarded his life as a Paris couturier and would-be actor, surely a coded life-history from a Faulkner who spent so much time hiding in costumes and roles (*Fable* 59). The aide's search for the meaning of the "old verities and truths of the heart" left nothing on which to pin a medal, but the William Faulkner who could look back from the Nobel dais to the road not taken (at least, not all the way) into poetry could boast of some justification, some epic success. He had not been blown up, at least not yet; there *was* something left of him to pin the Nobel to. Ironically, it was one of the old, fabricated selves. William Faulkner, waiting to receive his Prize from the King of Sweden, had to endure parts of his own apocryphal biography, read by the presenter from the Swedish Academy who hailed the Laureate as the young pilot-hero William Faulkner fancied he had been: "He himself grew up in the atmosphere created by warlike feats and by the bitterness and the poverty resulting from the never admitted defeat [in the Civil War]. When he was twenty he entered the Canadian Royal Air Force, crashed twice, and returned home, not as a military hero but as a physically and psychically war-damaged youth with dubious prospects, who for some years faced a precarious existence" ("Nobel" 4).

Gerald David Levine, one of the several protagonists of *A Fable,* embodies Faulkner's own design to cancel this "war damaged youth" self, the failed hero of a quest that was never actually there. Just a few days late for the glory of the Royal Flying Corps, like William Faulkner himself, Levine is a pathetic, youthful pawn in a game, not a warlike quest. He fires blanks at a foe who is not real. Levine is like Quentin Compson, the would-be hero in an ironically deflated age, and recapitulates Quentin's brief life and suicide in a world literally (for him) full of sound (and silence) and fury signifying nothing (*Fable* 289).

Faulkner canceled or garbled the epic motive most conclusively by putting his own Nobel address into the mouth of the Old General, Mama Bidet, whose fixation upon the anus (65) suggests that his every utterance (to give Hemingway his due) is shit, including the expanded Nobel address. The Old General, in the episode climaxing the allegorical plot of A Fable, takes his corporal-son to an eminence above the city of man and offers him "the mundane earth" (308). From this pinnacle in A Fable, the Old General, like "Faulkner," delivers the Nobel acceptance speech almost verbatim. In Stockholm Faulkner had declined to accept the end of man in mere endurance ("Nobel" 8). It was, he said, all too easy to rest with endurance alone, as the corporal does. Man must and shall prevail. But how? The Old General glosses the acceptance speech: Man will prevail as man, unspirited and nontranscendent, "planning still to build something higher and faster and louder" that will paradoxically "fail to eradicate him from the earth" (Fable 313). Like the cockroach and the earthworm, mankind will prevail. The poet is to save man from this benighted fate by "lifting his heart" ("Nobel" 8), but no such lifting is vouchsafed in A Fable. As he had canceled his youthful poet-self and his Quentin-self in the aide and Gerald Levine, respectively, Faulkner abdicates his office as Nobel Laureate by unwriting the affirmation in his own speech.

These abdications suggest William Faulkner's desire to evacuate "Faulkner." Although he had early thought the fable "an indictment of war," his unused preface to the novel holds the contrary. He stood as little for pacifism as for war, he wrote, and continued along the lofty but absurdist path mapped by Reinhold Niebuhr: "to put an end to war," Faulkner wrote, "man must either find or invent something more powerful than war and man's aptitude for belligerence and his thirst for power at any cost, or use the fire itself to fight and destroy the fire with . . . that the men who do not want war may have to arm themselves as for war" (Blotner, Biography 2: 1494). In Cold War terms, "Faulkner" accepted the necessity of a massive deterrent, a bomb. From the caboose of an afterthought preface, William Faulkner tried to steer A Fable into a position akin to the absurdist Christian position described by Niebuhr— we could possess power it would be un-Christian to use. Like Laöcoon, however, Faulkner got himself ensnared in the coils of this ironic thinking: the Old General represents the thoughts of the acceptance speech and the wordless undifferentiated materialism of the blind, inarticulate gut. It is difficult to imagine a set of aesthetic criteria that rescue A Fable from this paradox.

"Faulkner" could never seem to articulate his thinking on the age and the human predicament without becoming tangle-footed or paradoxical. In his Pine Manor graduation address, which he apparently wrote as he was finishing

A Fable (in the summer of 1953), he recommends to his audience (among whom was his own daughter) a sort of humanist theology in which man, not God, "completes" creation. The challenge, as Faulkner sees it, seems to be to resist the Lucifer in ourselves, to create a human "home" just beneath a level of the technological and ideological overreaching of which we are capable. It is paradoxical that Faulkner should have urged upon his audience a wish contrary to fact, for he surely knew of the technological end game initiated by the bomb and the ideological correctness preached by both West and East. Artists, "the articulate and grieving who have reminded us always of our capacity for honor and courage and compassion and pity and sacrifice" (*Essays* 138), somehow roll us back from the brink by stirring some feeling innately human and prepolitical. Like the corporal, they confound ideology by ignoring it.

Don't ask Faulkner to explain what this innately human sense is, where it comes from, where it leads. He only knows, it seems, that it stands opposite "government" of any kind. Accepting the National Book Award in 1955 (for *A Fable*), Faulkner tried again to describe this concept. All he could, or chose to, say, however, was that art was like breeding Dalmatians—harmless— and the State, "the giants of industry and commerce, and the manipulators for profit or power of the mass emotions called government" (*Essays* 144), should go about their business free of any suspicion that "our American right to existence" as artists or whatever was of any danger, clear, present, or potential, to the "geopolitical solvency" of states. The Old General could live out his reincarnations, as could the corporal, and nothing would change.

William Faulkner's coded unwriting of previous selves, against which he tried and failed to articulate an intellectual position commensurate with the status of "Faulkner," forced upon him an unwanted discovery: the end of the history of the Judeo-Christian tradition. Not, however, its end in history after the debacles of two world wars and the bomb but its end the instant it became "was" in the mind of man. Faulkner at a crucial moment in midhistory of the southern renaissance as a community-affirming idea, like Allen Tate at the beginning, came upon its impossibility. It would only work if no one thought about it. He had once thought of his fable as "an indictment of war perhaps" and later as "the greatest [book] of our time." *A Fable*, though, is not so much an indictment of war as testimony of an expert witness to the end of the possibility of community in the "first world's" cultural order. Our only defense against the "unavoidable" destruction of war is to become the mudlike undifferentiated mass — not to endure as something, just to endure.

Faulkner had obliquely acknowledged the presence of the "Christian legend [as] part of any southern country boy's background" (Blotner, *Biography* 2: 1500), and many critics have detailed the layers of reference by which *A Fable* operates along the allegory's lines. The "Christian legend" as a store of images and partial narrative form in *A Fable* is just that — consciously chosen form, horsepower rather than Tate's horse as he is. Contemporary intellectuals, like Hannah Arendt, were beginning to realize that the Christian legend no longer functioned as an explanation of history, past or present: "Whether we like it or not, we have long ceased to live in a world in which the Judaeo-Christian myth of creation is secure enough to constitute a basis and source of authority for actual laws, and we certainly no longer believe . . . in a universal cosmos of which man was a part and whose natural laws he had to imitate and conform to" (434). More strongly, ultimately, than Arendt, Faulkner in *A Fable* registers the breakdown and disintegration of the whole content and historical span of the western cultural tradition from the instant of its conception in history as an idea of history, but he does so not so much as *l'homme engagé* ready with a political alternative. He does so as the kind of artist he was — before "Faulkner" loomed above and before him. He rejects any and all public ideology, as he rejected the man from the Palmer Institute, by returning to self.

William Faulkner survives by subverting in large and small ways the power of the Christian legend to produce affirmation in *A Fable*. The central allegorical pairing in the novel, the Old General and the corporal, is so deeply compromised that to read the corporal as any kind of redeemer is foolhardy. His sweet martyrdom is void of meaning; he barely approximates the toughness in disputation of the Jesus of the gospels. Nor is he as serious in self-searching as Ludwig's Jesus; his death is merely the cap to a life that the text of *A Fable* represents bitterly as ineffectual and meaningless. The corporal leaves behind no church to perpetuate his wisdom and example. The nameless priest who tries to wrestle him into acquiescence to the institutional betrayal of the original Word bows out of the novel with a mockingly klutzy suicide that combines elements of both God and Caesar: wearing his collar he falls, Cato-like, upon a borrowed sword (326). And the maimed runner, who had in Faulkner's view the best shot at continuing the preaching of the corporal's simple gospel, is defeated by the monolithic preference of the masses for their own ignorance and the totalitarian image of the Old General apotheosized in death. It is better, A *Fable* would have us believe, that enterprises in institutionalizing religion fail. The best religion, like the best government and the best host, is the religion that leaves you alone.

Deeper than the level of textual motif, however, is the level on which William Faulkner evidences an unwillingness to believe in hope, to believe in terms of transhistorical meaning: meaning extended from original phenomenon into abstract and predictive patterns, traditions, or images of community. He seems to operate from what Arendt called "reckless despair," the conviction that "all traditional elements of our political and spiritual world were dissolved into a conglomeration where everything seems to have lost specific value, and has become unrecognizable for human comprehension, unusable for human purpose. To yield to the mere process of disintegration has become an irresistible temptation, not only because it has assumed the spurious grandeur of 'historical necessity,' but also because everything outside it has begun to appear lifeless, bloodless, meaningless, and unreal" (viii). Arendt's words are stunning parallel to Faulkner's engulfing imagery of mud, shit, and protoplasm: the reduction and digestion of all meaning and experience. For Arendt it was a kind of intellectual sin to succumb to disintegration. For William Faulkner there is no truer sign of authenticity, no more effective escape from the public.

Even though Arendt saw a world after World War II that was beset by paralyzing ironies ("though we have many traditions," she wrote, "and know them more intimately than any generation before us, we can fall back upon none, and . . . though we are saturated with experience and are more competent at interpreting it than any century before, we cannot use any of it" [434]), she nevertheless counseled hope in the first consciously planned beginning in human history, the previous myths of origins—each "supposing something was there, given, already established before human history actually began" (435) having been obliterated by evil and the knowledge of evil as beyond all existing canons. The Old General proposes such a restart for human history when he escorts the corporal to the promontory overlooking the city of man. The general claims he believes in man (307). Barely articulating his position in response, the corporal declines to join the Old General's party, is then executed, lost, enshrined and consigned to mankind's amnesia. Even though Arendt quotes Faulkner approvingly at the close of her treatise, hoping perhaps to enlist his prestige for her politics, the Faulkner who represents cultural wisdom cannot be so enlisted. He is AWOL.

"The all-pervasive, dominating presence of William Faulkner" is rather the imposition of "Faulkner," a set of literary behaviors, not the indwelling of a literary spirit, a common or communalizing voice or vision. As Vasari wished to enforce a set of High Renaissance standards by invoking the name of Michelangelo, southern literary critics and literary historians invoke the name of "Faulkner" to enforce *a* literary agenda. In his most flawed and enigmatic fiction, *A Fable*, William Faulkner undermined such projects by systematically unwriting the prestige of "Faulkner" and using the most powerful communalizing myth available to the Christian West, the redemption narrative of Jesus, to proclaim its termination as story and as community. William Faulkner is indeed a profound writer, but that is not the same as saying he was wise in seeing a summa sort of meaning above the contingencies of history that the rest of us could not glimpse.

As his work continued in what was to be the last decade of his life, self-parody became his modus operandi, and he passed on to southern literature in general the problem of how to follow a writer who, living in a period of concerted efforts to construct a southern literary history around "Faulkner," made erasing "Faulkner" the identifying mark of his late career. But no such confusion would stymie the critic. The perfection that might be the bane of creativity would be the strong framework of analysis and judgment. And so Dan Young, like Vasari, rejoices in "Faulkner" the Major Figure and finds in all other literary work only what "Faulkner" has left there.

VIII

PARODY AND POST-SOUTHERNNESS

"No," Shreve said, "you wait. Let me play awhile now."
WILLIAM FAULKNER, *Absalom, Absalom!*

The death of southern literature is no less a crucial trope than its origin. Both are fraught, in Lewis Simpson's articulate view, with issues of great pitch and moment historically and morally. "A major motive of the twentieth-century southern literary expression," he writes in *The Brazen Face of History*, "is a vision of social order at once strongly sacramental and sternly moralistic. The vision, integral with its source, the classical-Christian ground of Western civilization, has been fundamental to the moral history of the nation as a whole" (253). For any literary expression to legitimate its claim to being sacramental, the work in its analyzable parts must mean a whole truth beyond human fabrication. Humans can make the bread; we cannot make the Eucharist without help.

Parody is the expression of a suspicion or conscious conviction that as humans we can make nothing but analyzable parts; wholes are figments of the imagination. Moreover, parody arranges parts in ways that mock our wish for whole truths in such phrases as "moral history," "sacramental social order," "nation as a whole," and—not least—"Western civilization." The turn of southern literature into parody and postsouthernness is an emergency of the highest seriousness to believers in the whole. To others, it is a relief.

The problem of postsouthernness, its alleged inadequacy in imagining community, is, however, deeply embedded in the marrow of the Major Figure, William Faulkner, whose work is thought to summarize the moral and aesthetic order of the South. Quentin's anxiety in reaction to the events of *Absalom, Absalom!* is crushing when Shreve "plays" at the controls of the narrative system. The simulacrum of

South that Shreve produces is indistinguishable from the one Quentin thinks he knows as real. It is a good question whether the parodist is less dangerous to the order of the South than miscegenation and incest.

With a few exceptions (the work of Joseph Urgo, for example) critics of Faulkner's work do not like to write about the post-Nobel books because Faulkner in effect migrates from Quentin to Shreve. It is generally agreed that *A Fable*, *The Town* (1957), *The Mansion* (1959), and *The Reivers* (1962) represent a long tailing-off of the great vision and talent of the "acknowledged classics." Explaining these latter works requires that we admit that too often the rigors of "structure" are fudged, that the characters and incidents are too blatantly recycled (and often changed) from earlier works, and that characters uncomfortably "Faulknerian" utter speeches (often about gender and race) that make the Laureate seem misogynistic and racially unprogressive. The late Faulkner is almost as troublesome to the project of cultural legitimation of the South as the early Swinburnian Faulkner. Perhaps William Faulkner had his revenge on a public that would not leave him well enough alone.

But he wrote the books. Gary Stonum, in *Faulkner's Career: An Internal Literary History* (1979), maintains that in the final two-thirds of the Snopes trilogy writer becomes author by fulfilling the curve begun in *The Hamlet* (53). Such an approach ameliorates the obvious problems in *The Town* and *The Mansion*, and deftly shifts our attention from their particular "moments" in Faulkner's life and career to an earlier and, in many respects, freer "moment." The aesthetic motivation to complete the form promised in *The Hamlet* does not abolish the more immediate motivations of William Faulkner working in the last decade of his life to void "Faulkner," a cultural effigy he, at the very least, beheld with suspicion.

William Faulkner's return to his trilogy, I would argue, came about not because of a necessary desire to move into the status of author but because of his desire to void himself of "Faulkner." Certainly some degree of self-consciousness is inevitable and even necessary to make trilogies, or other extended and interlocking works, hold together. Proust, for example, achieves the art of representing Proust in *Remembrance of Things Past*. Joyce, an author whose work Faulkner knew well, turned to himself throughout his work. But "Faulkner" pushes self-representation to the brink of self-erasure in the final pieces of his trilogy. The second and third parts of "the Snopes trilogy" become a wax museum of "Faulkneriana" at odds with more flattering appraisals of the South in the family of man.

The Town begins erasure under the supervision of a tired William Faulkner who complained to Jean Stein, "[P]erhaps I have written myself out and all that remains now is the empty craftsmanship—no fire, force, passion anymore in the words and sentences" (*Letters* 391). Most of William Faulkner's late letters similarly lament his waning powers. Without, however, turning the words inside out, one can make the argument that William Faulkner had not completely finished the process of "writing himself out" of existence. There was still the other "Faulkner," known to many by the "craftsmanship . . . in the words and sentences" that continued to exact William Faulkner's time and attention.

Gavin Stevens, for instance, is presented in the trilogy as a windbag Quentin Compson who survived Harvard in 1910 to become a garrulous clown. Gavin's pronouncements on the South and mankind are less frequently invoked than Quentin's because they are more ironical. As a talking head (rather than a troubled oracle) on the South, Gavin seldom outplaces Quentin in literary criticism, history, or other professional fields in which numbers of citations are tallied. Perhaps for good reason. Gavin tends to see experience (primarily his in the South) as a script that has always already been played to the hilt. Race relations, southern history, the mythic past, community versus society, sex and gender—Gavin is a much more jaundiced source than Quentin on all of these issues and themes. He does not suffer in eloquent (comparative) silence, as does his predecessor; he talks far too much. Even his nephew Chick gets tired of the "hero-dinning" (*Mansion* 180–81).

In *The Sound and the Fury* Quentin had seen complex layers of "positionality" and cultural role playing among white and black, both in the South and between whites and blacks outside the South. Gavin settles for simplistic minstrelsy. The "clever slave" image seems to fit all the blacks of his acquaintance (*Town* 30). By implication, Tom Tom and Tomey's Turl (the only two Jeffersonians to skin Flem Snopes) are shown to be better off with their natural cunning; they would only be damaged by the civil rights and education urged by, for example, the NAACP, of whose policies William Faulkner disapproved (*Letters* 396). In *The Mansion*, after years of being hounded by questioners from *Life*, various other news organizations, and students in Japan and Virginia, "Faulkner," (as if) through Chick and Gavin, says for the record, striving for equality just robs "them, Negroes," of their natural tenderness, gentleness, and wisdom in dealing from a minority position with the powerful but crude white race (*Mansion* 223ff.).

As a clown, Gavin was a useful decoy. He could "say" much that "Faulkner" could not. Gavin was not good material for those using "Faulkner" to reimagine the South in the changing 1950s and 1960s. To a large extent, the survival of southern literature, institutionally in its adolescence in the late 1950s, would have been harmed, not helped, by having Gavin as its mouthpiece. William Faulkner could preserve some semblance of his "unapproachableness" through such scandalous figures. Yet he could reap the psychological benefit of Gavin's ventings and querulous complaints about the modern age, modern women, the "government." William Faulkner used such surrogates to "write himself out" of ideological debates into which he had been dragooned.

Race politics in the 1950s is relatively easy to read in the late Faulkner. Literary and cultural politics is less apparent, but William Faulkner seems to want to write "Faulkner" out of that discourse as well. In the 1950s, when such foundational literary-cultural southern works as Rubin and Jacobs's *Southern Renaissance* (1953), Rubin and Kilpatrick's *The Lasting South* (1957), and Davidson's *The Southern Writer in the Modern World* (1958) argue outright for the conservative, tradition-affirming powers of the southern community as vital to a meaningful literature and social life, Gavin is — at best — an ambivalent source. He delivers some potentially embarrassing messages on a southern "community" that habitually overrides law with custom (*Mansion* 13). Resort to "folkways" as a defense against change had taken a beating in recent Supreme Court decisions, but Gavin is not a true-blue defender of immemorial ways. In *The Town* Gavin explains that the community cannot be evaded, countered, or superseded. Yet there must be law too. A few years after Gavin tangled this issue, Atticus Finch arrived in *To Kill a Mockingbird* (1960) to appear to make it simple again. Atticus is the southern attorney we all prefer to remember, not Gavin Stevens.

The late "Faulkner's" campaign of self-quotation is even more stunning — or disappointing — in *The Mansion*. Gavin and Chick carry on their misogynistic myth making, begun on the body of Eula and continued on that of her daughter Linda Snopes. Pleas for racial status quo and complaints about government "Omnipotence" (242) put "Faulkner" on both sides of the state rights debate. Less obviously he continues to write himself out of earlier "Faulknerian" personae. Gavin's disavowal of Bayard Sartoris and his ilk (*Town* 140) is extended by Chick, who reduces all Bayardic heroism to simple "boredom" (*Mansion* 189–90). "Faulkner" makes his presence felt, too, in potshots at the literary competition. For most of his career Faulkner carried on competition in private or shunned it altogether. But he replies to Hemingway, and all that he had come to stand for in American Literature, in *The Mansion* through the character of Barton Kohl—a nice combination of Hemingway's Spanish Civil War experience and Norman Mailer's Jewish intellectual shtick.

"Academical gumshoes" (*Letters* 430) can make as full a roster of self-quotation, recycling, and literary one-upmanship as we like. The challenge is to posit a reason why the process of "writing himself out," begun in *A Fable*, continues in the other late works and becomes increasingly deliberate and designed. It is linked to the early, prepublic "Faulkner" through the constant and unresolved tension between "writing in" (the "fun" Faulkner wrote home about during *Soldier's Pay*) and "writing out," shrugging off the public obligation of *l'homme engagé*.

He repeatedly complained—to various correspondents and with various purposes—that he was tired, burnt out, scraping the "last minuscule from the bottom of the F. barrel" (*Letters* 433) to complete the trilogy. One character in the trilogy, Mink Snopes, seems to fit this "Faulkner" more neatly than the other ghost images. As Faulkner plotted and revised the chronology of Mink's life for the trilogy, he made his Parchman term thirty-eight years. Faulkner had, by his own reckoning, been at work on the trilogy for thirty-four years when the final volume was published in 1959. Mink was sixty-three when he was released; Faulkner was sixty-two when the book was published. Mink is moved toward his climactic murder of Flem—final liberation for both (or for all three)—by an intelligent fate that seems to deem it appropriate that the small man who just wanted to be left alone should kill a tireless accumulator who had turned the de Spain house, "jest a house: two-storey, with a gallery" (*Mansion* 153), into a replica of Mount Vernon, and not coincidentally of Rowan Oak too (154).

Faulkner reserves for V. K. Ratliff, however, the best eulogy for Mink-Faulkner, providing something like a tantalizing self-revelation of the William Faulkner within who was writing hard to expose the public "Faulkner" as the inauthentic double: "'He's tired,' Ratliff said [of Mink]. 'Even if he wasn't sixty-three or -four years old. He's been under a strain for thirty-eight years.... And now he ain't got no more strain to prop him up. Jest suppose you had spent thirty-eight years waiting to do something, and sho enough one day you finally done it. You wouldn't have much left neither. So what he wants now is just to lay down in the dark and quiet somewhere for a spell'" (*Mansion* 418). It had not been exactly thirty-eight years since an ebullient and much younger Faulkner had written to his mother that in the dark and quiet of his writer's cell he ran to his typewriter each morning to "sho enough . . .

do something . . . he one day finally done." But it had been thirty-eight years since he had written and made the book *Vision in Spring*.

William Faulkner became a commodity in ongoing, overlapping cultural projects that implicated him in career and history in public ways he deplored. If the pattern in/of his lifework suggests rounding, completion, closure, a positive response to the obligations of career, it also suggests something else: the usurpation of a living human's work for projects in which he did not necessarily want a part, followed by that writer's attempt to withdraw it all. The "meaning" of the late Faulkner for southern literary history is vexed: invoking the "late Faulkner" seems to indict the cause with postsouthernness, a consciousness of replica and parody.

Lately there has been a break in the more or less constant elegy for the death of southern literature. Both Fred Hobson and Lewis Simpson have expressed hope that southern literary history will continue on its classic, renaissance foundations, and that the African-American male writer will oversee restoration. John Lowe and Jefferson Humphries's *The Future of Southern Letters* (1996) suggests, by way of its title, that there is more to come. Both Oxford University Press and Norton have supplied volumes to the consumers of southernness.

Almost twenty years ago, however, in "The Closure of History in a Postsouthern America," Lewis Simpson had concluded that the "epiphany of the southern literary artist will not be repeated. The Southern Renaissence will not come again" (269). In early postmodern years (for southern literary history), Simpson had been puzzling over the novels of Walker Percy from *The Moviegoer* (1961) through *Lancelot* (1977), and it is no great surprise that in reading Percy's parody Simpson came to the melancholy conclusion that our common culture (if indeed there were such a thing, for Americans or for southerners) had reached the end of its tether. Its familiar way of making and maintaining meaning, its orthodoxy or consensus, had ceased functioning, except for the elaborate life-support systems in Dr. Percy's clinic. Will Barrett was the new hero, but he drifted in a funhouse of representations, not reality. He would not have registered at all on the southern scope if it were not for the category of "virtual southernness" or postsouthernness. Will does not extend southern literature, unless one is prepared to allow that by turning it back upon itself one "extends" it.

Simpson characteristically had picked up the symptoms of the postmodern/postsouthern before the rest of us. According to Umberto Eco, the postmodern condition is one in which meaning is so rich it disappears: Eco tells us he chose the rose for the title of his famous postmodern whodunit because "the rose is a symbolic figure so rich in meaning that by now it hardly has any meaning left" (3). Simpson, one might argue, thinks "southern" is also such a term, at risk in the postmodern climate because it is so multivalent it has no core.

In another essay, "What Survivors Do" (originally 1978), Simpson recalls the small Texas community where he grew up. His father, like many southern gentlemen of the turn of the century, "had aspired to at least a part-time literary career" (234) to gild his work as a lawyer that actually supported the family. The elder Simpson had mastered the standard Latin works, the Victorian poets, Emerson, and *The Library of Southern Literature* and, the son confesses, wrote instructive verse "of stultifying sentimentality" (235). Simpson's mother performed more pragmatic duties in the growth of the southern critic's mind: she doled out surplus milk from the family Jerseys to "a pathetic old man" who showed up for charity each week. This man, Simpson remembers, was thought to be a Confederate veteran, a survivor of the heroic and epochal struggle the boy had read about in *The Library of Southern Literature* and the works of Thomas Nelson Page. To the southern boy, meaning seemed to run unimpeded from text to world and back again.

One day—all instructional tales have such a day—the boy's grandmother (who knew the whole history of their community back through the Civil War) uttered the plain fact that the tattered hero had been only a forager, not a cavalier, and had never been in any battle at all, "big or little" (234). No one disputed her. As a boy, Simpson recalls, he had felt whiplashed in the collision of myth and history. What was missing in the southern education of his father and his father's books was suspicion of the sign, a habit of tolerating more than one mode of meaning at a time. "It was hard for a boy of a southern family," Simpson concludes, with his own late-twentieth-century deadpan, "to come by a sense of irony" (234).

Simpson, using himself as the main character, gives the reader of southern literature a motive for postmodern attention. It begins with skepticism: before the act of interpretation, the postmodern critic places quotation marks around the act itself and the terms on which it is founded. Eco writes succinctly, "[P]ostmodern discourse: it demands, in order to be understood, not the negation of the already said, but its ironic rethinking" (68). Linda Hutcheon, in *The Politics of Postmodernism* (1989), goes further: "[I]t seems reasonable to say that the postmodern's initial concern is to de-naturalize some of the dominant features of our way of life, to point out that those entities that we unthinkingly experience as 'natural' (they might even include capitalism, patriarchy, liberal humanism) are in fact 'cultural'; made by us, not given to us. Even nature, postmodernism might point out, doesn't grow on trees" (2). The first step of the postmodern critic of southern literature is to question the natural authority of the foundation term: *southern*. Like *rose*, it has been used so much, been invested with so much meaning, that we can no longer distinguish between what if anything is inherent and what other interests have attached over time. Fredric Jameson might say that "southern" has fallen victim to the inexorable critical-economic process of commodification: "Postmodernism is what you have when the modernization process [commodification] is complete and nature is gone for good" (ix).

The next step is a cautionary one. To put quotation marks around the real is not to efface the real; rather, it is to put it into a condition of multiple codes rather than the traditional realistic mimetic system of the one and only. History still exists; but we now acknowledge that we know it through a system of representations rather than in an unmediated, direct way. Simpson's naive ignorance and his father's elaborate, patriarchal authority are set at equal. Postmodernism does not deconstruct the past and meaning, except by interrogating the systems by which those entities have been known as such. Hutcheon reminds us that this road started decades ago, with Walter Benjamin's insights into the reproducibility of works of art. The postmodern world is "utterly mediated through representations" ([31]); acts of interpretive closure are therefore rare. Once the postmodern word is spoken, there can no longer be a "return to some older kind of machinery, some older and more transparent rational space, or some more traditional and reassuring perspectival or mimetic enclave" (Jameson 54). The act of the postmodern critic is more like juggling than archery. "Irony, metalinguistic play, enunciation squared" is Eco's formula (Eco 68). For better or worse, there is no escape from a world mediated through representations, no recourse to the totalizing and totally authoritative referent: capitalism, patriarchy, the novel, the South. This conclusion is not as radically upsetting as it sounds to anyone familiar with the "Disneyfication" of our history and culture(s).

The collision of the southern "immovable object" and the postmodern "irresistible force" did not occur this morning; as Lewis Simpson's work attests, it could have been seen almost two decades ago. But the consensus in southern literature is slow to change, especially in response to a movement that threatens its core. Better to try to fold the new into the established.

Fred Hobson's 1990 Lamar Lectures, *The Southern Writer in the Postmodern World* (1991), attempt to accomplish just that reconciliation. Hobson wants to ascertain the damage, if any, on the South and its literature in the encounter with postmodernism (Hobson [1]). Hobson's description of postmodernism, however, depends upon a nonironic, ideal southern identity—a formulation he borrows, with caveats, from Donald Davidson, the original Lamar Lecturer. Davidson proposed an "autochthonous ideal" of southern cultural conscious- ness: "By the term he meant a condition in which the writer was in a certain harmony with his social and cultural environments, was nearly *unconscious* of it as a 'special' environment, quaint or rustic or backward, and thus was not motivated by any urge to interpret or explain" (Hobson 80; emphasis in original). Hobson's updated interpretive principle is likewise not subject to mediation. An autochthonous ideal of the South is an unmediated entity, the arbiter of meaning above interrogation. Simpson's anecdote suggests that this "certain harmony" is in actuality neither natural nor pervasive but the product of cultural thinking and forgetting, saying and not saying. The em- bedded discovery plot in the story of the ragged vet claims its force because several caches of intelligence near the boy but silent to him hold back the "truth" until a collision will have its most telling result. The lesson of Simp- son's anecdote is not only parallel to the one in O'Connor's "A Late En- counter with the Enemy" but is also structural rather than declarative. Each and every act of thought proceeds on the probability of certainty. Unlike the boy in Simpson's story, however, the postmodern thinker must be aware that there is always something pertinent one does not know.

In Jameson's terms the autochthonous ideal qualifies as a "mimetic enclave." Yet Hobson strives to recover it. There are pitfalls. Hobson's adoption of an "*unconscious*," as it were, natural, southernness is akin to Simpson's preironic inscription into the southern "text" that spread outward from the books, poems, speeches, and general conversation he heard as a boy. For Simpson, such a stable southernness never was actually in place, except as a temporary condi- tion; the tattered vet was never someone genuinely heroic, then someone else. For Hobson, though, via Davidson, there was at one moment in history a South (a natural human artifact) that changed, was lost. Quentin Compson's "tragic sense" is the authoritative literary example of that loss; the Faulkner- ian literary character is universally invoked to substantiate the southern claim. The hermeneutic process is dangerously close to being circular.

Moreover, Hobson's theory of "influence" or continuity leaves insuffi- cient clearance for irony. In his critical model the "autochthonous" South is a huge cultural dynamo. One previous generation of southern writers, male writers of the southern renaissance, for instance, had the "power" (Warren, Styron, Faulkner), and most recent southern writers (under the age of fifty in 1990) seem "comparatively devoid of influence from past Southern literary giants" (9–10). The void appears because ironic (or any other kind of) parody cannot register on this critical seismograph. Parody, though, is power — perhaps the only type of power available (or desirable) to a writer or critic living in the post-conscious sequel to a successful age of inimitable originals, as mannerists followed Michelangelo.

Southern writers, more acutely than southern critics of their work, have known that post-began with "Faulkner," the great master code recognized for so long as synonymous with "literary" and with "southern" that it is now harvested in parody contests. Faulkner himself played the game of undoing his own code. Not only is the current atmosphere ripe for an "anxiety of influence"; it is also ripe for the most common response to such anxiety: parody. Hutcheon reminds us that "on the one hand, there is a sense that we can never get out from under the weight of a long tradition of visual and narrative representations and, on the other hand, we also seem to be losing faith in both the inexhaustibility and the power of those existing representations. And parody is often the postmodern form this particular paradox takes" (8). The question whether parody designs to restore "faith" and "power" is crucial to choosing one's stance in postmodernism. Hutcheon, for example, is content with the destabilization of sociopolitical and literary standards intrinsic to parody. Jameson finds postmodern parody, a term he disqualifies in favor of "pastiche," "without any of parody's ulterior motives, amputated of satiric impulse, devoid of laughter and of any conviction that alongside the abnormal tongue you have momentarily borrowed, some healthy linguistic normality still exists" (17). Diagnosis as parodically challenged seems, to Jameson, about the best one may hope for in "a world transformed into sheer images of itself and for pseudo-events and 'spectacles'" (18).

There is ample evidence that the southern culture which serves as the mimetic backup for southern literature has for some time been self-fascinated, addicted to images of itself and pseudoevents. Along with Elvis look-alike contests, there is the "Faux Faulkner Contest" cosponsored by Yoknapatawpha Press, *American Way* in-flight magazine, and the University of Mississippi's Center for the Study of Southern Culture (which also sponsors an annual conference on Faulkner and Yoknapatawpha [the master's own replica of an actual place]), where the winner of the parody contest is fêted. The first volume of *The Best of Bad Faulkner* (1991) even includes one of the master's self-parodies. Real and virtual coexist; "the master's unmistakable style, themes, characters or plot" move freely from "healthy linguistic normality" to an "abnormal tongue...momentarily borrowed" (Wells xii). We can all, potentially, like Shreve, play the Faulknerian keyboard.

Shrugging off "Faulknerian" influence is serious business aimed not so much at the writer himself as at the literary critics and historians who use his achievements to enforce southern literature. The history of insurrection is long. William Styron took on *The Sound and the Fury* (as well as fiction by Fitzgerald and Hemingway) in *Lie Down in Darkness* (1951). William Humphrey tried the coattails of the family saga in *Home from the Hills* (1958). Early Cormac McCarthy draws upon the "Faulknerian" grotesque of *Sanctuary* and *As I Lay Dying*.

Reynolds Price published his first novel, *A Long and Happy Life*, in 1962, a few months before Faulkner died. Reviews and blurbs for the book have reiterated the connection: a recent (1983) reissue of *A Long and Happy Life* in a single volume of all the Mustian family stories carries a jacket blurb that reminds us of Price's favorable ranking in the Faulkner derby and emphasizes the southern verisimilitude of his work: "he offers a penetrating, lively, and honest look at the lives of country people" (*Mustian*). But the first sentence of the novel, both praised and hooted at by reviewers, belies that claim. It is strategic parody. Whether it is a neutral ironic rewriting of "Faulkner" or yearning for a return of faith and literary power is a more difficult question. Here is the sentence, all of the first paragraph of the novel in fact, complete at the tail end with a send-off that readers of "Faulkner" could not mistake:

> Just with his body and form inside like a snake, leaning that black motorcycle side to side, cutting in and out of the slow line of cars to get there first, staring due-north through goggles towards Mount Moriah and switching coon tails in everybody's face was Wesley Beavers, and laid against his back like sleep, spraddle-legged on the sheepskin seat behind him was Rosacoke Mustian who was maybe his girl and who had given up looking into the wind and trying to nod at every sad car in the line, and when he even speeded up and passed the truck (lent for the afternoon by Mr. Isaac Alston and driven by Sammy his man, hauling one pine box and one black boy dressed in all he could borrow, set up in a ladder-back chair with flowers banked round him and foot on the box to steady it)—when he even passed that, Rosacoke said once into his back "Don't" and rested in humiliation, not thinking but with her hands on his hips for dear life and her white blouse blown out behind her like a banner in defeat. ([3])

Is this anxiety of influence — a younger writer has no voice but that of his predecessor? Or is Price demonstrating at the outset of *his* novel *his* command of compulsory southern figures? The convoluted, embedded sentences; the images of death and love; the echoes of "Faulknerian" staples in the name Isaac and the trip to the cemetery; finally, "flags in the dust." After Faulkner, can a southern writer be anything but self-conscious, attuned to southernness as a matter of metalinguistics, a subject matter never unmediated? Price's gambit in *A Long and Happy Life* seems an elegant turn: "All right, audience, I can do a Triple-Faulkner without hitting the ice. Can we now get on with *my* novel?"

Price's second novel, *A Generous Man* (1964), attracted even more divided attention because the author, far in advance of his audience, was aware that the lesson of the southern Major Figure was deeper (much thanks to critics) than imitable style. Well before the organizers of the Faux Faulkner Contest, Price knew that the original franchise had been extended to themes, characters, and plots. Was this young southern author bucking for the mantle of Faulkner, as John Wain suggested in a review, or was his literary repertoire so mortgaged to the past master and his language that Price, the apprentice, could do no more than imitate?

Price himself was the detonator of a second round of dispute on the issue of "influence" or parody. He put his explanation of *A Generous Man* into an essay, "News for the Mineshaft," a few years after the novel and the reviews had settled down. It had been his design in the novel, he wrote, to parody several of the hallowed pieties of southern fiction — many of which can be found in a book by Faulkner, *Go Down, Moses,* but go back into the frontier southern writing of Thomas Bangs Thorpe, "Madison Tensas," and William Elliott: a young male southern hero (an Ike McCaslin with no celibate tendencies) on the threshold of manhood; a hunt to represent the passage into adulthood; magic prey (a twenty-foot python named Death); rituals of male tribal bonding; encounters in the woods with mystical manifestations; an heroic dog. *A Generous Man* is built on parody; its relation to its South runs through literary representation at least as much as through "verisimilitude." These coded representations of the South, always already there, occupy cultural space where the "real South" is thought to be.

Price's wrestling match with the still-warm ghost of the southern master suggests that the postmodern/postsouthern condition had set in earlier than we thought, well before the "recent" southern writing that is customarily identified as postmodern. As usual, any periodizing — hasty or not — ends in objections. If we listen carefully to Eudora Welty in the 1950s, we can hear the subtle tones of "Faulknerian" parody in "The Burning." Welty was awarded an O. Henry second prize, and $200, in 1951 for her Civil War story, the most historically "southern" fiction she ever wrote. The O. Henry panel, though, praised Welty's story not for its historicity but for its "rhythmic patterns of word and symbol and idea" (Brickell xi). They liked it better than one of Faulkner's own short stories, "A Name for the City," which was to turn up later in *Requiem for a Nun* as the virtuoso fugue on the Jefferson jailhouse and its puissant lock. Oddly, Faulkner's story is one of his more untoppable Faulknerian performances, rich in "rhythmic patterns of word and symbol and idea." A later reviewer (Orville Prescott, in the *New York Times*), commenting on "The Burning" in *The Bride of the Innisfallen and Other Stories* (1955), actually faulted the story for being "Faulknerian," by which he meant, as early as the middle 1950s, parodic, imitative, southern-once-removed. That the appearance of Faulknerianness in Welty's story might have been parody seems not to have occurred to Prescott or his contemporaries. It is not an easy case to make today.

If "The Burning" is a southern literary standard bearer (it was acknowledged as such by the O. Henry panel), it was not without hints of parody. In one short story we have incest and miscegenation (a staple of the South created by Quentin and Shreve in *Absalom, Absalom!*), destruction by fire of the house that symbolizes the old regime and its sins, forcible intrusion by the offending invaders (Scarlett is never so alive as when she shoots the ugly Yankee in *Gone with the Wind*), the bifurcation of southern womanhood into active and passive, hardheaded practicality and dreamy gentility (Melanie and Scarlett). There is even a soupçon of faux Faulkner, the labyrinthine sentence with "breathless gerundives" (Jameson 16) and cumulative adjectives: "The sisters showed no surprise to see soldiers and Negroes alike (old Ophelia in the way, talking, talking) strike into and out of the doors of the house, the front now the same as the back, to carry off beds, tables, candlesticks, washstands, cedar buckets, china pitchers, with their backs bent double; or the horses ready to go; or the food of the kitchen bolted down — and so much of it thrown away, this must be a second dinner; of the unsilenceable dogs, the old pack mixed with the strangers and fighting with all their hearts over bones" ("Burning" 21). The O. Henry editors had not cared much for the "Faulknerian" rhetoric of Faulkner himself: "interminable sentences, which meander like one of his own Mississippi rivers, breaking all the rules of style but getting away scot free" (Brickell xvi). Under another signature, however, a parody slips by as southern literary language. "The Burning," anticipating postmodern parody, self-consciously displays its own southernness as literariness; in so doing, it adjusts or lightens the burden of southern literariness it must necessarily carry in the presence of "Faulkner" triumphant.

Did southern writers know they were in this fix? The complexity and self-referentiality of this condition, in which writing self-consciously addresses writing, then perhaps history or "life," was predicted by Flannery O'Connor in "The Grotesque in Southern Fiction": "The great novels we get in the future are not going to be those the public thinks it wants, or those that critics demand. They are going to be the kind of novels that interest the novelist. And the novels that interest are those that have already been written" (49–50). O'Connor's own short story, "A Late Encounter with the Enemy," parodies the public's fondness for replicas or representations ("sheer images . . . and pseudo-events") of southern history more broadly than "The Burning," its near-contemporary. In "A Late Encounter with the Enemy," Sally Poker Sash, mired in the mediocrity of a southern teacher's college — a situation for which the author had little sympathy — compels her grandfather, bogus Confederate General "Tennessee" Flintrock Sash, to attend her commencement: a pseudoevent described by O'Connor, a connoisseur of such folly. The "general's" Civil War experience only runs to its replica at the premiere of "Gone with the Wind" in 1939; he was even farther away from actual combat than Lewis Simpson's wandering vet. But his granddaughter insists that he act out the part, and her insistence leads to his death at the ceremony, attended symbolically by Old South (a uniformed Boy Scout) and new (a Coca-Cola machine).

O'Connor's point registers twice, once in her essay and once in the story: writers (including self-consciously southern writers like herself caught in the path of the Dixie Limited) work through previous writing, which replaces the "natural." For the southern writer that means self-consciously foregrounding southernness as a set of representations already in cultural place. And, in turn, that means some degree of "Faulknerian" parody, broad or subtle. O'-Connor, a cartoonist in her youth, wielded a broad brush; Price, a more subtle one; Welty, with her famous obliqueness, might even escape parodic detection in "The Burning."

Barry Hannah is a younger southern writer whose work seems aggressively postsouthern. Hobson sees Hannah in an agonistic relationship to "Faulkner": yearning for the powers of the father but lacking the Faulknerian "tragic sense, . . . high seriousness and social consciousness" that constitute paternal blessing (Hobson 34). Proposing a direct relationship might be a mistake in this case, for Hannah acts out a more complicated relationship to the master. After all, he has served as one of the judges of the Faux Faulkner contest. Literary parody is built into Hannah's situation, if not into his artistic temperament.

Geronimo Rex (1972), Hannah's first novel, appeared ten years after Faulkner's death, yet it bears many of the scars of an author trying to exorcise or redefine his southernness. Harriman Monroe, the young protagonist and self-proclaimed spiritual brother to Geronimo, is, like Cash's typical southerner under the savage ideal, a killer. Ironically, however, one of his first slayings in the novel is the clubbing of one of his wealthy neighbor's peacocks. Harry then tosses the carcass into a ditch and covers it with lime. The dead peacock's name — Harry had blocked it but later remembers he had known it all the while — is Bayard, a Sartoris name. Harry's mayhem is anything but gratuitous; it is, rather, redolent of postmodern parodic "meaning," for it has more to do with hostility to literary representations than with cruelty to animals. Harry's act is, in Jameson's postmodern lexicon, "transcoded": a reader may use the dynamics or modes of interpretation of one critique in another (54). A peacock named Bayard becomes a complex coded symbol or representation that means the work and stature of Flannery O'Connor (famous for her peacocks, real and literary), vying with "Faulkner" for pride of place in the southern standings. The lime is left over from Hazel Motes's self-blinding. "The novels that interest," O'Connor had written, "are those that have already been written" — and Hannah turns the prophecy upon the prophet.

Geronimo Rex is laced with transcoded tropes like the battering of the peacock. Harry's father, Ode Elann Monroe, parodies the type of gentleman-poet epitomized by William Alexander Percy, the Delta poet and stymied son of a southern Bayard in Lanterns on the Levee. Lewis Simpson's lawyer-poet father is a member of this troop as well. Harry's first meeting with his roommate at college, Bobby Dove Fleece, takes place during a meandering, paranoid monologue by Bobby Dove that lampoons the demented patriarchal figure (for example, Thomas Sutpen), raunchily dubbed Whitfield Peter, who stalks both young men. The scene parodies the extended episode in Absalom, Absalom! in which the two earlier college roommates, Quentin and Shreve, together concoct a similarly haunting patriarchal figure. Sutpen's predatory procreative activities are taken down a notch when Hannah demotes the phallic will-to-power to "Peter" and drops the name-of-the-father in favor of Whitfield, the Mississippi town where the state institution for the mentally "aberrant" is located. Later in the novel Harry wanders around the battlefield at Vicksburg, spoofing the fugue state of Walker Percy's Will Barrett in *The Last Gentleman*. Harry avoids the futility of identifying with the Lost Cause by adopting as his patron spirit Ulysses S. Grant, another "hairy man," prone, like *Harri-man* Monroe, to moods and funks and bouts with the bottle.

The transcoding that gives *Geronimo Rex* its parodic bite, or overbite, into southernness stems from Hannah's postmodern version of historical and literary "seriousness." "Seriousness" in the "post-" condition means thinking about thinking. The past and the South, Harry sadly realizes, are now a set of mediated representations. There is nothing natural. Not even sexual desire breaks free of commodification and belatedness. Once Harry sees a poster of a Revlonized woman in a local drugstore, he realizes that even his Jungian anima has been airbrushed. The yearning for the natural throbs like a severed limb, but nothing will bring it back.

Examples are too numerous; as Shreve yammered, once you watch you want to play. One more must suffice to make the point that reading southern literature in a postmodern condition calls for attention to structures of mediation, "intertexts" not necessarily named and identified. Peter Taylor's short story "In the Miro District" mirrors Simpson's anecdote of the wandering vet and O'Connor's "A Late Encounter with the Enemy." The story, like so much of Taylor's fiction, is so deeply nuanced that "mediation" itself seems his central, absorbing theme.

"In the Miro District" is a longish short story, as Taylor's usually are, narrated by a middle-aged Nashvillian remembering a crucial season in his youth in the 1920s when he was eighteen and his grandfather (with the tantalizingly symbolic name of Major Basil Manley) was seventy-nine but showing no signs of decrepitude. The narrator remembers himself as a boy in a crucial struggle with the "manly" archetype of the South, not so much a region as a psychosocial condition requiring careful negotiation. Like most of Taylor's plots of fierce generational and familial struggle, this one is oblique, offset.

At seventy-nine in the 1920s, the present-time of Taylor's story, Major Manley would have been born in the antebellum 1840s. He might have served the Confederacy in the Civil War. There is an actual local hero in Middle Tennessee (the Miro District, our narrator tells us in a meandering aside, is an earlier name for this region when it was the property of Spanish dons headquartered in Natchez in the late eighteenth century): Sam Davis, who, on a mission for the Confederate army, was captured and executed. Davis, "The Boy Hero of the Confederacy," is memorialized by a larger-than-life-size bronze statue on the grounds of the Capitol in Nashville. Major Manley, however, declines any hint that his similar exploits were heroic. He refuses to attend Confederate Memorial Days or reunions for fear he will be ceremoniously—and erroneously—promoted, like "Tennessee" Flintrock Sash. And he will not reminisce, except under limited and special circumstances, even though his capture and harrowing escape from "nightriders" years after the War is a tale everyone, including the grandson, seems to know. The grandson is in fact somewhat obsessed by this story, so obsessed that remembering it almost word for word becomes the great psycholinguistic burden of his coming-of-age. Taylor's narrator suggests that his growth to maturity necessitates driving a stake through the heart of *the story*.

Major Manley will not come to town to live with his daughter and son-in-law; he prefers his farmhouse in an adjoining, rural county. He does, however, have the habit of showing up "unheralded and unannounced." It is this unpredictability that brings about the crisis in the relationship between the grandfather and his actual history and the grandson and his Quentinian antagonism toward it.

The crisis builds through two episodes and explodes in the third. In the first, the narrator has invited several high school pals to the family home and liquor cabinet while the parents are away. All are earnestly drunk when the Major is heard in the foyer. Friends scatter, and bourbon is spilled. But the narrator is not satisfied until he drunkenly beards his grandfather in the latter's room and, like Ike McCaslin or Quentin Compson, demands to hear from history's own lips a story that could only belittle and crush him—the belated and non-heroic follower of the manly. "I had the sensation," the narrator remembers, "of retching or actually vomiting, not the whisky I had in my stomach but all the words about the nightriders I had ever had from him and had not known how to digest—words I had not ever wanted to hear" (166). The modern connection to history is deeply compromised by its antagonism to words: it is the only thing he wants to hear; it is the last thing he wants to hear. For his silence about the past Major Manley has his reasons: "*You don't want to hear such stuff as that,*" the narrator imagines his grandfather thinking. "*Not from me, you don't. You just want to hear yourself sketching in my old stories, giving them back to me. It makes you feel good. It helps you hide your feelings or whatever it is you've always wished to hide*" (166). In fact, the young man can tell the old story verbatim, and the aroma of the "Faulknerian" is curiously present in his own rhetoric (168).

The boy had heard all of these tales in a situation canonized in *Go Down, Moses*. In those stories Isaac McCaslin, the representative of the southern male coming-of-age in a test of words and courage, hears the old tales from the older men at Major DeSpain's hunting camp. So does Taylor's young man, at a duck hunting lodge on Reelfoot Lake (173). As he grows older, though, the grandfather's refusal to repeat the stories publicly — to step out of his own original proprietorship of the experience and surrender it to cultural possession and repetition — stymies the young man. Unable to live the experience by virtue of being born too late for heroic action, and prevented from possessing the words of the story by the Major's inaccessible silence, the young man is frustrated. If this sounds like Quentin's predicament, the similarity is not accidental. It is as if his life cannot proceed until and unless the grandfather relinquishes *his* life to parody, to the condition of irony. That an original must submit to the system of representations is a frequent theme in Taylor's fiction, perhaps most widely known in his mannerist story "Venus, Cupid, Folly and Time."

The next time the Major turns up "unheralded and unannounced" the grandson and three of his pals are surprised in separate bedrooms with young ladies of the town — each and every one buck naked. Like the drinking episode, this one fails to register very shockingly on the grandfather; he even seems to forge an immediate and friendly bond with the girls. He gallantly helps them to find articles of clothing; when they leave, they wave goodbyes to the grandfather — not to the grandson.

The final break comes when the grandson spends the night in his grandfather's bed with a college (Ward Belmont) girl with whom he has some sort of "relationship." She is not supposed to be the type to be found in a compromising situation, but Major Manley does find her, in his wardrobe and wearing not a stitch of clothing. The previous two "errors," the narrator concludes, must have fallen within the scope of the Major's tolerance; the third transgression does not. He leaves the house without unpacking, returns to a summer retreat where his daughter and son-in-law are spending a holiday, and thereafter surrenders to demands that he reenact a heroic past. He begins to wear a Confederate uniform (is even buried in one), attends all reunions and accepts honorary promotions, and even indulges (as if on cue) in sober discussion of the Great Confederate *IF* — Civil War gabbing on a grand but artificial scale. When the Major surrenders to parody, he enters the same sideshow as O'Connor's "Tennessee" Flintrock Sash and dismisses the actuality of Simpson's remembered vet for the stereotype of the romantic hero marketed by myth.

Is the Taylor plot one of winning the past or losing it? Has the grandson "won" by finally shocking the past into a costume-dummy version of itself? Has the narrator "lost" himself by selfishly insisting on a theme-park version of that self and its history? Would salvation have been genuine if the Major had held on to his history so that the "post-" generation had been refused easy digestion of its past through the enzymes of parody?

"In the Miro District," like so many of Taylor's short stories, relies on asking questions rather than answering them. Nevertheless, the story strongly suggests that a southern writer's engagement with his past is a self-conscious challenge, that it takes place mediated by already written stories, ritually composed and reenacted scenes, and that ironic rethinking (and rereading) are necessary if the southern writer in the postmodern condition is to have any voice at all — even such a faint and fading voice as so many of Taylor's narrators possess.

If there are writers and readers in the South for whom parody is the appropriate language, there are many who insist upon the South without irony. Even though Toyotas are built in Kentucky, Nissans in Tennessee, BMWs in South Carolina, and Mercedes-Benzes in Alabama — the first home of the government of the Confederate States of American and the state whose Governor George Wallace proclaimed "Segregation forever" — a strongly conservative minority still dedicates itself to preserving the South as a cultural refuge from the excesses and wrong turns of modern life. This loosely organized "movement" attempts to drive southern identity back into the arena of U.S. cultural politics.

IX

THE INVENTION
OF THE SOUTH
AND THE
CULTURE WAR

Our future as Southerners is
threatened. . . . But if we, as the remnant
of Western Man, are to survive to enjoy
our voluntary associations, we must
temporarily rigidify them, close ranks, and
require of ourselves service to the cause
of southern independence.
SOUTHERN PATRIOT, 1995

The culture wars that have consumed so much media and political
attention in the last decade have
thrown the meaning of "nationness"
for the United States into question.
Polarization in the battle over "values" has brought the South as region and tradition back into the spotlight. Recently, Eugene Genovese has thrown down the gauntlet in his writing on the unquiet
southern front in these culture wars. With Confederate flag controversies in several states, a racially motivated killing and subsequently
guilty verdict in Robert Penn Warren's hometown, a recent presidential primary season in which one candidate on the Right cultivated
southern identity and issues, and the short history of the Southern
League (founded in 1994 to reinvent southern cultural identity along
"cracker" [that is, populist] lines counter to the elite lines of the literati
and intelligentsia), the theater of war — so to speak — is busy. What
Genovese has to say on this topic, in fact, obligates each one of us to
take a position. With both brio and subtlety, his reinterpretation excludes the middle ground.

As Genovese sees "the southern front," one is either victim or war
criminal. The metaphorical language is not gratuitous; the martial
vocabulary is as natural to the discourse of southern cultural identity
as gravy is to rice. In his preface to *The Southern Tradition: The Achievement and Limitations of an American Conservatism* (1994), the presti-

gious William E. Massey, Sr., Lectures in the History of American Civilization at Harvard (1993), Genovese draws a clear line in the sand: "We are witnessing a cultural and political atrocity — an increasingly successful campaign by the media and an academic elite to strip young white southerners, and arguably black southerners as well, of their heritage, and, therefore, their identity" (xii). As Genovese makes clear elsewhere in his recent writing on the South, he does not use the word "atrocity" lightly or even metaphorically. We, whose recent historical memory includes the Holocaust and whose headlines bring news of mass graves in the former Yugoslavia and the once-and-future Congo, know atrocities all too well. In a review of Genovese's work, David Brion Davis quotes him as seeing the experiment with Marxism as having nothing to show for its seventy-year run but "tens of millions of corpses" (qtd. in Davis 43). Slave trading and slave holding, Genovese implies, were never so bloody. In the current moment of cultural crisis, Genovese's conservative salvo admonishes us, we risk the loss of historical perspective in an offensive of cultural and identitarian rhetoric. Elemental values hang in the balance. There is nothing "imagined" (*pace* Anderson) about the crisis, as Genovese places the South centrally in it.

A necessary and preliminary step in the discourse of the culture war is and (especially on the southern front) has been to inject martial rhetoric into the conversation and to ratchet-up the tension to the breaking point. Southern literary and cultural "forms and styles" are hammered out in this forge. As Faulkner wrote in *Intruder in the Dust*, it is always a few minutes before two o'clock on July 3, 1863, and Pickett is always about to give the fateful order to charge: southern identity is always about to be achieved and obliterated in the same fateful instant.

The "heritage" or tradition of which young southerners are being shorn (or, to be precise, are always about to be shorn) is both identitarian (holding it bestows southernness) and political (it is conservative). Once again, in the preface to *The Southern Tradition*, Genovese writes: "I speak and write on the southern (conservative) tradition" (ix). "Conservative" appears in parentheses, injected by stealth into the discourse not as a modifier but as a synonym for southern. There is only one southern tradition, and it is conservative. In the introduction Genovese goes further: "Understandably, liberals seek to silence a southern conservatism that has, from its origins, constituted America's most impressive native-born critique of our national development, of liberalism, and of the more disquieting features of the modern world" (1–2). In a few following lines the southern (conservative) tradition is connected to a theme broached by the Agrarians and made central by their disciple Richard Weaver: southern culture is "a worthy embodiment of Western Christian civilization" (2). The lines for a full-scale culture battle are fairly completely drawn. Southernness, as construed by Genovese, is a nearly exact structural counterpart to Benedict Anderson's concept of "nationness." My purpose in *Inventing Southern Literature* parallels Anderson's, colliding head-on with Genovese: "My point of departure is that nationality, or, as one might prefer to put it in view of that word's multiple significations, nation-ness, as well as nationalism, are cultural artefacts of a particular kind. To understand them properly we need to consider carefully how they have come into historical being, in what ways their meanings have changed over time, and why, today, they command such profound emotional legitimacy" (Anderson 4).

The conduct of my argument in this book—a consideration of the ways and means by which southernness has come into being and been sustained there, along with the attempt to measure how and why the meaning of the term has changed over time—progresses along lines conservative culture critics deplore in stereotypical "left-liberal" postmodernists.

First, I postpone responding to the drawing of the lines as and where Genovese has located them, choosing first to historicize his strategy as more or less continuous with the ongoing strategy emerging in the Agrarian project, moving through Richard Weaver, and emerging (until recently) in the anthologies defining and supporting the curriculum of the southern heritage. Genovese did not, for example, choose the title *The Southern Tradition* by accident—Weaver's posthumous *The Southern Tradition at Bay* is invoked as precursor—and Genovese's construction of the southern tradition borrows more from this precursor than merely a title. Positioning Weaver as precursor means running all the risks inherent in his argument—or, surreptitiously deflecting them.

One of the biggest of these risks looms in a central disjunction between Weaver's legacy to southern culture and Genovese's mode of receiving it. Whereas Genovese accepts sets of social relations (for example, master/slave, capitalist/worker) as determining "limits to what may be accomplished in the polity and in the culture" (8–9), Weaver forged his idea of southern culture in a more metaphysical medium in which "universals" constituted the language of thought. Even though Weaver, like Genovese, began his intellectual career on the Left, when he departed for the Right he jettisoned much more of his past. Weaver ignored, whereas Genovese elides, two fashionable but powerful *idées fixes* of "social democracy" (x), the social relations of black/white and male/female. Race and gender are, and historically have been, muffled in official enunciations of the southern tradition. It had to be so, for as I hope I have shown in the course of my argument, attention to either "idea" produces "consequences" for the southern tradition that seriously threaten its powerful (conservative) symmetry.

Postponing response to an argument is mere stalling if there is nothing closing the gap. Conservative cultural critiques (as the chapters on the Agrarians and Weaver, respectively, attempt to show) are often ahistorical even as they invoke history. The amnesia often alleged to be part and parcel of southernness is most often attributed to the southern habit of preferring "the past" to the varied circumstances of day-to-day history. Historical context is in order, then, for the perception of threat to the southern tradition (posed by Supreme Court, Left-liberal academics, or "the media") is not unique to the present, fin de siècle intellectual climate. Indeed, as Anderson roughly encompasses his study of imagined communities of "nationness" within "the past two centuries" (7), I position *Inventing Southern Literature* in the second two-thirds of this one. The invention of the American South is hardly thinkable without the Western movement to invent nations; the invention of southern literature is unthinkable without the historical circumstancing of the Tennessee Valley Authority, racial desegregation, the realigning of gender power in society, and a myriad other historical prods.

The "stripping" of a generation of southerners of their "heritage" is not in the offing. Indeed, if the implicit cultural "arguments" in the fiction of Kennedy, Simms, and lesser antebellum writers is admitted into the conversation, the contemporary cultural emergency has more than a century to its life span already. John Pendleton Kennedy fretted, in *Swallow Barn* (1831; rev. 1852), that his traditional southern gentleman, Frank Meriwether, master of Swallow Barn plantation, was to be replaced by a less stable Romantic type, Ned Hazard, who might not protect and preserve the old ways. William Gilmore Simms's Captain Porgy, insofar as he roundly embodies traditional southern ways, is always about to surrender them as he is always on the brink of bankrupting his plantation in *Woodcraft* (1854). It was this theme of loss of or danger to southern tradition from within—not only or even primarily from beyond the pale—that Allen Tate retrieved from the plantation legend (an earlier incarnation of "the southern tradition") for his only novel, *The Fathers* (1938).

Postbellum southern writers through Ellen Glasgow in the first half of this century kept up the theme, although some (Glasgow herself) saw it with more nuance than the straightforward propagandists—Stark Young, for example, in *So Red the Rose* (1934) or Margaret Mitchell in *Gone with the Wind* (1936). To allege that now the definitive denuding is to take place is, in view of the longevity of the cultural psychomachia (or "narrative of identity"), to miss the point. The southern tradition is held and in fact affirmed under conditions of alarm that it is about to be squelched. We act in rituals designed to dramatize affirmation of identity by decrying the enemy: flying the battle flag, joining the Southern League, proclaiming an emergency and demonizing "the other" (in this case "liberals") who seek to impose silence rather than tolerate dialogue.

Southern cultural self-consciousness has historically expressed itself in such terms of anxiety of invasion and takeover. Henry Grady's New South/Old South dilemma metastasized, in a sense, into William Graham Sumner's sociological view of folkways and stateways (especially as regards racial beliefs and behaviors in the South) and thence into the Agrarian/Industrialism—traditional/modern dichotomy of the Twelve Southerners who undertook *I'll Take My Stand*. As nuances shifted, the same us/them antagonism endured. In the 1990s it is liberals/conservatives.

Although *I'll Take My Stand* has, since its publication, been taken as a kind of sacred text and its message a kind of revelation, in fact it serves as a script for inventing southern identity through anxiety. The identity the Agrarians unconsciously dramatized (as opposed, perhaps, to the one they consciously outlined) is an identity of anxious doubt. This is not to say that each was equally ravaged by the same identity crisis; it is to say, though, that the essays by those whom we tend to quote most frequently (Ransom, Davidson, Tate, Warren) register self-doubt.

Allen Tate is the most anxious southerner, one who is most deeply in doubt as to whether being self-conscious of the content of southern character can coexist with actually being a southerner. In his enigmatic essay in *I'll Take My Stand*, "Remarks on the Southern Religion," Tate worries this point incessantly: "For abstraction is the death of religion no less than the death of anything else [southern identity and tradition perhaps, in the essay's immediate context]. Religion, when it directs its attention to the horse cropping the blue-grass on the lawn, is concerned with the whole horse, and not with (1) that part of him which he has in common with other horses, or that more general part which he shares with other quadrupeds or with the more general vertebrates; and not with (2) that power of the horse which he shares with horsepower in general, of pushing or pulling another object. Religion pretends to place before us the horse as he is" (156–57).

The problem of thought, as we see it traced in Tate's metaphor, is that it begins general and continues to be ever more generalizing—comparing and comparing in a widening spiral until all that is left is the outline of the similarities: the loathed "abstraction." You cannot think (much less write) the phrase "quadrupeds or . . . the more general vertebrates" and not be implicated in the scientific, Linnaean, abstracting mind. The horse as he is—religion, southern tradition, identity in a culture—is subverted in the instant the intellect subjects it. Through the course of his essay on southern identity, thinly disguised as religion, Tate can neither live with this problem nor live without it. The mythic or concrete mind, the one seamlessly integrated into its history and moment ("the horse as he is"), is radically different from the modern mind, especially when the modern mind makes the concrete mind its target. And Tate, as well as his brother Agrarians, was a modern mind identified by anxiety and estrangement. When Tate concluded his essay with a final tantalizing prophecy, he defined southern tradition and identity—at the very least for modern times—as process rather than finished product: "We are very near an answer to our question—How may the Southerner take hold of his Tradition? The answer is, by violence. . . . The Southerner is faced with the paradox: He must use an instrument, which is political [self-conscious and programmatic "reaction"], and so unrealistic and pretentious that he cannot believe in it, to re-establish a private, self-contained, and essentially spiritual life. I say he must do this; but that remains to be seen" (174, 175).

For Tate southern identity lay (or rather oscillated) in this condition of never possessing itself, never believing in the intellectual and political means used to possess itself in an act of thought. In a very real sense, Tate lived a generation too soon—or he should have been granted two consecutive lives. He made a quintessential modern; he would have made an equally adept postmodern. He could not deny that southern identity was invented in certain historical circumstances; he knew himself to be doing this very thing when he merely thought about the South as subject matter to his intellect.

Tate defined southern identity as the internalization and psychologization of the sociological phenomena Sumner had defined as folkways and stateways. The latter (stateways standing for abstraction) is always just about to strip the former of its status in human society, to render it an anachronism just now disappearing around the corner. Tate made this liminal, vanishing condition *the* condition of southern identity. His elder, John Crowe Ransom, constructed a more elaborate (but static) table of this dichotomy, opposing pairs of terms such as American and southern, industrial and agrarian, pioneering and stable, urban and rural, progressive and traditional, male and female.

Genovese, then, is right to say that a current generation of young southerners is about to be stripped of its heritage; every generation of southerners since the one of 1861–65 (and perhaps several prior to this crisis) has lived through or contrived circumstances that would strip it of identity and tradition. And each cultural warrior, and the collective group expressing itself through acceptance of such things as texts, is forever poised at the moment of violently seizing (or losing) his or her pure identity. Genovese is mistaken, though, to think an academic elite or a liberal media campaign is doing the deed. As Robert Penn Warren knew, and explored deeply in *Brother to Dragons* (quoted much earlier), affirmation and its opposite coexist in every moment of thought. A somewhat less alarmist voice in *I'll Take My Stand*, Herman Clarence Nixon, reported, for example, that agrarianism and industrialism historically and presently coexisted in the South, that they were (by implication) not antithetical but symbiotic, and that there was nothing "distinctive" about southern culture that geography and economics could not account for. Nixon's essay serves as an illustrative counterexample to the rallying cries of Ransom, Davidson, Tate, and Lytle. Although this economist does express the requisite warning ("The South is no longer conquered territory, not quite conquered, but a protest, articulate and constructive, is needed against another conquest, a conquest of the spirit" [20].), the tenor of his essay in general is that of the "constructive protest," not the rebel yell as the culture flings itself toward its tradition against all odds.

The Agrarian version of southern cultural defense and identification passed from the first generation of the Twelve Fathers to Richard Weaver in the 1940s and 1950s (Weaver died prematurely in 1963), and it is from Weaver's version of the discourse that Genovese primarily derives his "southern tradition." The original Twelve were, with some exceptions, consciously engaged in hand-to-hand combat for immediate cultural-political advantage with the southernists at the University of North Carolina at Chapel Hill in the 1920s an 1930s, and with the Humanists orbiting Irving Babbitt and Paul Elmer More in the North—cultural yankees. Later, in the early 1930s, hard times brought them into conflict with American Communists and Socialists; but they probably had more in common with their latter adversaries than either would care to admit. Weaver was also engaged in battle against particular foes, and his antagonists (and his rhetoric) seem more germane to Genovese's work than the Agrarians', although as founders they are still acknowledged.

Genovese takes, as I have already mentioned, the title of *The Southern Tradition* from Weaver's posthumously published doctoral thesis (1943), *The Southern Tradition at Bay* (1968). Weaver's work bears many of the marks of a dissertation; it is full of the findings of his excavations among the archives of southern periodical and book publications from antebellum times to the eve of the First World War. There is a section of hortatory prose, serving as a coda to the historical work, that anticipates the later phase of Weaver's intellectual career. This latter phase, as embodied in *Visions of Order: The Cultural Crisis of Our Time* (1964), is really where an alignment with Genovese's work takes place. The "cultural crisis" Weaver diagnoses in the late 1950s and early 1960s is, in his view, a misconstruction of the nature of democratic society, and of societies in general; in this general aspect his earlier work and Genovese's are very compatible. Both critics warn of imminent moral and cultural chaos and counsel an immediate return to a central enclave of value and meaning—an "imagined community" less politically than metaphysically "sovereign" (Anderson 6–7). This community is similar for both writers: religious (Christian), conservative (that is, informed by an awareness of human error rather than perfectibility), and southern.

In several parts of *Visions of Order* Weaver seems to have foreshadowed Genovese's appearance. The cultural prophet is, Weaver predicted, a kind of outsider whose experience of the culture to be defended might have originated on the inside but is informed by experience of the outside. This savant figure is in his society but not wholly of it: "[H]e has acquired knowledge and developed habits of thought which enable him to see it in perspective and to gauge it. He has not lost the intuitive understanding which belongs to him as a member, but he has added something to that. A temporary alienation from his culture may be followed by an intense preoccupation with it, but on a more reflective level than that of the typical member. He has become sufficiently aware of what is outside it to see it as a system or an entity. This person may be a kind of doctor of culture" (7). Prophet, savant, doctor: Weaver juggles his metaphor, but the operating form of the cultural narrative is return from alienation. As Genovese sets forth in "In Lieu of an Introduction: Personal Reflections," the first section of *The Southern Front*, he also has returned to "the south" (the quotation marks are called for: Genovese is not a native southerner and the South he returns to, as if from exile, is a historical/ cultural assemblage). By virtue of his alienation on the outside he is equipped to diagnose and prescribe what Weaver calls the "culture that is weakening" (7). And Genovese's prescription is much like Tate's in "Remarks on the Southern Religion"; the southerner (white and "arguably" black) must recognize and seize his culture as "a worthy embodiment of Western Christian civilization" in two senses of that term: cultural and religious (2).

By virtue of filtering the substance and the role of the self-conscious southerner as conservative cultural "doctor," Genovese affirms the inevitability of conservatism as *the* southern cultural position. He also shows a touch of sensitivity when that cultural position is subjected to examination. The original Agrarian group suffered the slings and arrows of negative criticism from the likes of such "progressives" as W. J. Cash and Gerald Johnson. These two critics were allied with the North Carolina *barbaroi* and so could be expected to be negative. When Seward Collins, brought on board primarily for his financial resources (he owned the *American Review*, a journal that Tate saw as a kind of official organ of the movement [see Chapter II), allowed himself to be quoted as saying that he admired Hitler and thought neither Jews nor blacks were entitled to certain privileges in the polity, the Agrarian movement went into damage control and then into dormancy. When it emerged, with the 1962 reprint of *I'll Take My Stand* introduced by Louis Rubin, its message was reinterpreted as metaphorical, not programmatic. Its real-time political agenda has been downplayed since.

Genovese has had his own critics, and their duels bear resemblance to those between the Agrarians and their antagonists, and Weaver and his. Genovese has vehemently objected to David Brion Davis's review in the *New York Review of Books* on the grounds that it contains unfair implications of racism in its comparison of Genovese's views with those of others claiming to speak for the conservative southern cultural tradition, notably Michael Hill, president of the Southern League.

Genovese has anticipated the criticism he sees in Davis's review: that embracing southern tradition is also embracing racism. Early in *The Southern Tradition* he makes it very clear that "those who wish to take southern conservatism seriously must recognize that the widespread political identification of men like Bilbo with the conservative movement exposes grave weaknesses in its theory and politics" (20). Students of the southern tradition must separate the husk from the kernel: "Historically, their [southern conservatives'] viewpoint has often accompanied racism, but it has no necessary connection to it" (27). This darker tint to southern conservatism Genovese attaches to excessive veneration of the yeomanry, the icons of so-called cracker culture studies. "The greater part by far of southern conservatism's political principles," Genovese insists, "derive decisively from the gentry and its claims to natural aristocracy" (80). "Men like Bilbo," and by association their cultural and political thinking, have contributed only "weaknesses" to the southern (conservative) tradition. Underneath Genovese's thinking here is a class elitism: synecdochically "Bilbo" represents the mass of southern poor whites from which he came, and they are the causes of racism in southern cultural practices. This is a shadow argument by no means unique to Genovese. In *To Kill a Mockingbird*, "men like Bilbo," but considerably less determined, petition Atticus Finch for permission to lynch Tom Robinson. They are turned away, departing sheepishly, by Atticus's stern refusal and Scout's innocent conversation. The "invention" at work here is that the race hatred virulent enough to result in lynching flows from the lower southern classes, not from the bourgeoisie or the gentry—and especially not from the intellectual work they produced in inventing themselves.

Genovese discloses, and in part exacerbates, a turf war within southern cultural studies—a turf war at least as old as *I'll Take My Stand*, in which some essays extol the yeomanry (crackers) and others the elite. If southern cultural identity (any cultural identity for that matter) is jeopardized by an "academic elite," it is also invented and promulgated by one—or by more than one, who fight with each other to carry the standard.

Genovese's anticipation of criticism and his response to Davis are germane to my case, for at issue is whether or how racism can be divided from the narrative system of southern cultural identity. Genovese, not surprisingly, knows this full well: "With the proslavery theorists, as well as with Marx, I believe social relations, whether master/slave or capitalist/worker [not male/female?—see below], set definite limits to what may be accomplished in the polity and the culture. . . . Rather [than delve into the 'racist legacy of the southern tradition'], I have suggested that the realization of the finest values of the southern tradition requires a total break with its legacy of racism" (8–9). The issue dogging the resurgence of southern cultural forces is whether the "finest values" can be surgically excised from the main body of the culture. Can a total break with the legacy of racism be accomplished without severing the culture from its processes of discrimination, distinction, hierarchy, and self-definition? More vulgarly: is a southern tradition "cured" of its racism any longer interesting?

Not in calling for a resurrection of "southern tradition" but in carving it out of the rough stone of precedent does cultural infighting begin. Genovese's letter to the *New York Review of Books* protests Davis's alleged implication that scholars associated with the Southern League are racist; it is revealing. Having read the original review, including its footnotes, several times looking for Davis's implication that members on the new southern cultural Right, or their platform, are racist, I have found no such evidence.

One should not, however, expect to find the more virulent and obvious racism of some of the essays in *I'll Take My Stand,* ranging from the sincere attempts of Warren and Herman Clarence Nixon to find some intellectually, culturally significant role for African-Americans in the (white) southern agenda to the more strident racism of Frank Owsley. Both of the former essayists not only mention the verboten subject of race, which a diehard like Davidson wanted banished from the document altogether, but they also identify an African-American intellectual (if not a culture) in Booker T. Washington. There are, in some bands of the intellectual rainbow these days, voices to ask why Washington and not Du Bois? There is a form of latent racism even in trying not to be racist. Owsley uses his essay, "The Irrepressible Conflict," to push a racist cultural image in the guise of history. The American Civil War failed to attract the respectful notice of "Europe," according to Owsley, until "Anglo-Saxons stood within ten paces of one another at Chickamauga and fired point-blank" (61). At that mythic moment—a moment previously commemorated by Thomas Dixon and filmmaker D. W. Griffith—a nation was born, an Anglo-Saxon nation basking in the gaze of its elder predecessor: Europe. The African-American had no part in this cultural rebirth. They were relegated to mass identity: "three millions of former slaves, some of whom could still remember the taste of human flesh and the bulk of them hardly three generations removed from cannibalism. These half-savage blacks were armed," Owsley warned (62). One cannot deny that Owsley's "Willie-Hortonized" rendition of southern history is racist and—more importantly—that his view of southern culture, with its emphasis on the cracker rather than the aristocrat, depends on a racist segregation of the Anglo-Saxon and the African-American. One must argue more carefully about Ransom's lone statement on slavery and race: "Slavery was a feature monstrous enough in theory, but, more often than not, humane in practice; and it is impossible to believe that its abolition alone could have effected any great revolution in society" (14). Something as yet unstated and unacknowledged must then have motivated masses of African-Americans to want to reject chattel slavery for freedom. Like most of Ransom's arguments, this one scarcely leaves traces of having been made. From denial through careful choosing of the ground to outright stereotyping, the southern intellectual and cultural tradition, as it is represented by *I'll Take My Stand*, is inextricably coiled in race. That does not make every individual who seeks identity in its narrative a racist, but it does make the question of breaking with the legacy of racism extremely relevant.

Conservative defenders of the southern tradition have apparently always known the subtle rules of this game. We can return to Weaver for an important example of the way from the Agrarians to the more recent Southern League. Closing his essay "The Image of Culture" (in *Visions of Order*), Weaver takes the contemporary bull by the horns:

> But "integration" and "segregation" are two sides of the same operation. A culture integrates by segregating its forms of activity and its members from those not belonging. The right to self-segregate then is an indispensable ground of its being. Enough has been said to show that our culture today is faced with very serious threats in the form of rationalistic drives to prohibit in the name of equality cultural segregation. The effect of this would be to break up the natural cultural cohesion and to try to replace it with artificial politically dictated integration. Such "integration" would of course be a failure because where deep inner impulse is lacking cohesiveness for any length of time is impossible. This crisis has been brought to our attention most spectacularly in the attempt to "integrate" culturally distinct elements by court action. It is, however, only the most publicized of the moves; others are taking place in areas not in the spotlight, but all originate in ignorance, if not in a suicidal determination to write an end to the heritage of Western culture. (21)

Weaver has been called many things as a champion on the southern side of the culture war (including "quietly ironic" by Davis [46]), but it seems to me that statements such as the one above are not whimsical, profound, coy, or ironic. In reserving ahistorical meanings for the words *integration* and *segregation* in the early 1960s Weaver is doing the rhetorician's equivalent of flying a Confederate battle flag on his pickup truck. It is not so much "culturally distinct elements" that Weaver wishes to segregate but racial ones, and in this aim he is only more urbane in verbal skill than a writer like Owsley. The code becomes, over time, more difficult to decipher.

The southern intellectual tradition is riven by such denial and assertion by coding. The struggle of the Southern League to gain numbers and visibil-

ity as a paleoconservative inventor of the southern tradition is the most recent appearance of this desire for voice and power. Genovese undercuts the
premise of this paleoconservative movement by disparaging their foundation
assumption that the yeomanry is the historical basis of authentic southern
culture (*Tradition* 80). His objections to Davis's review continue this disavowal.
But there is much to argue that the mass of southerners, and apprentice
southerners from other regions, respond to the paleoconservative array of
positions and images much more deeply than they do to the elite intellectual
culture of the Agrarians. Patrick Buchanan's measured success in 1996 southern presidential primaries suggests the same conclusion.

The drivers of the Southern League agenda have a fairly clear grasp of the
basic tenets of southern intellectual tradition. They reinvented the killing of
a young white man, Michael Westerman, on January 17, 1995 (the day following Martin Luther King Day), as a mythic sacrifice. Motorcades to his
burial, commemorating eulogies, fund drives for his widow and fatherless
twins, even a country-music CD, have been used to invent that "community"
and "deep, horizontal comradeship" that Anderson cites as crucial in imagining community (Anderson 7). In rally speeches and other statements, spokes-
persons for the League have lifted the nineteen-year-old Westerman to the
symbolic status of Western Man. His death is represented as an apocalyptic
strike in an ongoing racial war. In the words of Michael Hill, president of
the Southern League, the victim was "allegedly murdered . . . by two carloads
of black males who objected to his flying of the Confederate flag from his
truck" (Hill [9]). The flag is cherished as the stainless symbol of ethnic southern nationalism; and, to borrow again from Anderson, it ambiguously represents "not so much [the potential] to kill, as willingly to die for such limited
imaginings [as nation/community]" (Anderson 7). The actual participants —
the good yeomen involved — might have possessed a different understanding. One of the dead man's friends confessed to an interviewer that they
knew "the flag sent a message to blacks. . . . We knew it made them mad" (Horwitz 68). Any hope for recouping the communicative power of the symbol is
lost, though, when it is disclosed that one of the convicted men, Freddie Mor-
row, says that he thought the Confederate flag was just "the 'Dukes of Haz-
zard' sign" that meant to whites "white pride and continued slavery" (Horwitz 68). The widow can do little better, for she thought her dead husband
flew the flag because its color "matched his truck and . . . made it look sharp"
(Horwitz 76). Two years later, the events are still too hot to touch. The Met-

ropolitan Arts Commission (Nashville) declined to grant developmental funds to a group seeking to create an original dramatic work based on the events on the grounds that "the potential for controversy was too great" (Bostick 4B).

The discrepancy between the meanings participants place upon events and symbols, and those meanings championed by culture critics engaged in maneuvers, clearly reveals the process of inventing traditions, of constructing meaningful narratives from merely serial incidents. From the Agrarian agenda to that of the Southern League one propelling force of the southern tradition has been the overcoming of one element of the network of social relations within which it has come into being: the social relations evolving in and through slavery, then continuing in postslavery race relations. No conservative southern tradition has yet developed a way to acknowledge the defining characteristics of race relations upon southern cultural identity without simultaneously acknowledging the shaping influence of race on the "finer" aspects of southern cultural accomplishment. Nor has any southern cultural stance faced the question of the extent to which the culture's defining habits of discrimination and distinction have been actually formed in the practice of racism. The paleoconservative southern thinkers of the Southern League rally with the Celtic clans, affirming the historical existence of an indigenous southern Anglo-Saxon cultural heritage that is defined as prior to and uninvolved in racial issues. The aristocracy owned slaves, this argument asserts; on them and their heirs be the stigma. Genovese's southern conservative culture occupies the high road, bracketing such representative figures as Theodore Bilbo with adherents of "cracker culture" theory and any other signs of "the racist legacy of the southern tradition" (*Tradition* 9) and attempting to salvage what is imagined to be left: limited acquisitiveness, a skepticism of the messianic pretensions of science, the inviolability of the family, faith in Christian religion (*Tradition* 12–18).

Just as the vexed issue of race relations as significant in the shaping of the southern tradition requires careful management, the issue of gender does as well. Genovese does not foreground this issue in his recent writings on the South but it is there, and his scrupulous respect for its controversial potential is obvious in his quarantine of it. Central to the finer aspects of the southern tradition, in Genovese's view, is "above all, the family" (*Tradition* 14). If shunning the racist element of southern culture is the strongest negative obligation of the definers of that tradition, then affirming family is the strongest positive: "The southern-conservative critique of individualism shares much with that of other Christians who have refused to capitulate to theological liberalism. Spokesmen for the Catholic Church and the Ortho-dox Presbyterian Church, among others, have drawn on Saint Augustine's denunciation of self-love and the contempt for God inherent in the claim that he is a limited Being. In particular, they have stressed the inviolability of the family—'the society of a man's household,' as Pope Leo XIII described it—as anterior to state and nation, with the individual head of household as the authoritative officer of its members" (*Tradition* 14).

Genovese is careful not to use the word so obviously present under the cover of a substitute: patriarch. What Pope Leo XIII, and all of the other pontiffs before and since, have urged upon the world has been a version of the patriarchy at the head of which they sit. The inequalities in and stem-ming from that "natural" model of community are, then, handed off to the Supreme Being; appeals are postponed for Parousia. In urging the stability of the patriarchal family as the basis of "state and nation," Genovese also rec-ommends a hierarchy of social power and activity that places the white male at the apex of a pyramid, followed by his female mate, and so on down through children and the infantilized.

There are inequities built into this system, and *patriarchy* is one of a few words used to denote them. So powerful, however, is the importance of the southern-conservative tradition to Genovese's model of the South that he confronts these inequities without blinking: "Second [in his list of positions common to northern and southern conservatives in the antebellum period], northerners defined the household as the family, narrowly construed, whereas southerners defined the household to include independent laborers. The slave holders meant precisely what they said when they referred, privately as well as publicly, to 'our family, white and black'" (*Tradition* 69). Clearly, the vast majority of those "independent laborers" were slaves, persons wholly owned by the "authoritative officer" of the household, who could sell them at his pleasure. As clearly, even allowing for rhetorical extremism, slave holders meant precisely, if not always overtly, what they said when they referred to some of those wholly owned persons as "family," for many masters were bio-logical as well as figurative fathers. That Genovese can push his argument for the viability of the southern-conservative tradition nose-to-nose with the volatile issues of sexual predation and the subjection of women of all races, and then swerve as if they are not there in his path, indicates that is-sues of sex and gender, along with issues of race, confront the inventors of the southern community at every twist. As southern studies develops in the future, the impact of sexuality and gender will doubtless be the most important area of growth and change.

The phantom accusation of racism in Davis's review of Genovese and the latter's volcanic demand for recantation amount to a kind of diversionary spectacle. The sexism that is not mentioned is just as crucial to the argument as the alleged racism that is. In the literary record of the southern tradition, as I have shown, these two "isms" bide their time in the repressed mind of the South until, awakening, they present inventors and reinventors with problems that render the continuity of the South — and its literary practices — all but impossible.

My narrative of the invention of southern identity in the literary record moves to no happy ending. I have neither reassuring news that despite the appearance of discontinuity and confusion all will go on as before, the same yet different; nor do I have the proclamation of a new southern canon to replace the old one and inevitably to repeat the errors of the old one in the very act of believing itself to be a canon. What I have found in this study of literary maneuverings and reinventions — and have striven to explain in the book — is that "the South" is the richest site yet discovered in the U.S. cultural terrain for the study of and participation in the reinvention of culture. We should not wish this activity shut down; the process is our collective life.

WORKS CITED

[Adams, Henry]. *The Education of Henry Adams*. Boston: Houghton Mifflin, 1918.

Agar, Herbert, and Allen Tate, eds. *Who Owns America?* Boston: Houghton, 1936.

Alderman, Edwin Anderson, et al., eds. *The Library of Southern Literature*. 16 vols. New Orleans: Martin, 1908–13.

Allison, Dorothy. *Bastard out of Carolina*. New York: Dutton, 1992.

Althusser, Louis. *Essays on Ideology*. 1971, 1976. London: Verso, 1984.

Anderson, Benedict. *Imagined Communities: Reflections on the Origins and Spread of Nationalism*. 1983. Rev. ed. London: Verso, 1991.

Andrews, Raymond. *Appalachee Red*. 1978. Athens: U of Georgia P, 1987.

Arendt, Hannah. *The Origins of Totalitarianism*. New York: Harcourt, 1951.

Auerbach, Nina. *Communities of Women: An Idea in Fact and Fiction*. Cambridge: Harvard UP, 1978.

Ayers, Edward L., and Bradley C. Mittendorf, eds. *The Oxford Book of the American South: Testimony, Memory, and Fiction*. New York: Oxford UP, 1997.

Babbitt, Irving. "Humanism: An Essay at Self-Definition." Foerster 25–51.

Baker, Carlos. *Ernest Hemingway: A Life Story*. New York: Scribners, 1969.

Barr, Stringfellow. "Shall Slavery Come South?" *Virginia Quarterly Review* 6 (1930): 481–94.

Baskervill, William Malone. *Southern Writers: Biographical and Critical Studies*. Nashville: Publishing House of the Methodist Episcopal Church, South, 1897.

Bate, Walter Jackson. *The Burden of the Past and the English Poet*. Cambridge: Harvard UP, 1970.

Beatty, Richmond Croom, and William Perry Fidler, eds. *Contemporary Southern Prose*. Boston: Heath, 1940.

Bennett, William J., ed. *The Book of Virtues*. New York: Simon, 1993.

Berlin, Isaiah. *The Crooked Timber of Humanity: Chapters in the History of Ideas*. Ed. Henry Hardy. London: John Murray, 1990.

Betts, Doris. Introduction. *Southern Women Writers: The New Generation*. Ed. Tonette Bond Inge. Tuscaloosa: U of Alabama P, 1990. 1–8.

Blotner, Joseph. *Robert Penn Warren: A Biography*. New York: Random, 1997.

———, ed. *Selected Letters of William Faulkner*. New York: Random, 1977.

———. *William Faulkner: A Biography*. 2 vols. New York: Random, 1974.

———. *William Faulkner's Library, A Catalogue*. Charlottesville: Bibliographical Society of Virginia, 1964.

Bostick, Alan. "Play about 'flag' slaying denied grant." *Nashville Tennessean* 18 July 1997: 4B.

Bové, Paul. "Agriculture and Academe: America's Southern Question." In *Mastering Discourse: The Politics of Intellectual Culture*. Durham, NC: Duke UP, 1992. 113–42.

Brickell, Herschel, ed. *Prize Stories of 1951: The O. Henry Awards*. Garden City, NY: Doubleday, 1951.

———. Introduction. *Prize*. vii–xxvi.

Brooks, Cleanth, R. W. B. Lewis, and Robert Penn Warren, eds. *American Literature: The Makers and the Making*. 2 vols. New York: St. Martin's, 1973.

———. "Southern Literature: The Wellsprings of Its Vitality (1962)." In *A Shaping Joy: Studies in the Writer's Craft*. New York: Harcourt, 1972. 215–29.

———. *William Faulkner: The Yoknapatawpha Country*. New Haven: Yale UP, 1963.

Brown et al. v. Board of Education of Topeka et al. 347 US 483. 1954.

Buell, Lawrence. "Literary History as a Hybrid Genre." In *New Historical Literary Study: Essays on Reproducing Texts, Representing History*. Eds. Jeffrey N. Cox and Larry J. Reynolds. Princeton: Princeton UP, 1993. 216–29.

Cable, George Washington. *The Grandissimes*. New York: Scribner's, 1880.

———. *Dr. Sevier*. Boston: Osgood, 1884. [Scribner's after 1887.]

———. *John March, Southerner*. New York: Scribner's, 1894.

Canby, Henry Seidel. "The School of Cruelty." Rev. of *Sanctuary*, by William Faulkner. *Saturday Review of Literature* 21 March 1931: 673–74.

Cash, W. J. *The Mind of the South*. New York: Knopf, 1941.

Chase, Richard V. *The American Novel and Its Tradition*. Garden City, NY: Doubleday, 1957.

Christian, Barbara. "Trajectories of Self-Definition: Placing Contemporary Afro-American Women's Fiction." Pryse 233–48.

Collins, Carvel, ed. *William Faulkner: Early Prose and Poetry*. Boston: Little, Brown, 1962.

Core, George, and M. E. Bradford. Preface. Weaver, *Southern Tradition* [9]–12.

Crews, Harry. *Karate Is a Thing of the Spirit*. 1972. New York: Quill, 1983.

Cofield, Jack. *William Faulkner: The Cofield Collection*. Oxford: Yoknapatawpha, 1978.

Conkin, Paul. *The Southern Agrarians*. Knoxville: U of Tennessee P, 1988.

Couch, William Terry, ed. *Culture in the South*. Chapel Hill: U of North Carolina P, 1934.

Cowley, Malcolm, ed. *The Portable Faulkner*. New York: Viking, 1946.

Davis, David Brion. "Southern Comfort." Rev. of *The Southern Tradition, The Southern Front,* and *The Slaveholders' Dilemma,* by Eugene D. Genovese. *New York Review of Books* 5 October 1995: 43–46.

Davis, Richard Beale, C. Hugh Holman, and Louis D. Rubin, Jr., eds. *Southern Writing: 1585–1920.* New York: Odyssey, 1970.

Davidson, Donald. Introduction. Weaver, *Southern Tradition* 29–46.

———. Letter to Howard Mumford Jones. 21 Oct. 1930. Donald Davidson Papers.

———. Letter to John Crowe Ransom. 5 July 1929. Donald Davidson Papers.

———. *Southern Writers in the Modern World.* Athens: U of Georgia P, 1958.

———. "The Trend of Literature." Couch 183–210.

Donald Davidson Papers. Special Collections. Vanderbilt University Library. Nashville, Tennessee.

Donaldson, Susan V. "Songs with a Difference: Beatrice Ravenel and the Detritus of Southern History." *The Female Tradition in Southern Literature.* Ed. Carol S. Manning. Urbana: U of Illinois P, 1993. 176–92.

Douglas, Mary. *Purity and Dangers: An Analysis of Concepts of Pollution and Taboo.* New York: Praeger, 1966.

Du Bois, W. E. B. *The Souls of Black Folk.* 1903. Ed. Herbert Aptheker. Millwood, NY: Kraus-Thomson, 1973.

Eco, Umberto. *Postscript to The Name of the Rose.* Trans. William Weaver. San Diego: Harcourt, 1984.

Edmonds, Irene C. "Faulkner and the Black Shadow." Rubin and Jacobs, *Renascence* 192–206.

Ellison, Ralph. *Invisible Man.* New York: Vintage, 1952.

———. *Shadow and Act.* New York: Random, 1964.

Escott, Paul D., and David R. Goldfield, eds. *Major Problems in the History of the American South.* 2 vols. Lexington, MA: Heath, 1990.

Evans, August Jane. *St. Elmo.* 1866. Tuscaloosa: U of Alabama P, 1992.

Fain, John Tyree, and Thomas Daniel Young, eds. *The Literary Correspondence of Donald Davidson and Allen Tate.* Athens: U of Georgia P, 1974.

Faulkner, William. *Absalom, Absalom!* 1936. New York: Vintage International, 1990.

———. "Afternoon of a Cow." Wells 135–50.

———. *Essays, Speeches, and Public Letters.* Ed. James B. Meriwether. London: Chatto, 1967.

———. *A Fable.* 1954. New York: New American Library, 1968.

———. *A Faulkner Miscellany.* Ed. James B. Meriwether. Jackson: UP of Mississippi, 1973.

———. *The Hamlet.* 1940. New York: Vintage International, 1991.

———. *Helen: A Courtship* and *Mississippi Poems.* Ed. Carvel Collins. Oxford, MS, and New Orleans: Yoknapatawpha P and Tulane U, 1981.

———. "Landing in Luck." Collins 42–50.

———. *Light in August.* 1932. New York: Vintage International, 1985.

———. *The Mansion.* 1959. New York: Random, 1965.

———. *The Marble Faun and A Green Bough.* 1933. New York: Random, 1965.

———. "A Name for the City." Brickell 98–115.

———. "Nobel Prize Acceptance Speech." *Essays* 119–21.

———. *Sanctuary.* 1931. New York: Vintage International, 1985.

———. *Soldiers' Pay.* 1926. New York: Liveright, 1997.

———. *The Sound and the Fury.* 1929. New York: Vintage International, 1990.

———. *Thinking of Home: William Faulkner's Letters to His Mother and Father, 1918–1925.* Ed. James G. Watson. New York: Norton, 1992.

———. *The Town.* 1957. New York: Random, 1961.

———. "To the Graduating Class, Pine Manor Junior College, 1953." *Essays* 135–42.

———. *Vision in Spring.* Ed. Judith Sensibar. Austin: U of Texas P, 1984.

Flagg, Fannie. *Fried Green Tomatoes at the Whistle Stop Cafe.* New York: McGraw, 1988.

Foerster, Norman, ed. *Humanism and America: Essays on the Outlook of Modern Civilization.* New York: Farrar, 1930.

Forkner, Ben, and Patrick Samway, S.J., eds. *A Modern Southern Reader.* Atlanta: Peachtree, 1986.

———. *A New Reader of the Old South.* Atlanta: Peachtree, 1991.

Fried Green Tomatoes. Dir. John Avnet. Perf. Kathy Bates, Jessica Tandy, Mary Stuart Masterson, Mary Louise Parker, and Cicely Tyson. Universal, 1991.

Gaines, Ernest J. *Bloodline.* 1968. New York: Norton, 1976.

———. *In My Father's House.* New York: Knopf, 1978.

———. *A Lesson before Dying.* New York: Knopf, 1993.

Gaudet, Marcia, and Carl Wooten, eds. *Porch Talk with Ernest Gaines: Conversations on the Writer's Craft.* Baton Rouge: Louisiana State UP, 1990.

Genovese, Eugene D. *Roll, Jordan, Roll: The World the Slaves Made.* New York: Pantheon, 1974.

———. *The Slaveholders' Dilemma: Freedom and Progress in Southern Conservative Thought, 1820–1860.* Columbia: U of South Carolina P, 1992.

———. *The Southern Front: History and Politics in the Culture War.* Columbia: U of Missouri P, 1995.

———. *The Southern Tradition: The Achievement and Limitations of an American Conservatism.* Cambridge: Harvard UP, 1994.

Graff, Gerald. *Professing Literature: An Institutional History.* Chicago: U of Chicago P, 1987.

Grattan, C. Hartley, ed. *The Critique of Humanism: A Symposium.* 1930. Port Washington, NY: Kennikat, [1968].

Gwynn, Frederick L., and Joseph Blotner, eds. *Faulkner in the University: Class Conferences at the University of Virginia, 1957–1958.* 1959. New York: Random, 1965.

Hannah, Barry. *Geronimo Rex*. New York: Viking, 1972.

Harrison, Elizabeth Jane. *Female Pastoral: Women Writers Re-Visioning The American South*. Knoxville: U of Tennessee P, 1991.

Harvey, David. *The Condition of Postmodernity*. Cambridge, UK: Basil Blackwell, 1989.

Heilman, Robert. "The Southern Temper." Rubin and Jacobs, *Renascence* 3–13.

Hill, James Michael. *Celtic Warfare 1595–1763*. Edinburgh: Donald, 1986.

———. "President's Message." *Southern Patriot* March–April 1995: [9]–10.

Hobsbawm, Eric. "Introduction: Inventing Traditions." In Eric Habsbawm and Terence Ranger, eds. *The Invention of Tradition*. Cambridge: Cambridge UP, 1983. 1–14.

Hobson, Fred. *The Southern Writer in the Postmodern World*. Athens: U of Georgia P, 1991.

———. "Surveyors and Boundaries: Southern Literature and Southern Literary Scholarship after Mid-Century." *Southern Review* 27 (1991): 739–55.

Hoeveler, J. David, Jr. *The New Humanism: A Critique of Modern America, 1900–1940*. Charlottesville: UP of Virginia, 1977.

Horwitz, Tony. "A Death for Dixie." *New Yorker* 18 March 1996: 64–77.

———. "Rebel Voices." *Wall Street Journal* 28 April 1995, eastern ed.: A1, A6.

Howe, Irving. *William Faulkner: A Critical Study*. 2nd ed. New York: Random House, n.d.

———. *A World More Attractive: A View of Modern Literature and Politics*. New York: Horizon, 1963.

Hubbell, Jay Broadus. *American Life in Literature*. New York: Harper, 1936.

Humphreys, Josephine. *Rich in Love*. 1987. New York: Penguin, 1988.

Humphries, Jefferson. Introduction. *Southern Literature and Literary Theory*. Athens: U of Georgia P, 1990. vii–xviii.

Humphries, Jefferson, and John Lowe, eds. *The Future of Southern Letters*. New York: Oxford UP, 1996.

Hutcheon, Linda. *The Politics of Postmodernism*. London: Routledge, 1989.

Hyman, Stanley Edgar. *The Promised End: Essays and Reviews, 1942–1962*. Cleveland, OH: World, 1963.

Irwin, John T. *Doubling and Incest/Repetition and Revenge: A Speculative Reading of Faulkner*. Baltimore: Johns Hopkins UP, 1975.

Jackson, Blyden. *"Growing Up Black in the Old South and the New: or, Mr. Wheat Goes with the Wind."* Rubin, *American South* 101–09.

Jameson, Fredric. *Postmodernism; or, The Cultural Logic of Late Capitalism*. Durham, NC: Duke UP, 1991.

Jelliffe, Robert A., ed. *Faulkner at Nagano*. 1956. N.p:. Folcroft Library, 1973.

Johnson, Charles S. *Shadow of the Plantation*. Chicago: U of Chicago P, 1934.

Jones, Anne Goodwyn. *Tomorrow Is Another Day: The Woman Writer in the South, 1859–1936*. Baton Rouge: Louisiana State UP, 1981.

Jones, Howard Mumford. "The Future of Southern Culture." *Southwest Review* 16 (1931): 141–63.

————. "Is There a Southern Renaissance?" *Virginia Quarterly Review* 6 (1930): 184–97.

————. Letter to Donald Davidson. 25 July 1929. Donald Davidson Papers.

————. Letter to John Crowe Ransome [*sic*]. 25 July 1929. Donald Davidson Papers.

————. Letter to Donald Davidson. 7 Oct. 1930. Donald Davidson Papers.

King, Richard. *A Southern Renaissance*. New York: Oxford UP, 1980.

Kreyling, Michael. "Ellen Glasgow and the Dismantling of Heroic Narrative." In *Figures of the Hero in Southern Narrative*. Baton Rouge: Louisiana State UP, 1987. 76–102.

Ladd, Barbara. *Nationalism and the Color Line in George Washington Cable, Mark Twain, and William Faulkner*. Baton Rouge: Louisiana State UP, 1966.

Lauter, Paul, et al., eds. *The Heath Anthology of American Literature*. 2 vols. 1990. 2nd ed. Lexington, MA: Heath, 1994.

Lee, Harper. *To Kill a Mockingbird*. Philadelphia, Lippincott, 1960.

Logan, Rayford W., ed. *What the Negro Wants*. Chapel Hill: U of North Carolina P, 1944.

Ludwig, Emil. *The Son of Man*. Trans. Eden and Cedar Paul. Garden City, NY: Garden City, 1928.

Lumpkin, Grace. "I Want a King." *Fight against War and Fascism* Feb. 1936: 3, 14.

Lytle, Andrew Nelson. *Bedford Forrest and His Critter Company*. 1930. Nashville, TN: Sanders, 1984.

————. "Regeneration for the Man: Faulkner's *Intruder in the Dust*." In *Southerners and Europeans: Essays in a Time of Disorder*. Baton Rouge: Louisiana State UP, 1988. 172–79.

Malraux, André. *Man's Fate*. Trans. Haakon M. Chevalier. New York: Random, 1934.

Mannheim, Karl. *Ideology and Utopia*. Trans. Louis Wright and Edward Shils. New York: Harcourt, [1959].

Manning, Carol S. Introduction. *The Female Tradition in Southern Literature*. Ed. Carol S. Manning. Urbana: U of Illinois P, 1993. 1–12.

Mattheissen, F. O. *American Renaissance: Art and Expression in the Age of Emerson and Whitman*. New York: Oxford UP, 1941.

McCorkle, Jill. *Tending to Virginia*. 1987. New York: Ballantine, 1988.

McMichael, Andrew. "Nashville Eye: Slavery's Civil War role can't be ignored." *Nashville Tennessean* 24 March 1997: 13A.

Menand, Louis. "Books: The Hammer and the Nail." *New Yorker* 20 July 1992: 79–84.

Mencken, Henry Louis. "The Sahara of the Bozart." In *Prejudices: Second Series*. New York: Knopf, 1924: 136–54.

Mitchell, Broadus. "A Survey of Industry." Couch 80–92.

Moon, Bucklin, ed. *A Primer for White Folks*. Garden City, NY: Doubleday, 1945.

————. *Without Magnolias*. Garden City, NY: Doubleday, 1949.

Moses, Montrose J. *The Literature of the South*. New York: Crowell, 1910.

Myrdal, Gunnar. *An American Dilemma: The Negro Problem and Modern Democracy.* New York: Harper, 1944.

Niebuhr, Reinhold. *The Irony of American History.* New York: Scribner's, 1952.

Nixon, Herman Clarence. "Whither Southern Economy?" Twelve Southerners 176–200.

O'Brien, Michael. *Rethinking the South: Essays in Intellectual History.* Baltimore: Johns Hopkins UP, 1988.

O'Connor, Flannery. "A Late Encounter with the Enemy." In *The Complete Stories.* New York: Farrar, 1972: 134–44.

———. *The Habit of Being.* Ed. Sally Fitzgerald. New York: Farrar, 1979.

———. "Some Aspects of the Grotesque in Southern Fiction." In *Mystery and Manners.* Ed. Sally and Robert Fitzgerald. New York: Farrar, 1969: 36–50.

Owsley, Frank Lawrence. "The Irrepressible Conflict." Twelve Southerners 61–91.

Pfaff, William. "A Critic at Large: *L'homme engagé.*" *New Yorker* 9 July 1990: 83–91.

Phillips, Ulrich Bonnell. *Life and Labor in the Old South.* Boston: Little, 1929.

Pinckney, Darryl. "The Drama of Ralph Ellison." *New York Review of Books* 15 May 1997: 52–60.

Podhoretz, Norman. "Southern Claims." *Partisan Review* (Jan./Feb. 1954): 119–23.

Polk, Noel. "Enduring *A Fable* and Prevailing." *Faulkner: The Nobel and after.* Eds. Michel Gresset and Kenzaburo Ohashi. Tokyo: Yamaguchi, n.d.

Prenshaw, Peggy Whitman, ed. *Conversations with Eudora Welty.* Jackson: UP of Mississippi, 1984.

Prescott, Orville. "Books of the Times." *New York Times* 8 April 1955: 19.

Price, Reynolds. *A Long and Happy Life.* New York: Atheneum, 1962.

———. *Mustian.* 1983. New York: Ballantine, 1984.

———. "News for the Mineshaft." *Virginia Quarterly Review* 44 (1968): 641–58. Rpt. in *Things Themselves.* New York: Atheneum, 1972. 70–90; *A Common Room: Essays 1954–1987.* New York: Atheneum, 1987. 40–53.

Pryse, Marjorie, and Hortense Spillers, eds. *Conjuring: Black Women, Fiction, and Literary Tradition.* Bloomington: Indiana UP, 1985.

Ransom, John Crowe. *God without Thunder: An Unorthodox Defense of Orthodoxy.* 1930. London: Gerald Howe, 1931.

———. "Land! An Answer to the Unemployment Problem." *Harpers Magazine* July 1932: 216–24.

———. "Poets without Laurels." In *The World's Body.* New York: Charles Scribner's Sons, 1938. 55–75.

Raper, Julius Rowan. "Creating Modern Southern Literature: A Postmodern View." *Southern Literary Journal* 22 (1990): 3–18.

Reed, Adolph, Jr. "Tokens of the White Left." *Progressive* Dec. 1993: 18–20.

Reed, Ishmael. "Steven Spielberg Plays Howard Beach." In *Writin' Is Fightin': Thirty-Seven Years of Boxing on Paper.* New York: Atheneum, 1988. 145–60.

Ripley, Alexandra. *Scarlett: The Sequel to Margaret Mitchell's Gone with the Wind.* New York: Warner, 1991.

Roberts, Elizabeth Madox. *The Time of Man.* New York: Viking, 1926.

Rubin, Louis D., Jr. *The American South: Portrait of a Culture.* Baton Rouge: Louisiana State UP, 1980.

———. "'Begum of Bengal': Mark Twain and the South." *William Elliott* 250–70.

———. *The Curious Death of the Novel: Essays in American Literature.* Baton Rouge: Louisiana State UP, 1967.

———. "The Dixie Special: William Faulkner and the Southern Literary Renascence." Rubin, *Mockingbird* 37–62.

———. *The Edge of the Swamp: A Study in the Literature and Society of the Old South.* Baton Rouge: Louisiana State UP, 1989.

———. *The Faraway Country: Writers of the Modern South.* Seattle: U of Washington P, 1963.

———. "The Historical Image of Modern Southern Writing." *Journal of Southern History* 22 (1956): 147–66.

———. "An Image of the South." Rubin and Kilpatrick, *Lasting* 1–15.

———. "Introduction: Torch Book Edition (1962)." Twelve Southerners xxiii–xxxv.

———, gen. ed. *The History of Southern Literature.* Baton Rouge: Louisiana State UP, 1985.

———. "Letter to the Editor." *Mississippi Quarterly* 45 (1992): 189–93.

———, ed. *The Literary South.* New York: Wiley, 1979.

———. *Mockingbird in the Gum Tree: A Literary Gallimaufry.* Baton Rouge: Louisiana State UP, 1990.

———. "Notes on a Rear-Guard Action." Rubin, *Curious* 131–51.

———. "Politics and the Novel: George W. Cable and the Genteel Tradition." Rubin, *William Elliott* 61–81.

———. "Second Thoughts on the Old Gray Mare." Rubin, *William Elliott* 250–69.

———. Memo: "The Southern Novel and the Southern Community." N.E.H. Summer Institute at the U of North Carolina, Chapel Hill. 1989. [1].

———. "The Way It Was with Southern Literary Study." *Mississippi Quarterly* 43 (1990): 147–62.

———. *William Elliott Shoots a Bear: Essays on the Southern Literary Imagination.* Baton Rouge: Louisiana State UP, 1975.

Rubin, Louis D., Jr., and Robert Jacobs, eds. Introduction. *South: Modern Southern Literature in Its Cultural Setting.* Garden City, NY: Doubleday, 1961. 11–25.

———. *Southern Renascence: The Literature of the Modern South.* Baltimore: Johns Hopkins UP, 1953.

Rubin, Louis D., Jr., and James J. Kilpatrick, eds. *The Lasting South: Fourteen Southerners Look at Their Home.* Chicago: Regnery, 1957.

Ruland, Richard. "Art and a Better American." *American Literary History* 3 (1991): 337–59.

Sartre, Jean-Paul. "American Novelists in French Eyes." *Atlantic Monthly* 178 (1946): 114–18.

Sass, Herbert Ravenel. "Mixed Schools and Mixed Blood." *Atlantic Monthly* 198 (Nov. 1956): 45–49.

Schwartz, Lawrence. *Creating Faulkner's Reputation*. Knoxville: U of Tennessee P, 1988.

Segrest, Mab. "Southern Women Writing: toward a Literature of Wholeness." In *My Mama's Dead Squirrel: Lesbian Essays on Southern Culture*. Ithaca, NY: Firebrand, 1985. 19–42.

Shofner, William E. "The Nashville Eye." *Nashville Tennessean* 10 March 1997: 11A.

Simpson, Lewis P. *The Brazen Face of History*. Baton Rouge: Louisiana State UP, 1980.

———. "The Closure of History in a Postsouthern America." Simpson, *Brazen* 255–72.

———. *The Fable of the Southern Writer*. Baton Rouge: Louisiana State UP, 1994.

———. "The South and the Poetry of Community." In *The Poetry of Community: Essays on the Southern Sensibility of History and Literature*. Atlanta: Georgia State U, 1972. xi–xxvi.

———. "What Survivors Do." Simpson, *Brazen* 237–54.

Singal, Daniel Joseph. *The War Within: From Victorian to Modernist Thought in the South, 1919–1945*. Chapel Hill: U of North Carolina P, 1982.

Smith, Lee. *Oral History*. 1983. New York: Ballantine, 1984.

Smith, Lillian. "Addressed to White Liberals." *Primer for White Folks*. Ed. Bucklin Moon. New York: Random, 1945. 484–87.

———. *Strange Fruit*. Foreword by Fred Hobson. Athens: U of Georgia P, 1985.

"Southern Authors." *The Nation* 17 Oct. 1953: 317.

Spencer, Elizabeth. *The Voice at the Back Door*. 1956. New York: Avon, 1986.

Spiller, Robert. *The Cycle of American Literature*. 1955. New York: Mentor, 1957

Spiller, Robert, et al., eds. *Literary History of the United States*. 3 vols. New York: Macmillan, 1948.

Stewart, Randall, gen. ed. *The Literature of the South*. Ed. Richmond Croom Beatty, Floyd C. Watkins, and Thomas Daniel Young. Chicago: Scott, 1952. 2nd ed. 1968.

Stonum, Gary Lee. *Faulkner's Career: An Internal Literary History*. Ithaca, NY: Cornell UP, 1979.

Streitfield, David. "Eudora Welty, In Her Own Words."*Washington Post* 4 Dec. 1992: D3.

Sumner, William Graham. *Folkways: A Study of the Sociological Importance of Usages, Manners, Customs, Mores, and Morals*. Boston: Ginn, 1907.

Surowiecki, James. "Genovese's March: The Radical Reconstructions of a Southern Historian." *Lingua Franca* (Dec./Jan. 1997): 36–52.)

Tate, Allen. "A View of the Whole South." *American Review* 2 (1934): 411–32.

———. "Humanism and Naturalism."Tate, *Memoirs* 170–84.

———. "*The Fugitive*, 1922–1925: A Personal Recollection Twenty Years After." Tate, *Memoirs* 24–34.

———. *Memoirs and Opinions*, 1926–1974. Chicago: Swallow, 1975. 170–84.

———. "The Profession of Letters in the South." In *Essays of Four Decades*. Denver: Swallow, 1968. 517–34.

———. "Remarks on the Southern Religion." Twelve Southerners 155–74.

———, ed. *A Southern Vanguard: The John Peale Bishop Memorial Volume*. New York: Prentice Hall, 1947.

Taylor, Peter. "In the Miro District." In *In the Miro District*. 1977. New York: Carroll, 1987. 157–204.

Thorpe, Willard. Rev. of *Southern Renascence*, by Louis D. Rubin, Jr., and Robert Jacobs, eds. *American Literature* 26 (1955): [575]–78.

Tindall, George Brown. "The Central Theme Revisited." In *The Southerner as American*. Ed. Charles Grier Sellers. Chapel Hill: U of North Carolina P, 1960. 104–29.

Trent, William Peterfield, John Erskine, Stuart P. Sherman, and Carl Van Doren, eds. *Cambridge History of American Literature*. 4 vols. New York: Putnam's, 1917–21.

———. *Southern Writers: Selections in Prose and Verse*. New York: Macmillan, 1910.

Twelve Southerners. *I'll Take My Stand*. 1930. Baton Rouge: Louisiana State UP, 1977.

Urgo, Joseph R. *Faulkner's Apocrypha: A Fable, Snopes, and the Spirit of Human Rebellion*. Jackson: UP of Mississippi, 1989.

Vance, Rupert B. "The Profile of Southern Culture." Couch 24–39.

Vanderbilt, Kermit. *American Literature and the Academy*. Philadelphia: U of Pennsylvania P, 1986.

Vasari, Giorgio. *Lives of the Artists*. Trans. George Bull. 1568. New York and London: Penguin, 1965.

Voegelin, Eric. *Israel and Revolution*. Baton Rouge: Louisiana State UP, 1956.

Wagner-Martin, Linda. "'Just the doing of it': Southern Women Writers and the Idea of Community." *Southern Literary Journal* 22 (1990): 19–32.

Warren, Robert Penn. "The Briar Patch." Twelve Southerners 246–64.

———. *Brother to Dragons*. New ed. New York: Random, 1979.

———. *Segregation: The Inner Conflict in the South*. New York: Random House, 1956.

Wasson, Ben. *Count no' Count: Flashbacks to Faulkner*. Jackson: UP of Mississippi, 1983.

Weaver, Richard M. "Albert Taylor Bledsoe." 1944. *Southern Essays* 147–58.

———. "The Confederate South, 1865–1910: A Study in the Survival of a Mind and a Culture." Diss. Louisiana State U. 1943.

———. *Ideas Have Consequences*. Chicago: U of Chicago P, 1948.

———. "The Older Religiousness of the South." 1943. *Southern Essays* 134–46.

———. "The Revolt against Humanism." Master's thesis. Vanderbilt U. 1934.

———. "Southern Chivalry and Total War." 1945. *Southern Essays* 159–70.

———. *The Southern Essays of Richard Weaver*. Eds. George M. Curtis III and James J. Thompson. Indianapolis: Liberty, 1987.

———. *The Southern Tradition at Bay: A History of Postbellum Thought*. Eds. George Core and M.E. Bradford. New Rochelle, NY: Arlington, 1968.

———. "Up from Liberalism." *Modern Age* 3 (1958–59): 21–32.

———. *Visions of Order: The Cultural Crisis of Our Time*. Baton Rouge: Louisiana State UP, 1964.

Wells, Dean Faulkner, ed. *The Best of Bad Faulkner*. San Diego: Harcourt, 1991.

Welty, Eudora. "The Burning." Brickell, 17–31.

———. *Delta Wedding*. New York: Harcourt, 1946.

———. "Must The Novelist Crusade?" *Atlantic Monthly* 216 (Oct. 1965): 104–08. Rpt. in *The Eye of the Story: Selected Essays and Reviews*. New York: Random, 1978. 146–58.

White, Hayden. *Metahistory: The Historical Imagination in Nineteenth-Century Europe*. Baltimore: Johns Hopkins UP, 1973.

Williamson, Joel. *William Faulkner and Southern History*. New York: Oxford UP, 1993.

Woodward, C. Vann. "The Search for Southern Identity." In *The Burden of Southern History*. New York: Vintage, 1961.

———. "The South and the Fury." Rev. of *William Faulkner and Southern History*, by Joel Williamson. *New Republic* 23 and 30 August 1993: 41–45.

———. "Why the Southern Renaissance?" *Virginia Quarterly Review* 51 (1975): 222–39. Rpt. in *The Future of the Past*. New York: Oxford UP, 1989. 203–20.

Wright, Richard. *Black Boy*. 1945. New York: Harper, 1966.

———. *The Long Dream*. 1958. New York: Harper Perennial, 1987.

———. *Native Son*. 1940. New York: Harper Perennial, 1966.

———. *Uncle Tom's Children*. 1940. New York: Harper, 1965.

Wyatt-Brown, Bertram. *The House of Percy: Honor, Melancholy and Imagination in a Southern Family*. New York: Oxford UP, 1994.

INDEX